ONE FOOT ON THE PLATFORM

ALSO BY PETER GODDARD

NONFICTION

Frank Sinatra: The Man, The Myth and The Music

The Rolling Stones: The Last Tour (with Philip Kamin)

The Who: The Farewell Tour (with Philip Kamin)

David Bowie: Out of the Cool (with Philip Kamin)

Van Halen (with Philip Kamin)

Michael Jackson & The Jacksons: Live on Tour in '84 (with Philip Kamin)

The Police Chronicles: From Beginning to End (with Philip Kamin)

Genesis: Peter Gabriel, Phil Collins and Beyond (with Philip Kamin)

Springsteen: Live (with Philip Kamin)

Duran Duran: Live (with Philip Kamin)

Cyndi Lauper (with Philip Kamin)

The Video Hits Book (co-editor, with Philip Kamin)

Triumph: The Book (with Philip Kamin)

The Cars (with Philip Kamin)

Ronnie Hawkins: Last of the Good Ol' Boys (with Ronnie Hawkins)

Shakin' All Over: The Rock 'n' Roll Years in Canada (co-editor, with Philip Kamin)

The Great Gould

FICTION

The Sounding

Praise for *One Foot on the Platform: A Rock 'n' Roll Journey*

"Peter Goddard was always the 'King of Cool' to me: His brilliant rock reporting helped define an era, as he educated and entertained us all with his savvy observations of a scene we could never get enough of. Peter's amazing stories take me back to a time of passion and idealism, when we all believed that music could really change the world." —JEANNE BEKER, television host and author of *Heart on My Sleeve: Stories from a Life Well Worn*

"Reading *One Foot on the Platform* is like rediscovering a long-lost album by your favourite band. For an instant they are alive again: the Beatles, Zeppelin, Janis, the Doors, Bowie—the gods that birthed rock music. So venture up to Peter's attic, let him unspool his tapes and dust off his records, and lose yourself in the music and stories of all these magical artists." —ELLIOTT LEFKO, AEG/Goldenvoice Concerts (promoter for Leonard Cohen, Nick Cave, Sigur Rós, and Courtney Barnett)

"Peter Goddard always had his finger on the pulse of popular music, writing fluidly and thoughtfully about artists who stood out from the pack. This illuminating collection confirms his place among the world's finest critics." —NICHOLAS JENNINGS, author of *Lightfoot*

"A testament to the power of print, *One Foot on the Platform* captures the joy of diving into the daily papers, when the Entertainment section was a secret conduit to underground culture. It's also a wormhole to a lost Toronto, as you're transported to a smoke-filled room on Yonge Street or Yorkville Avenue, watching a musical legend play for a few dozen bodies. At the set break, your seatmate explains what you just heard with rapid-fire blasts of bon mots and literary references. In real time, Peter Goddard documented an era when rock wasn't just a subset of "modern music" but the centre of popular culture—without forgetting its roots in blues, jazz, and folk. Through Goddard's eyes, we witness rock's ascendance from teen trash to adult art, an evolution he playfully interrogated throughout his career. Essential reading for those who want to understand not just where today's music came from, but the long, hard-earned shadow of the Sixties Generation." —JONNY DOVERCOURT, author of *Any Night of the Week: A D.I.Y. History of Toronto Music, 1957–2001*

PETER GODDARD

ONE FOOT ON THE PLATFORM

A ROCK 'N' ROLL JOURNEY

WRITINGS ON MUSIC

EDITED BY J. A. WAINWRIGHT

ANANSI

Published in Canada in 2025 and the USA in 2025 by House of Anansi Press Inc.
houseofanansi.com

House of Anansi Press is committed to protecting our natural environment. This book is made of material from well-managed FSC®-certified forests, recycled materials, and other controlled sources.

House of Anansi Press is a Global Certified Accessible™ (GCA by Benetech) publisher. The ebook version of this book meets stringent accessibility standards and is available to readers with print disabilities.

29 28 27 26 25   1 2 3 4 5

Library and Archives Canada Cataloguing in Publication

Title: One foot on the platform : a rock 'n' roll journey : writings on music / Peter Goddard ; edited by J.A. Wainwright.
Names: Goddard, Peter, author | Wainwright, J. A., 1946- editor
Identifiers: Canadiana (print) 20240441419 | Canadiana (ebook) 20240441443 | ISBN 9781487010430 (softcover) | ISBN 9781487010447 (EPUB)
Subjects: LCSH: Rock musicians—Biography. | LCSH: Rock music—Canada—History and criticism. | LCSH: Popular music—Canada—History and criticism.
Classification: LCC ML394 .G578 2025 | DDC 782.42166092/2—dc23

Cover design: Greg Tabor
Cover image: Toronto Rock and Roll Revival, Varsity Stadium, September 13, 1969 (Boris Spremo / Toronto Star via Getty Images)
Interior design: Alysia Shewchuk

House of Anansi Press is grateful for the privilege to work on and create from the Traditional Territory of many Nations, including the Anishinabeg, the Wendat, and the Haudenosaunee, as well as the Treaty Lands of the Mississaugas of the Credit.

Canada Council for the Arts   Conseil des Arts du Canada

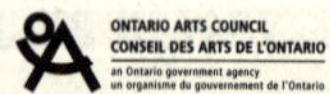

With the participation of the Government of Canada
Avec la participation du gouvernement du Canada | Canadä

We acknowledge for their financial support of our publishing program the Canada Council for the Arts, the Ontario Arts Council, and the Government of Canada.

Printed and bound in Canada

for Kate Woudenberg

CONTENTS

FOLK

POP/COUNTRY/JAZZ

SINGER-SONGWRITERS

PERFORMANCE ROCK

3. OUT OF TIME

EDITOR'S NOTE

AS INDICATED IN THE introduction to this volume, the fusion of forms and expressions that have constituted rock 'n' roll over the past seventy years or so has been vast and varied. Anyone interested in a thorough and sequential revelation of rock's history should access one or more of the many encyclopedias on the subject, as well as particular studies of individual genres, figures, and groups. My selection of Peter's material from the mid-sixties on is not intended to be all-inclusive, but to provide a sense of his personal immersion in the unfolding of rock's development—from its relatively humble blues- and folk-based origins, on through the poetic articulations of a range of singer-songwriters, and into the electric chords of band and single-artist performance that revealed undeniable musical and lyrical brilliance, as well as often over-the-top stage antics. My choices of his reviews and essays are also meant to be a testimony to his evident writing skills and consistent ability to place rock in a larger cultural context: "For if you consider Bob Dylan to be the Dostoevsky of popular music and the Beatles the James Joyce, then [Jerry Lee] Lewis is its Edward Lear: incomprehensible, apparently slightly mad, yet likeable beneath all the insanity." —JAW

INTRODUCTION

IN JUNE OF 1967, I returned home to Toronto from a two-month stay in California where, among other things, I'd attended the Monterey International Pop Festival held in a small rodeo arena outside of town. For the most part, my fellow citizens, including the ones from my generation, weren't yet familiar with the west coast sounds of Jimi Hendrix, Janis Joplin, the Grateful Dead, and Jefferson Airplane, or attuned to the almost unearthly r & b tones of Otis Redding. Other Festival performers like the Mamas & the Papas, the Who, and Simon & Garfunkel were already widely accepted denizens of the unfolding Summer of Love that would share headlines with the violence in Vietnam and civil rights protest lines.

The year 1967 was a huge one in rock 'n' roll and other forms of popular music that contributed to its remarkable ascendancy. Landmark albums hit the charts, not only by those musicians who had highlighted Monterey, but also by soon-to-be legends like Jim Morrison and the Doors, Cream, Pink Floyd, and at least three Canadian singer-songwriters whose lyrics would only grow more complex and influential: Gordon Lightfoot, Leonard Cohen, and Joni Mitchell (her first album was released in March 1968).

Already-established figures like Bob Dylan, the Beach Boys, and the Rolling Stones would throw creative fuel on the rock fire that summer and fall, but the most notable and ultimately influential album was the Beatles' *Sgt. Pepper's Lonely Hearts Club Band*, released as I settled back into the Toronto scene. I thought my California experience would put me at the head of any Canadian response to this cultural cornucopia, but I soon learned who the real leader of the pack was—a classically trained musician who was the first on-staff popular music critic for the *Toronto Telegram*, a freelancer for the *Globe and Mail*, and later a full-time writer for the *Toronto Star*. His name was Peter Goddard.

The area around the University of Toronto campus (including the folk clubs on Avenue Road and Yorkville Avenue), was in many ways like a small town in those days, and word of my Monterey experience quickly got around. Out of the blue, Peter called me up to ask if I'd like to write a review of the festival for the student newspaper, *The Varsity* (whose entertainment pages he edited). It was the beginning of a fifty-five-year friendship.

I wrote the thousand-word review, which he judiciously edited, toning down my somewhat hippie-like enthusiasms and encouraging me to be more critical in my assessments of what I had seen and heard on the rodeo arena stage. Monterey aside, at that point my rock 'n' roll knowledge came out of private responses to individual albums and occasional concert attendance (I'd skipped my high school graduation in the fall of 1964 to witness Dylan's solo performance at Massey Hall), but Peter's awareness was much deeper and broader.

At the time of his death from brain cancer in early 2022, he was compiling what was intended to be a twenty-essay volume to be titled *My Private Rock 'n' Roll*, which would emphasize how "rock is idiosyncratic and personal and unfathomable at its best. Raphael and the High Renaissance, a pretty decent group, should have had as many certified hits over such a stretch." His intent, as he wrote in a provisional introduction, was to reveal and emphasize "the humanness of rock, its inherent if crazy humanity which is best understood as narrative—multiple stories actually, as the lives and careers of rock's several generations of musicians criss-crossed one another, leaving me to witness all the comings and goings and their influences."

Several of these new essays—longer, probing pieces on Dylan, the Beatles, John Lennon, and k.d. lang—and briefer portraits of such disparate characters as Pete Townshend of the Who, Robbie Robertson and The Band, Neil Diamond, Jim Morrison, David Bowie, and even Liza Minnelli, are printed here as he left them on the page. Within these portraits of individual rock/pop lives and creativities at the top are memorable considerations of their cultural surround, including (as backdrop to the British Invasion of the mid-sixties) an appreciation of the socially and politically loaded *The Goon Show* humour from the fifties, and a compelling assessment of Dylan's America in his Rolling Thunder Revue and his masked place in it as presented in his film *Renaldo and Clara*.

That was as far as Peter got before his "telling stories as though we had gathered at a bar or party" was silenced forever. But he did leave behind a plethora of reviews for three Toronto-based newspapers and other venues that reveal the range of his knowledge of the origins and efficacies of rock, particularly the ongoing impact of the American blues ethos, folk music lyricism, pop music refrains, and rock-related jazz rhythms and innuendos revealed in the brilliant trumpet abstractions of Miles Davis and performances of the ageless Josephine Baker that anticipate the song-and-dance explosiveness of Tina Turner.

While the music commentaries reprinted here cover the late sixties through the seventies and into the eighties, they begin in 1967. Significantly, Peter saved many of his newspaper reviews from that seminal year, a clear indication of its place for him in the development of popular music and of the significance of his first days as a full-time rock critic. He insisted his book-to-be was "not about nostalgia" but rather the genre's "unsettled history" and its participants (artists and audience) who contributed to what a memorable voice from another era called "a moveable feast."

We can only imagine, had he lived, what he would have done with the cornerstone contributions of the blues to rock as we read about Sonny Terry and Brownie McGhee at the Riverboat club on Yorkville Avenue playing "old backroom, sex and soul" music whose roots lie, as McGhee said, in the lived experience of "picking cotton and chopping corn"; or we encounter in his prose the "simple, twelve-bar blues" of Buddy Guy (such a powerful influence on Hendrix and Eric Clapton, and still performing today), that's "like looking at a cubist portrait of your next of kin." While we miss a vital overview of Joni Mitchell's movement from "flowery and fanciful" expression into a "peaceful expansion of microscopically observed detail," as well as a developed portrait of Gordon Lightfoot's ongoing and eventually successful struggle to transcend surface hipness and do more than simply sing his own songs better than anyone else, we do gain from the reviews of their performances a distinct sense of their progression and special creative qualities. We are also reminded of the contribution to rock of various pop/country stars who attracted a phenomenally large audience to the centre or edges (depending on how you looked at it) of rock's amalgam. Figures such as Neil Diamond, Glen Campbell, Johnny Cash, and Anne Murray.

Peter offers crucial insight into both the short and extended lives of rock 'n' roll—the former encapsulated by the monied performance of the Monkees, and the all-too-brief time at the top of talented groups like Jefferson Airplane, the latter bound up in the refusal-to-die qualities of James Brown, Jerry Lee Lewis, Chuck Berry, Bo Diddley, Ronnie Hawkins, Fats Domino, and the determined efforts of John Lennon to remain relevant long after the Beatles' reign was over.

All this leads into the performative rock cauldron of the late sixties and early-to-mid seventies containing supergroups of one kind of metal or another like Blind Faith and Led Zeppelin; the country inflections of Creedence Clearwater Revival and The Band; and such individual giants as Hendrix, Joplin, Jim Morrison, Bowie, Paul Simon, Springsteen, and others caught by Peter in expressive flight during individual concerts and one-on-one interviews.

Peter was unable to complete his personal rock 'n' roll project. From the measured insights he has left behind, however, there is sufficient evidence of his clear-eyed vision of a musical form whose undeniable strengths he recognized, but never overestimated, and whose high-priest representatives he often challenged and questioned. Even the king of his own cool and skilled evasiveness:

"Here's Bob Dylan [in Santa Monica, 1978] surrounded by agents, reporters, and friends, and no one has anything to ask him.

"'So,' he says. We're standing near the couch.

"'So,' I say back."

J. A. Wainwright
Toronto, 2023

1.
CONTEXTS

MY PRIVATE ROCK 'N' ROLL (2020)

I WAS WALKING IN A polished part of Toronto, a real estate boom having shined up the slum it once was, when I noticed a crane angled skyward to dangle a wrecking ball over 134 Yorkville Avenue. And I realized it was about to obliterate the Riverboat, one of the world's pioneering coffee houses in the late sixties and early seventies, which closed in 1978. I once watched Neil Young perform solo to an audience of three people there.

The ball was terrifying, medieval even, poised over the building like bait waiting to catch something. Sensing a story, I phoned the city desk of the *Star*, the paper which had run many hundreds of my Riverboat reviews, to inform them of the historical disaster I was about to witness.

"What's the place again?" said the editor down the line.

"The Riverboat," I shouted into the wind.

"Never heard of it."

"But Phil Ochs played there, and Gordon Lightfoot," I bellowed.

"Phil who?"

"He wrote 'Changes.'"

"I love that song."

At the beginning of my fifty years spent writing, I soon learned that pop critics working in mainstream media were expected to cover anything that fell under the rubric of popular music. I might review the Benny Goodman band one night—and try to coax an interview out of him—and then Creedence Clearwater Revival two nights later, before hopping into an early morning taxi to a television studio to talk with an openly hostile Bobbie Gentry, squeezed into a pair of jeans, who glumly refused to talk about the story behind the events described in "Ode to Billie Joe."

Nevertheless, rock—and folk and the rest of its ancillaries—occupied more and more time, more taxis, more late nights, more visits from record industry folks bearing the latest vinyl "product." In time, fewer and fewer newspapers or radio or TV outlets noted anything but rock. Few of them noticed that Louis Armstrong was in town for a week, or even cared.

But I'd turn up. I wanted to see what was going on at the end of the line for some old band or some old kind of music before it had entirely passed by. I caught several Armstrong shows for the reason, as I told him backstage, that he played okay trumpet and, besides, catching one of his concerts years before had cost me my summer job selling fairground programs. "Ahhhhh," he smiled.

I spent more hours than I can remember talking to one balding jazz legend or another as they waited out their time for the night's job: Bobby Hackett, the superlative jazz trumpeter, nattily dressed in a cheap hotel room; Chet Baker, a nervous wreck early one Sunday morning that had yet to see him sleep; or guitarist/fiddler Lonnie Johnson waiting for audiences, which often didn't show up at his Home of the Blues club. One night, a silvery-handsome, poised gentleman hosted a big band concert I was to review. Buddy Rogers, just in from Los Angeles, told the sparse crowd that Mary sent her love. Rogers, a former bandleader and movie star, was talking about his wife, Mary Pickford, the silent film star. Time travelled. I clapped as if it were 1929, just like everyone else.

Hackett's burnished solos were famous. (They took the mush out of Jackie Gleason's fifties-era moody LPs, like *Music to Make You Misty*.) Johnson invented the electric violin, no less. Now they coasted along on nostalgia. Would rock end up the same? The question never came up then. It was impossible to imagine. Rock was too big too, well, too much everything else for anything else to keep up.

Its fabulosity was in its ever-expanding scale of things, sky-filling light shows almost unimaginable, buffers against the ordinary like the mythic offshore accounts filled with cash that Alice Cooper called "fuck-off money." Rock's transcendency wasn't just in the atmosphere high over downtown Los Angeles where Alice would watch sports scores running across the bottom of his giant poolside TV screen. It was in the atmosphere everywhere.

Then, what? Downloading came.

The sheer bigness of rock's bigness became negligible in the context of a new digital hegemony. Numbers became counted in the billions, not millions, and were rung up by downloads that ran up the wealth of the proprietors, like Spotify's Daniel Ek. These are numbers without end, as music-bingeing audiences increase exponentially captured by newly minted technologies. No comparison is possible between the estimated 66 million copies of Michael Jackson's "killer" (his word) 1982 album, *Thriller*, and the one billion downloads of Max Richter's eight-hour-long *Sleep*, a music-to-slumber-by conceptual download.

The very use of the word "sales" dates its user. Merely talking about rock sales is inherently nostalgic. While *Thriller* earned Jackson a fortune, each sampling of *Sleep* earns Richter a barely calculable figure. ("I'm not going to buy a yacht," he tells me.)

In fact, what we're talking about is not about music at all.

We've arrived at a moment when the commodification of music, or any art form, is no longer a cultural concern. We now commodify desire and demand. Amazon knows what I'll buy before I do. My needs are an open book. The act of buying and selling merely seals the deal. That's not all. The medium, any medium, is no longer the message. The message is the need for the medium. (Actually, there's already a word just waiting for this: porn, where desire is turned into video.)

This is where this book comes in. It's not about nostalgia, although it goes back to pop's halcyon early days. Rock 'n' roll may not unsettle folks much these days, but its history remains unsettled and up for interpretation to a degree, starting with its roots origins and such existential considerations as the role of the Coasters' 1959 hit "Charlie Brown," with its chorus of "why is everybody always pickin' on me?"

Rock is idiosyncratic and personal and unfathomable at its best. It has remained so, staying quirky and alive despite decades of lavishly intrusive media attention. Raphael and the High Renaissance, a pretty decent group, should have had as many certified hits over such a stretch. In short, rock has individual life—many, many individual lives. It may be more intimate than ever before. Linda Ronstadt told me during a telephone interview that what she missed most from home while on the road was nice sheets, sleeping in her own bedsheets. I wanted to hug her. After hanging up, I remembered I'd heard almost the same thing from Janis Joplin.

This book is about the humanness of rock, its inherent if crazy humanity, which, to my mind, is best understood as narrative—multiple stories, actually, as the lives and careers of rock's several generations of musicians criss-crossed each other, leaving me to witness all the comings and goings and their influences.

Nostalgia, as they say, ain't what it used to be. The art of re-living eras is something equally progressive and regressive, like selling turntables to people born generations after the old ones were trashed in favour of the Walkman. The very idea of nostalgia feels out of step when faced with a spectral digital universe where nothing gets a chance to grow old, leaving us faced with competing nostalgias overlapping and mutating in front of our eyes.

This book is about public space, stadiums, ice rinks, farmlands, and the spaces found between the concerts when the interviews are finished and the deadlines met for the grumbling editors looking for real news. Empty hours and vacated seats only serve to magnify what happens in private spaces too, interviews beyond counting in hotel suites where I interviewed Art Garfunkel giggling behind his bedroom door. Where I sat opposite Prince sitting ramrod-straight in a fancy wing chair in a Four Seasons, clearing up rock history. "Michael Jackson is an entertainer," he announced. "I am a musician."

This is neither an all-inclusive history nor an encyclopedia. I'm telling stories—as though we had gathered at a bar or a party—but the facts are right. I attest to that. If a case of fiction breaks out, it's from the imagination of those whose imaginations I recorded.

RETURN OF THE SIXTIES

MAY 1982
QUEST

THE CBC IS ON the line, wanting to do a piece on me. Well, it's only the local affiliate, CBLT, and the segment is for a pre-prime-time show. Still, three minutes on air. I feign what I feel is that appropriate amount of modest interest ("Really, I'm more concerned about the, uh, issues involved that, ah, you understand... me") and wait impatiently for that sweet moment when, as deftly as Fred Astaire's first entrée in *Top Hat*, I'll leap for my main chance and say yes, yes, oh, YES! I'll do it. But let me explain this bald face for exposure. It's nothing psychoanalytical. I am a rock critic. Or, as my wife says at times of marital duress, only a rock critic. In terms of status, this ranks me with, say, a utility infielder for the Blue Jays who's often used as trade bait—or that woman who fishes those numbered balls out of the wire cage during national lottery shows on television. A bit of TV never hurts—until now, it seems.

You see, as my role in this segment is explained, it becomes clear that they want to make sport of me and the fact that I'm not just a rock critic, but one on into his thirties—not just a "sixties person," as the voice on the phone said, but a living symbol of the entire Day-Glo "epoch," to quote him again, "It'll be fun," the voice soothes, "we'll have you in a car, stalled by the side of the road and some younger people will be along, you know, kids and …"

Knowing a setup even when it only comes before prime time, I decline. The show eventually uses a rock critic who's just quit the gig and tells them what they want to hear. And I go back to sorting out the intricacies of the New Romantic look in recent British rock, trying to explain to everyone why a generation of moderately well-educated young chaps from the lower middle class would want to wear pirates' gear, complete with sword, and smear Cherokee makeup on their faces. And that's that, I think.

But it isn't. I find hours later I'm furious and days later I know exactly why. It's not because my feelings were hurt. It's because he missed the point entirely and the sixties are more at issue now than ever before.

How this comes about can be explained simply enough: the baby boom generation, you see, is the biggest generation in recent years, and as it moves *through* history, growing older and richer if not wiser, its effect on everyone behind it, in front of it, just near it, continues to be enormous. The crucial question, then, is not why it's happening, but why we took so long to come to terms with this … well, unwielded power? We're starting to work it through in private ways—hence such "personal" movies as *Kramer vs. Kramer* and *Ordinary People*—and in public, as the number of movies dealing with Vietnam would indicate. We're no longer even being tentative about it. It's as if we were all at a party that went on far too long and we ignored the cleaning up as long as we could. But all around me are friends and former friends working it through: Bernie, who wants to leave it all behind and go from music to computers; Marie, who thought her future was in television only to discover it was in video; and Liz, who still wonders about singing in that pub in Paris, although she's now doing public relations for big money tennis. The sixties generation is like the one that fought in the Great War and came home to find an entirely new England—and had to work out what was lost and what was found.

Admittedly, the sixties as idea, style, art, and generation have been under attack for some time now as this century's Silly Season, and the target is certainly big, fat, and tempting enough, not unlike one of those vermillion-and-lime-green Technicolor fifties Biblical extravaganzas, where the religiosity now seems camp and one has heard that Caesar was played by a transvestite. I've done my own bit of sixties-bashing, too. Some fifteen years ago I was told right on Toronto's Yorkville Avenue, and by the owner of the Riverboat Coffee House no less, that I "didn't hang out enough." *Zut alors*—I was deemed un-hip. I cringed and sulked then, but use the anecdote with some pride now, as Reagan Republicans must talk about their loss at the 1968 Miami convention to Richard Nixon.

The owner—Bernie Fiedler, to start naming names here—is now bald and manages Dan Hill, which says something about hanging out. Still, being a bit of a schlump in the sixties made entrée into the zippy anti-sixties style proportionally easier. I fell into pace with the brisk new quickstep. I've had my hair cut to the scalp trying to macho-gay-Mitteleuropa and have passed the time talking technologies in chrome-fitted lounges where waiters named Chuck hover about you like a swarm of gnats. From this perspective, attacking the longhairs, especially when they're in law or dentistry, has its pleasures.

But this is going too far, I think, twisting in bed at night. *Now they're after me*, I fume. I phone the CBC back to explain the situation, that with plays, books, movies, and music all dealing with the sixties suddenly showing up, more than nostalgia is happening. Besides, I point out, what they're doing, dividing is in its own way pure sixties. They listen, then choose another rock critic, this one who says he feels "burned out" at twenty-seven. I phone one more time and mention the nastiest, heaviest, loudest bands I can think of: Saxon, Judas Priest, Black Sabbath, AC/DC, Ozzy Osbourne—yargh! They are not impressed. I think of Ricky Nelson and feel a bit calmer, though. Ozzie and Harriet's smiling young son had a breakdown worrying about all of this. He said so right on Merv Griffin one night. *This is not going to happen to me*, I decide.

In truth, a lot of anti-sixties feeling out there—tight, hard lines in design versus the luxurious, blowsy effect in the sixties, minimalist tendencies in art versus the all-embracing, amorphic styles fifteen years ago—is just yin to the sixties yang, part of the same basic impulse. As a generation, sixties people—and by those I mean those baby boomers who can remember most of the lyrics to at least one Beatles song—are now reacting against their own past the way they once reacted against their parents. *We are, in short, still up to our old tricks.* And it's the style, the *exaggerated* style, of this rejection that gives us away. We've not just reacted, we've overreacted. And with style. We weren't born to be wild; we were born to need élan. It's *high*-tech, not just plain old technology. It's the new elegance and conspicuous consumption; moneymaking as a new art form, not for something as banal as necessity. The reason behind this overreaction, the key to understanding it, is the sheer pleasure we've taken in the rejection. Ours has likely been the first sensual counter-revolution in history. We continue to take pleasure in our pleasure. And this gets us down to the very nub of the thing: we're becoming aware that what we thought was radical change was, in fact, original growth. Just when everyone began to think the sixties were nicely, *safely*, in the past as so much unfinished business, it's becoming more and more apparent that they're back in our minds—and you may not like this, but they're here to stay. Time, as Mr. Jagger sings, is on our side.

Barry H. and I are in the bar at the Ritz in Paris, comfortable, English-style, right on Place Vendôme, with freshly cut *jacinthe* and, as far as I can tell, the best Bloody Mary in the world. Barry, who looks the way F. Scott Fitzgerald wanted Dick Diver to look, is a broker, a partner in his own company, and is about to tour selected wineries with one of the younger Eatons. Another Bloody Mary arrives, prompting me to lean confidentially over to him to discuss my modest portfolio of stocks in the hope of making it slightly less modest when, quickly, he too grows confidential. Ah.

"I've been meaning to ask you something rather personal," he says, "about the Everly Brothers."

My mind's an absolute scramble. Has he got their account, too?

"I've been trying to get some of their early stuff," he says. "Do you know where?"

The fact is, the effect of the sixties and the baby boom has never lessened, no matter what fashionable notion would have otherwise. To take this further—until well into the twenty-first century, the fate of North America and a good part of Europe will hang on the whims and plots of that generation of kids born during or after the Second World War, "the result of all the old soldiers coming back from the war and screwing until they were blue in the face," as the Who's Pete Townshend succinctly puts it.

For the past two *centuries*, the world's birthrate has been in general decline, with one exception: the baby boom years. Generally, it's agreed—and my sources here range from whoever wrote the Bible to contemporary sociologists—that each century is affected by three different generations. For instance, the relatively small-in-numbers generation that preceded the baby boomers had, however, a profound and lasting effect because its general optimism was matched and mirrored by North America's unprecedented economic growth. With the baby boomers, it's something more basic: what we have going for us is numbers. There are more of us than anyone else before or, likely, after. Other generations have been formed and influenced by external pressures; the hard, cruel world, for one. Not us. We have a buffer: it's us. *We* are our world or, as Landon Jones puts it in *Great Expectations: America & the Baby Boom Generation*, "the baby boomers *are* their environment."

If we've remained blissfully unaware of this until now it's only because the fashionable rulers of the sixties were generally elitist, no matter what they said about "power to the people." Signs that the broader spectrum of sixties people is making itself and its ideas noticed again come in the most vintage sixties ways. Take protest. Just last September, a march against Ronald Reagan's economic programs attracted more than 250,000 people to Washington, D.C., and the sheer size of the crowd reminded police of the peace marches of the Vietnam War of the sixties and early seventies. A resurgent peace movement has jolted Europe with massive antinuclear protests.

There are signs in Canadian and American politics of a swing to the left, and it would appear to come from a far deeper impulse than the inevitable midterm reaction away from a U.S. president, in this case, one on the right. There's already a crisp counter-revolution: neo-liberalism ("cool pragmatists ... economic issues first, social programs second," in *Esquire* magazine's description). What was inevitable, I suppose, was for all the neo-rhetoric bundling up of neo-conservatism to be peeled away revealing the oldest of economic master plans: it's my money and you can't have it. All that was needed was for someone, a conservative economist, say, to admit this on paper so the neo-liberals (that is, sixties pols) would have something to sink their teeth into. There's nothing sixties folk like better than a good argument and we can pick nits with the best. Remember that trial of the Chicago Seven and the exchange between Judge Julius Hoffman and Abbie Hoffman?

JUDGE: "Can you tell the court and jury your present age?"
ABBIE HOFFMAN: "My age is thirty-three. I am a child of the sixties."
JUDGE: "When you were born?"
ABBIE HOFFMAN: "Psychologically, 1960."

In *American Politics: The Promise of Disharmony*—a real chart-buster among the cheerleaders for Reaganomics—neo-conservative academic Samuel P. Huntington, a founding member of the Trilateral Commission, suggests that our problems stem from "an excess of democracy" and that "democracy will have a longer life if it has a more balanced existence." *The Village Voice*, using the favourite hate word of the sixties, "fascism," calls this "neo-conservative mischief." It's great stuff, all right, almost as good as Reagan himself suggesting that all European anti-nuke marchers were funded by the commies. It's given the sixties generation what it hasn't had since the Vietnam War: something to fight. And they say the son of Richard Daley could be the next mayor of Chicago. I hope this perks Ricky Nelson up a bit.

Politics has just caught the surface ripples of deeper currents and the sign of the sixties' massive presence in our midst comes from nearer the heart of things. The mourning for John Lennon two winters back caught most of us in the media by surprise, not because of the depth of the feelings expressed (nostalgia for one's youth could have accounted for that), but because of the breadth of the feeling. Everyone seemed to react, and some of the most cynical people were spouting foolishly sentimental nonsense about the least sentimental of men. It seemed everyone was shaken awake.

Publishing caught this drift early on and has been following the quiet success of Toby Thompson's *The '60s Report*, a book more often passed around than bought, with a slew of Elvis books. The theory here, it would seem, is to cash in on the current rage for explanatory journalism and explain the sixties away, as you might explain the fins on a 1963 Chrysler Imperial to someone who thinks a Toyota Celica is pretty darn fancy.

The theory in publishing is wrong, too, at least in this case. The sixties can't be explained because they were not about anything as observable or explicable as long hair or hallucinogenic banana peels. It was a system—of approaching all these and everything else—and this system continues. It's the way the system is worked through that gives its uniqueness. The method is always personal, the attitude, sensual, and the results usually confessional. Only the reasons for this working through change. Once it was fuelled by concern for everything all around. Now it's being fuelled by worry.

About what, exactly, is another matter. You can try the future, for starters. Two editors I know around town are plotting some form of magazine for the aged, hoping to match the success of those already out in the United States. It's a good plot. There'll be a lot of buyers. The sixties generation will go on to be the largest, best-educated, healthiest, most rambunctious, and least predictable group of old codgers and codgerettes ever. No one will know what to do with them—*us*, I mean. Predictions are that we'll have to stay on the job longer, to seventy, at least. This is only the first of many ironies to come our way: all our dropping in and out and general pleasure seeking will result in our need for more work because the children we *didn't* have—they got in the way, remember?—won't be there to pay for our retirement and social security benefits.

And what about sixties women, the first generation to smoke almost as heavily as men and also drink considerably? Will they go on to live longer than their men, as is the norm in most generations, or will these expressions of freedom come back to haunt them? Of course, fear of the future is not particular to the sixties generation and despite what sociologist Daniel Yankelovich calls the sixties "psychology of entitlement," diminishing expectations were built right into sixties thinking, as any Vietnam vet will tell you or as can be understood by listening to that sweet melancholy in most of the Beatles' last songs. "Vietnam and post-armistice economy has made everybody old," Toby Thompson wrote years before we pretended disco had made everyone young again. "It was like the 1930s downtown, a new sophistication distinguishing those who held jobs from those who shuffled raggedly on the dole."

To get this "new sophistication" we ransacked the past; with all those white linen suits, 1940s New York bars and 1920s heads-back boozing parties, it seemed for a while as if the seventies were a permanent flashback. But it got us by and explains in part our restrained approval of Ronald and Nancy Reagan, who, it must be said, know more about mixing a martini dry than did Jimmy Carter. But don't for a moment believe we've really disengaged ourselves from all of the proletarian aspects of our sixties past to leave in our wake those not so upscale as ourselves, who, to borrow a line from Thackeray in *Vanity Fair*, "we will leave to grumble anonymously." Yikes! Look around. We're the ones grumbling.

Typically enough, though, we've grafted our need for sophistication on to our need for some sort of pop figure and, as readers of the *Globe and Mail* in particular will know, we've come up with Corporate Chic. "Business itself is regarded with a new veneration. Once it had been considered less dignified and distinguished than the learned professions, but now people thought they praised a clergyman highly when they called him a good businessman." Although this description by historian Frederick Lewis Allen suits these times perfectly—it could, in fact, replace any number of paragraphs in George Gilder's *Wealth and Poverty*, the Reagan supply-siders' Bible—it was written to describe "Coolidge Prosperity" of the 1920s. The dynamic young entrepreneur, particularly one from the West and involved in some way with oil, may be the new glamour figure, but that's just because we're only responding to ourselves again—ourselves in offices, in suits. *Rolling Stone* magazine saved its highest praise for Mick Jagger until the Rolling Stones had finished their American tour. The evaluation? That he was more flamboyant than ever? Tougher? No, it was that Mick "stands revealed as a master career strategist of the first order—and the toughest, shrewdest businessman to emerge on the entertainment scene since Bob Hope and Frank Sinatra."

Well, doo-be-doo-be-dooo.

Among my friends, there's a sense of something gone wrong. Most are doing well, at least "okay," as they'll say, although some will work throughout a weekend. Most drink too much, although otherwise they worry about their health. Some jog, play tennis;

many have stopped smoking. They like their kids. They're not above slipping it to someone who gets in their way at work, but morality is not on their minds. Sex is not a particular problem, nor is companionship, nor access to culture, nor, although they'll never admit this, is money. What's wrong, then, is beneath our starched adulthood. It has to do with faith, I think. Or rather, it has to do with the loss of a particular *kind* of faith—a faith in that what we grew up with, just some of it and certainly not the more harebrained portions, was true. My parents and the parents of my friends have never seemed to worry about this. They survived the Depression and several wars and are bloody well glad it's all behind them. I'm probably more interested in the 1920s or 1930s than they are. None of them ever believed Glenn Miller and his orchestra might save the world.

It's this public testing of faith that's suddenly made the sixties so visible—and has made many of us feel so vulnerable again. The Cockroach trilogy by Alan Williams, an emaciated, twenty-seven-year-old chain-smoking British actor (who uses the stage name Alan Aldred), was one of the hits at last spring's Toronto International Theatre Festival due to its unrelenting stripping away of a lot of prime sixties teases.

He begins by going after ego: "I'm not going to give in to the egotistical indulgence of telling you my name." Later he detonates the twin notions of being hip and of being hip because of a certain rock band: "You've never heard of them," he says of one supergroup. "But they mean a great deal to me." John Gray's show *Rock and Roll*, which toured the country before settling down in Toronto for a run pretty much opposite Williams's three plays, deflates some high-flying sixties myths too, although in a far more sentimental way. Williams works like a surgeon, performing open-heart surgery on himself without anesthetic, and the rawness of his approach is reason enough behind his successful run. Another factor is involved, though, one critics failed to notice. His method is monologue, his mood, confessional. It's as if he's talking to himself, scraping away the unreal, unworthy and just plain absurd to see what's left. I think we're all doing this now to some degree.

Mick Jagger included. We're in his New York office, stratospherically high above New York City's Rockefeller Center, and he's explaining for the nth time just how he feels about growing old. Why, he wonders, does everyone feel compelled to ask him about it? Can he imagine, he's suddenly asked, doing what he's doing forever—or for the next ten years? "Wa-ll, why not," he snorts in his best Cockney, which he then modulates into something closer to Mayfair. "As long as it didn't appear unseemly."

As long as he wouldn't be made vulnerable, this most impeccably poised of men, our Duke of Windsor. I've met veterans of wars who were not afraid to admit their terror, their vulnerability. But for the sixties generation, it can be the substance of everything they do. Some time later, I spend an afternoon with Marianne Faithfull, Jagger's ex-girlfriend, and she too brings up fears about being found out, about being vulnerable. She tells me of the night not long ago she saw herself in an old film on the telly—"I started to cry; I couldn't believe that beautiful creature had been me"—and how she'd been trying to work out a sense of guilt and failure in her albums. "You see," she says, her voice as smoky as a cigarette, "the problem was that at one time we all—Mick, everybody—did believe we could change the world. We believed the sixties were real in that sense."

Vulnerability seems to be a rather common condition among sixties-generation performers these days. Survival requires craft, if not craftiness, though, and this provides a unique problem for a generation of artists whose very work was once praised for, among other things, its apparent lack of craft.

There's Murray McLauchlan, for instance. Some time back he was quoted widely as saying that he was never going to go out on the road again playing his old songs, "Honky Red," "Farmer's Song," and the like. He had yielded to the technological wizardry of a Toronto-based record producer named Bob Ezrin who'd actually convinced him to change the way he sang. The album that resulted was glorious sounding, yet little to do with McLauchlan. And because he'd left himself open to criticism, when it came (from me, as well as others), he seemed to take it particularly hard. We met at a cocktail party recently, but instead of smirking in my direction, his usual reaction when he was put off with me, he walked the other way instead. *That* hurt. But there are others, all finding themselves looking for resources they aren't sure are there, who are reversing that much-used warning of George Santayana: "Those who cannot remember the past are condemned to repeat it." It seems for some sixties artists, those who will not repeat the past are condemned to be remembered by it.

Or to put it another way, there's no way out, no excuse, no escape—no war to slice your life in two, no revolution to force a new start. There's you and more of you, your generation behind you, before you, all around you. No wonder the ever-thicker cocoon of technology we are aiming to wrap around ourselves, from the stereo at home, to Sony Walkman just about everywhere else, to huge home projection TV screens or the quartz-synthesized stereo projection sets complete with multidimensional digital speakers so that in private you can mimic Bruce Springsteen as he's up there on the screen—so, in short, you can be your own sixties image.

That's what irks me most about that CBC program, the way it forced me to recognize that I *had* no way to hide behind anything, especially behind what I did—and how many others in roles or professions that came along with the sixties are trying to explain the "humanistic base" of it all to a Harvard MBA? I realized that my basic faith in the sixties and my generation has had nothing to do with any sense of community, but, quite the opposite, that there was always *a way out.* IT wasn't a question of how (drugs, tai chi, the Unification Church) or to where (Tangiers, that forty acres of scrub brush just north of Parry Sound, marketing at Procter & Gamble). In fact, the very lack of definition of this escape route was its essential appeal.

And with it now gone? I know how McLauchlan feels, although that doesn't make his album any better. The one failure of Williams's Cockroach trilogy comes, genuinely enough—he is, after all, under thirty and since 1979 more than half of North America's population for the first time has been *over* thirty—from his apparent belief in the supposedly communal nature of the sixties. And here's where another irony comes in: we sixties people are probably more united now (at parties you often hear the word "survivor" being bandied about) than we were years ago.

It's this, not the fear of growing old, that has flushed the great sixties mass out from under cover—and has prompted a still younger generation, kids born *in* the sixties, to stage a cartoon version of what we're going through. "If you missed the sixties, you can catch them at the Ritz," runs a flyer for a New York club, which also asks, "Have you ever seen a *liquid light show*?—50 cents off if you are barefooted."

"*Trop d'idées neuves, pas assez d'idées communes*," said Germaine de Staël about the wild-eyed, middle-class radicals of the late eighteenth and nineteenth centuries in Germany—the period of *Sturm und Drang*, so-called, and one not unlike the sixties. Right. There were too many individual ideas. Maybe. Now, however, they're all coming together—and being heard.

Goethe, whose early novel *The Sorrows of Young Werther* had an impact on his generation not unlike Bob Dylan's "Blowin' in the Wind" did on his, came to realize that what he had accomplished as a young man was not to be sneered at, even if he were out of favour. That's something I should tell Ricky Nelson.

He'd worry less.

HAS THE ROCK ROCKET BURNED OUT?

JULY 1971
TORONTO TELEGRAM

WE WERE LOOKING AT a stadium glutted with post-festival garbage. "I tell you," said the promoter glumly, "it's coming. It looks like they're just cracking down on rock festivals. But there's more to it. They're going to go after rock itself... it's in the air."

I wanted to tell him that he was too late, that rock was already under pressure and that what he sensed was about to come down had already landed. But I didn't. If he wanted to sound pathetic at $60,000 per year, that was his business.

Three years ago, I might have shared his anger. Then, the counter-culture protected its own, rallying around its own myths and music. The pressure was external: the cops, the straights, the politicians, the rednecks. Now, it's different. Disenchantment with the counterculture is being registered internally, as the kids watch promotor after festival after band shock and jive away with their money.

Today, rock culture stands at the opposite pole from its peak years. Woodstock was an Indian Summer for a generation warmed cozily by Haight-Ashbury. Altamont, where the Rolling Stones sang while a young black man was stabbed—although generally ignored by the media that thought "revolution" was a word in a hair commercial—showed the sudden chill of change.

The old rock culture failed to take care of its own business; Toronto's last stab at a rock hall, Fillmore Market, collapsed through poor planning: two major Maple Leaf Gardens concerts were mish-mashes when Sly and the Family Stone showed up hours late at one, and Chicago's equipment arrived four hours late at another.

What was implied at the Winter Pop concert, last New Year's Eve, where kids mixed drugs with cheap wine, was not fully realized until the Cheap Thrills 2 concert last month when one man died from an overdose of MDA.

Writing in the *New York Review of Books*, Ellen Willis, rock critic for the *New Yorker*, lamented that "at this point, hate and love seem to be merging into a sense of cosmic failure, a pervasive feeling that everything is disintegrating, including the counterculture itself, and that we really have nowhere to go." Anyone with an overview of the scene might have reached the same conclusion. For others, however, until a pattern became obvious, each bad vibe seemed isolated. Hope grimaced eternal. So, it didn't really matter that the Fillmore East in New York City closed down, and its owner, Bill Graham, felt "the scene had changed." There'd be other halls, other promoters.

It didn't really matter that at least twenty major bands now cost over $20,000. Cheap bands would come along and, besides, we'd get the money from somewhere. It didn't matter that the sound at last Saturday's Beggars' Banquet failed. It would improve next time around. The point was, however, none of it seemed to matter anymore. Supposedly, 1970 was the terminal date for rock festivals. Strawberry Fields bounced from New Brunswick to Nova Scotia to wind up at Mosport. The Festival Express, which started in Toronto and ended in Calgary, lost $350,000 and its various promoting factions are still arguing. Three festivals held in Saskatchewan drew only a total of just over three thousand people. In British Columbia, the Aldergrove Beach Rock Festival (1969) and Strawberry Mountain Fair (1970) drew well but were called by one mayor "nothing other than an excuse for drugs, sex and liquor."

"We don't like the word 'festival' anymore," said one of the promoters for the Rock Hill Park camp-in that started last night, near Orangeville. "Besides, we have to be careful with what people up here think of it. As soon as they hear the word festival, they balk."

"It's hard to say what's happening," explained John Brower who, after successfully helping to promote both the Toronto Pop Festival and Rock and Roll Revival in 1969 saw his Toronto Peace Festival with John and Yoko Lennon fall apart. Then, this past week the Celebration of Life Festival, near McCrea, Louisiana was shouted down as a ripoff.

The Celebration of Life was to have been the rock culture's extravaganza of the year. But instead of a week of top bands, there were several days of bad planning. The medics on the site claimed to have no facilities, the promoters no money. The festival was the scene of two drownings in the nearby Atchafalaya River bordering the seven-hundred-acre site and one shooting death when a youth got into a scuffle with narcotics officers. "That sense of struggle around rock festivals is sometimes a good thing," explained Melanie last year (she'll be at Stratford this Sunday afternoon). "You have the feeling of working together to overcome something. But it can get a bit too heavy, a bit too much."

Rock, of course, has tried to realign itself. "To be any good," said Roland Paquin, who worked on a free festival in High Park this spring, "a festival has to seem spontaneous. And it should be kept one a smaller scale. The bigger they are the harder they are to handle."

"And that," said Dick Flohil recently, as he was lining up acts for next weekend's Mariposa Folk Festival on Toronto Island, "is one of the reasons we like Mariposa relatively small. It's better for both the performers and the public." Mariposa's organizers were clearly frightened last year when, during several of the evening converts, kids tried to break in for free. This year's three-day event as a consequence won't have evening concerts. Mariposa's success in the past—and probably, in the future—is less due to the vagaries of rock culture than to its own tightly run organization.

"You sense that's what people demand more than ever before," Paul Lane of West Side Promotions, who produced the All Canadian Rock Show two weeks ago today. "Hall owners want to know how something's going to be run. Small club or hall owners, a year or so ago, would rent to anybody. Now, the promoters have to have a good rapport. The owner has to know what his place is going to be left like."

"Our big problem," explained Peter Larsen, of the attractions department in Maple Leaf Gardens, "is with the promoters who don't know what they're doing. They haven't got the money to pay off when there isn't a crowd; they don't know how to keep a band in line. We've had some frightful messes at the Gardens. The day after a concert on May 30 was the messiest the building has ever been. Now, there's no official policy against rock, but I know some of our directors are getting upset."

"In the end," explained a spokesman for the University of Toronto Athletic Association that rents out Varsity Stadium and Varsity Arena," it all depends on who wants our areas. We judge each application separately."

But festivals and rock concerts are mere surface symptoms of something happening deeper inside the entire rock culture. It might have been the deaths of Janis Joplin, or Jimi Hendrix, or the recent Federal Communications Commission's drug-lyrics ban that has resulted in the music industry feeling a slight recession. It might be the fact that the old entrepreneurs like Bill Graham, or Albert Grossman are in semi-retirement, and that newer groups like Mott the Hoople have to resort to old rock to get crowds on their feet. "But," wrote rock critic Albert Goldman in his just-published book, *Freakshow*, "as the ideals and myths that had sustained rock began to crumble, into the gap rushed the banished swarm of parasite producers and wheeler-dealers. In no time rock was computerized into the stalking zombie it is today, lurching along without a thought, a purpose, or a plan beyond that offered by the record rating charts and airline timetables."

For the sound and the scene, at least in pop, are too intertwined for one to improve without the other. The rich hippie, not the musician, is the current idol. And the record companies, not the kids, are determining what's what.

Three years ago, I walked into a little underground paper, and found the place swarming with freaks, but it was a casual, joyful sort of chaos, and things got done. Just a week ago, I walked into another underground pop magazine, and it seemed like the entrance to a mausoleum. A promoter walked in, then out. So did an agent. Then a record company executive. And, in the corners, were piles of the magazine, still unsold.

THE HYPED GENERATION

NOVEMBER 1970
TORONTO TELEGRAM

ONE MORNING LAST SPRING, Paul woke up and found he didn't like himself very much. Worse yet, he didn't know why. With a double-breasted sincerity, he'd outfitted himself with a wife (young, pretty), a super curvy GTO (younger, prettier), an apartment appropriately austere for someone starting in stocks and bonds, and a job. But here he was with his mind buzzing discontent; things weren't connecting. Inside, Paul searched for the frantic fact: *Such a klutz*, he thought, *such a klutz*.

One morning, just this fall, Paul woke up loving everything. Incredible things have happened to him! The car was gone, the wife was going, and the apartment had become a Day-Glo wonder, lush with psychedelia and the appropriate prints. For Paul had found the scene. No, there was none of this artificial hipness for him; I mean. He was dipping into pot, and digging rock, and had long ago cancelled his subscription to *Playboy*. But he was into other things, as well. He had been watching the scene, you understand. He'd seen police clubbing kids. He'd seen moratoriums. He'd abandoned discotheques for rock concerts. His hair was still long—but it was messy-long, not neat-long. He read *The Village Voice*, and *Harbinger*, and *Guerilla*, and the *Whole Earth Catalogue*. He knew the mysteries behind gentle words of love and peace. Paul was in the scene; he could believe the things he's always wanted to believe.

But let's ruin the illusion a bit. Paul, in short, had been hyped dizzy. He's been conned into believing that what he wanted was what he needed. The liberal press had hinted that the old Paul was both doomed and damned ("What have you done for the Panthers?"). All and all, it was easy. Paul could mortify his head, share his white guilt, and sniff at the tracks of a new elite. *These people*, Paul thought of the rest of the scene-makers, *are beautiful. Besides, they're intelligent, they're well-read.*

Hype—the word isn't in any dictionary (although it's probably a diminutive of "hyperbole") not because it's new, or too complex for instant understanding, but because it's essentially meaningless. Ostensibly, it represents the logical outgrowth of advertising: Hype isn't in selling the product (this type of advertising went out as soon as mass media came in), nor is it in making the particular product absolutely necessary (the new styles of ads—"buy this product; buy this way of life.").

No. Hype plays with the truth. It rearranges values. Hype says that this record, this pantsuit, this revolution, this prime minister, really represents what you want; that it (or he) is really an extension of yourself. So, listen, why don't you go out and buy one? Feed your head. Once you could advertise something by implying that it would, somehow, in some vague way make you a better person. You added the product to yourself, like a wristwatch. It became a shield to deflect criticism and at the same time to add status. It kept you safe inside, and other people outside. But the new advertising, hype, realizes one essential and modern fact: We are too close nowadays, psychologically and physically, to hide anything. So don't go after a man's surfaces, go after his insides. Where the old advertising methods may have tried to convert you to the product, hype attempts to convert the product to you. You don't wear long hair just because it might make you more attractive. Now it curls and loops down to the ruffles on your shirt because ... because, why, it is you.

"The Moody Blues' *To Our Children's Children*. Perhaps the greatest musical achievement of the past decade!" Ahh, pop music. Are you going to miss the greatest musical achievement of the past decade? Would anyone? What would happen if you did miss it? Listen. I don't want you to buy this LP just because I'm selling it. Hell, no. It's a great album. In fact, the only reason I'm listening this way, is because I'm a friend. And I know you're into things like this. Dig? This is a great work of art. You can't miss it! So it goes. But no generation has ever been so awash in hype as ours. Anything can be hyped; a message, a president, a revolution, or rock 'n' roll. And we never really notice it—but that's just a clue to its success.

With San Francisco in 1967 we learned that a counterculture was forming, that it wasn't rejecting commerce, but was using it, subverting it. And when you're going to San Francisco, "be sure to wear some flowers in your hair." Thus, flowers, beads, beards, and psychedelic baubles became the key to your psychic consciousness. With the Beatles *Sgt. Pepper* album in the summer of 1967, we were informed that it was a "concept" album. It was an intelligent work of art, not just one of your run-of-the-mill pop beats. Intelligent. So in a current ad for Santana's new LP called *Abraxas*, Columbia Records quotes Herman Hesse's *Demian*. Heavy.

Again, the appeal is to the hidden corner of the listener/buyer's consciousness. This just isn't a piece of music, it's a "reflection of the times." It appeals both to the listener/buyer's ego (he too knows what "the times" are all about) and his—lately developed—social consciousness. ("The times"—yes, revolution, dope, love, peace, etc. etc. etc.) The new hype doesn't appeal to us because we have smelly armpits and would be social meatheads until we sprayed out little troubles away. The hypester comes to us with nirvana in his mouth and the word *revolution* in his copy. The old hip slogans, peace, love, psychedelia, turning on, have been replaced by new ones. *Share the Land* runs the title of the latest Guess Who LP. All of which makes social action and politics the latest hypable commodity. A group that doesn't claim to be "peoples' group," is in for a major problem from radical groups like the May Fourth Movement. But radicalism and the revolutionary stance had found new cachet lately, *Vogue* magazine will use shots of the rads to bolster fashion layouts. General Motors for its Chevy ads carefully emphasizes that "the people wanted changes, so Chevy changed."

Record promotion men, boutique owners, head shop managers, publishers, ad men, and movie executives all know where we live. We are a sensitive generation, oh yeah. Open. Gentle. Peace-loving. And believing. "So what I try to do," says a promotion man for a major movie company, "is to tell kids on campus that this movie is their movie. That it's about them, and since everybody is against them, they had better see this movie." But beneath this, something else is going on: We hear that New York City's young fashionables gave a party for the Black Panthers, an event described by Tom Wolfe as "radical chic." Yes, we see that, and think that the Panthers are finally starting to make it. Our willingness to be hyped just falls a little short of the media's ability to hype us. As Daniel J. Boorstin wrote in his book, *The Image*: "The deeper problems connected with advertising come less from the unscrupulousness of our 'deceivers' than from our pleasure in being deceived; less from the desire to seduce, than from being seduced.... Thus our heroes become more attractive than our lovers or friends." Only Judy Collins, says the ad, "has captured and isolated a fragile moment." Believe it. "The most important music in this country today is coming from Detroit." Believe it; it's "important."

Today's hype no longer communicates a product (we're all too clever for that) nor a context (we all know that drinking Coke won't necessarily make us any more beautiful or free). It communicates what we think is our belief: only Eugene McCarthy can save the country ... only in the Who's rock opera *Tommy* can you find something to satisfy your intellect ... you only make it with bell-bottoms ... part of the revolution ... dig the land ...

I met Paul a couple of days ago and told him I was going to write something on hype. "Listen man," he said, "there are better things you could get into. That's so old. There are new things ..."

2.
THE CRUCIBLE

BLUES

SONNY TERRY & BROWNIE MCGHEE

MARCH 1967
GLOBE AND MAIL

THE BLUES ARE SLOWLY slipping away. The stroboscopic pounding of the Byrds' or Bob Dylan's electric guitars have lacquered the blues with a commercial veneer. But the blues of blind Sonny Terry & Brownie McGhee, who opened their two-week stand at the Riverboat last night was the old backroom, sex and soul brand that evokes that age when American Negro music was suspended at the moment of turning into jazz.

McGhee sang, "I've had my fun with my guitar," and sounded like Jack Teagarden with congested sinuses as he gasped into a hybrid half kazoo, half flugelhorn, and Sonny Terry blew a strangled harmonica wail into the room, they still managed to moan, and shout out the bourbon bitterness of the blues. No vocal inanities of some of Tin Pan Alley's teen troubadours were there to veil the simplicity of the words or the starkness of the ideas as McGhee sang, "I've had my fun—If I don't get no mo'—My health is fallin' me—And I'm goin' down slow, whooooo."

"Ooooh, it's cold up here," McGhee said before the show. "But when you have been doing the same things for thirty years, not many things bother you. We've merely substantiated things we have been doing all this time. We've been playing them longer but liking them better all the time. You could write down and read our music, but you couldn't play it. Not everyone can play the blues. They are a true story, and sometimes I get so involved I break down and cry, but I don't like doing that. But I don't mind the younger singers changing our stuff," he added. "There is no harm in using electric guitars—people have to keep up with time. Our music is for people to use if they know how to use it. They have to follow somebody and I don't mind them following me. But do they understand our rhythm? They might use our musical form for their rhythm and blues, but their content is much different. Things have changed, and the younger kids don't know what it is like to pick cotton or chop corn."

The blues for Sonny Terry and Brownie McGhee is the blues of Lester Melrose, Tampa Red, Big Maceo, Big Bill Broonzy, Washboard Sam, and many others. And for these men who have lived the blues, lived with the blues and sing them, it is not merely an unsophisticated sundae with a rustic funky topping, but a highly developed art form originating from a way of living. As Terry supplies a shrill harmonica obbligato to McGhee's gravelly baritone, it seems as if the blues have had a temporary reprieve.

JULY 1969
TORONTO TELEGRAM

SONNY TERRY & BROWNIE McGHEE, to me, were always the Laurel and Hardy of bluesmen. As their personalities bump together on stage, sparks of music are lit. But, like the two comics, they seem trapped up there in all innocence. Brownie leans back, eyes shut, the hardening muscularity of his style barely concealing the softness beneath. Blind Sonny, as he jokes guilelessly, nevertheless reveals the toughness of his will.

It was still like that at the Riverboat last night where they started another two-week stint. Their personalities blend as one sings harmony over the other, then clash, as Sonny's babylike wailing on the harmonica, jabs across Brownie's soft, deft guitar chords. The one acting as a foil for the other, then acting as a crutch. Together, they still keep trying to re-distill an essence of their music, an essence now muddied. What is it, then, that makes things go so much smoother? What accounts for the almost jubilant nature of their playing? Rather than slipping into the uniformity most audiences expect, there seems to be a deliberate loosening of personalities now. Too often they've been typed as some protean embodiment of some collective nerve—of *all* Negroes, of *all* the blues experience, of *all* the suffering. They sing: "The Blues. Mommy had 'em and daddy had 'em too. The rocks have been my pillow and a hollow log my bed. I've been living with the blues and I ain't ashamed. Now ain't that news." Writers from Norman Mailer to James Baldwin have seen in this hardship and ennobling suffering. Bashed and belittled, they say the blacks sing the blues as a purge for their misery. Now, ain't that news?

For as Sonny and Brownie started the now famous "Rock Island Line," it became a little secular sermon on the poetry of rhythm. It was a folksy, funky kind of music. The metre, pulsed by hidden motors, drove the lyric ahead of it.

"Ohhhh ... the Rock Island Line," Sonny would sing, then gasp in a breath through the harmonica. "It's a mighty fine line," Brownie would answer. The tempo accelerated almost beyond their reach; the harp waiting like it was lost, the guitar chasing chord changes, pushing everything faster. In the quality of their self-respect, in the sense of deserved joy, Brownie and Sonny made out of this song a miniature anthem, brimming with life. This partly explains their openness in singing: The thirty years they've been together have taken them from wandering the streets of New York, playing for nickels until, recently, a stint at commercial making for Alka-Seltzer, for which each got $25,000 for one minute's airtime on radio and TV.

But perhaps there's something else, a sense of successful self-preservation. Sonny, born in Durham, North Carolina, lost his sight at sixteen. Still, he had to pick cotton and plough. And Brownie, too, after being lamed by polio as a kid, had to hustle in any way he could. Perhaps the quality of their blues were blue then. Gradually, however, the blues for both became more a frame of reference than a frame of mind. And last night they could celebrate, dignity, joy, kicks, and some jive, a self-preservation now complete. For most of us, having only to battle downtown traffic, self-preservation begins to smell of formaldehyde. It's becoming an academic matter. For Sonny and Brownie, it has unleashed a magic that can't be felt by most of us and understood by even fewer. It can only be listened to.

JUNIOR WELLS

MARCH 1967
GLOBE AND MAIL

AS IF IT WAS his last contact with reality, Junior Wells clutched the microphone and sent his voice wailing above the sluggish, droning blues of the band behind him. After a three-day delay in Chicago (car trouble he called it) singer Wells and his Chicago Blues Band started what was left of a two-week engagement at the Riverboat at the weekend with a head-back, yelling, frenetic type of South side Chicago blues.

It was like this: Tom Crawford's bass would send the vibrations shuddering along the floor, Wells would stop singing and gasp through his dented harmonica like a strangling child. Lefty Dizz's electric guitar would splutter a flurry of nervous squeaks, and the blues would come through in ultrasonic Technicolor. Although the sidemen in his band change from job to job, Wells brings to the Riverboat a larger group than usually performs with him. Yet the addition of a tenor sax (Doug Fagen) and another singer (Woody Williams) to the nucleus of bass, lead guitar and drums (Levi Warren) does not—could not—detract from Wells's presence on stage. His singing did more than create excitement; it was excitement. He didn't merely sing the blues, he committed them. And the yelps, vocal glissandos, and moans with which he punctuated each otherwise lugubrious four-bar blues changes meant at the climax it was difficult to tell the singer from the song.

With Wells the Riverboat, in its own non-licensed way, became a descendant of the long line of blues and gin joints—from Memphis in the 1920s and New Orleans in the 1930s to the Apollo Theater in New York in the sixties—where rhythm and blues is the funk folk music of the urban underground. Some of the blues he sang were standards (Ray Charles's "What'd I Say"), some Junior Wells ("Tribute to Sonny Boy") and some new. Yet all were of a genre, too repetitious and far too earthy for the Beatles-brainwashed, high school hippies, with transistors plugged into their skulls.

BUDDY GUY

JULY 1967
GLOBE AND MAIL

WHILE TORONTONIANS STROLLED IN the evening quiet of Avenue Road this week, around the corner at the Riverboat Buddy Guy's Chicago Blues Band was singing, wailing, and moaning the down-and-out music of the Negro outcast, the blues. The band, opening a week's stay, is in Junior Wells, rock-hard Chicago blues tradition. That city's ghetto culture acted as a crucible for a style rather than for individuals, and Guy, while not being radically different from other bluesmen, is intense, flamboyant, and diverse. His blues singing shows the split personality of the genre. The saddest numbers revealed a kind of rueful smile while the bright ones were tinged with melancholy. Yet the simplicity of the material belied the artistry of the performance, for listening to what Guy does to each simple, twelve-bar blues tune is like looking at a cubist portrait of your next-of-kin.

He is typical of many not-so-young—he's thirty-one—blues-oriented Negro artists today. "I can play whatever I'm told to," he said, "and I've done jazz and rock as well as the blues. But I like watching people dance to my music. It seems more a part of me than any other type." Yet the unusual mixture of his Louisiana-born earthiness and his desire for conventional respectability jostles uneasily in the singer-guitar player. "Critics expect blues players to be drunks. They think that it is an inferior form of music. Well, I've got a beautiful home that I earned from my career and if I can go this far playing the music I want to, I will just keep on doing it."

While the blues are the indigenous folk music of America, few serious classical composers have shown that they recognize its potentialities. Part of the trouble lies with the material itself. For the blues are in a continual state of becoming; the bluesman never really finishes a number, he merely leaves it for someone else. Because the basis of the blues is improvisation, serious, jazz-influenced compositions (Aaron Copland's *Piano Concerto*, for example) or the pseudo-classical works of [Duke] Ellington are stilted when compared with their origins.

After hearing the bawdy blues lyrics censured by critics who confuse morality with art, and seeing its simplicity overshadowed by modern pop music incubated in recording studios, I found the happy ham-fisted forcefulness of Buddy Guy's blues like a breath of fresh air in a musical world characterized by brute skill.

JAMES COTTON

SEPTEMBER 1967
GLOBE AND MAIL

JAMES COTTON, who opened a week's stay at the Riverboat last night, articulated his artistic experience through the medium of electric guitars, a raucous, pulsating beat and frenetic blues singing. There was little of the impotent cynicism and skepticism of many of the young white singers in Cotton's music. Artistically secure, he portrayed the clown, a Don Quixote riding across a neon-lighted jungle, mocking its foibles, singing of its common human affiliations.

His musical aesthetic is simple: "We try not to sound like any other band. We're loud, bold and brassy; we play blues, rock, and jazz; but it always sounds like us." And what a deafening blare it was! The eruptive solos taken by the other members of his Chicago Blues Band blurred the singer's voice; the jagged, rhythmic patterns laid down by drummer Francis Clay all but obliterated the sound of the electric piano.

The band seemed to strive for a final climax. Each song, such as "Somebody Gotta Go," "My Baby," "You Know That I Love You," grew from a sheer outpouring of noise to constant instrumental fireworks. There was little subtlety, little alternation in mood between the various songs, and even less variation from one constant, pulsing tempo.

Although Cotton is from the same Chicago environment that produced two recent Toronto performers, Junior Wells and Buddy Guy, his style is radically different than theirs. But while he hasn't Wells's emotional or vocal power, nor Guy's showmanship, his music comes from similar roots. "I was born with the blues," he says, "I've missed meals, been broke, had my women leave me, and been forced to leave my home. I don't know what else I could do if I didn't sing the blues."

For the thirty-three-year-old Cotton, blues singing seems less of a financial consideration than an artistic compulsion. To hear him is to be moved by the importance of this feeling to him.

THE PAUL BUTTERFIELD BLUES BAND

NOVEMBER 1967
GLOBE AND MAIL

THEY'RE YOUNG; their leader is a lawyer's son; they play the blues in a way that would cause coronaries among blues purists. Yet the Paul Butterfield Blues Band, at Massey Hall last night, produced in their music what traditional blues lovers claim a white band can't: a natural excitement, unity, and prolonged inventiveness.

The Butterfield band's performance was (no other word fits) fantastic in idea and execution. Their guitar sound churned the air like giant eggbeaters. They cut through preconceptions of what the new blues should be; and, more pertinently, they involved the listener directly in the experience of each number. Although they tended to be brutal at their loudest, their music was constantly controlled, expertly executed, and precise in attack. At their softest, the sound was stark and bleakly emotionless. So great was the moderately sized audience's response that the octet (two saxes, trumpet, drums, bass, guitar, organ, and Butterfield's harmonica) seemed to play the crowd as well as their instruments. After each number, the roar of the audience filled in the spaces left by the notes.

Until the mid-fifties, the blues were played mostly by Negros. But the arrival of Elvis Presley, whose style was based on that of bluesman Arthur Crudup, changed that. The blues, if not yet acceptable, were profitable. Bob Dylan began to cultivate blues chord changes. The Beatles learned from singer Chuck Berry.

Butterfield served his five-year apprenticeship in Chicago's East Side well. His blues resembled the traditional form in its external features: twelve-bar songs with three-bar refrains, and lyrics extolling the hardships of travelling, loneliness, and ghetto life—all eternal variations on a scream. But Butterfield's scream was not unmusical. Through his razor-edge voice, sounds and emotions interacted. His singing was suffused with the same defiance first heralded in the 1920s by the wordless revolt of jazzmen's trumpets.

If any young blues band can blend the shrieks and groans of the all-electric rock 'n' roll era with the blues, can break modern popular music away from the seductions of the mass market, and can create art for juke boxes, it will be the Butterfield Blues Band.

B. B. KING

FEBRUARY 1969
TORONTO TELEGRAM

"SHO, SHO. HE'LL BE HERE—don't you fret now."

The boys in the band! Cool as always. But out front Kingston's Palace Theatre was packed. Haunch to paunch, kids were gaping into the open maw of the stage. But … okay, okay … "play it cool. He'll show." Still, you wonder, how strange. How did these kids know? When did they hear about him in this grey, sloping, almost-city. Outside there is a sullen darkness, trees hanging over the snow like some apathetic fate. But tucked away inside, between plywood renovations, the kids' doldrum fury can almost be felt.

By now the anticipation had distilled into impatience. A little band, Sonny Freeman and the Unusuals, riff aimlessly. Waiting. One of them walks casually to the mic. Suddenly: "It's show time, ladieees and gentlemen. And here's the star of the show, the KING OF THE BLUES … Mr. B. B. … KING!!!!" And there, green three-buttoned suit, arms outstretched in the big-beat benediction ("the black Messiah," someone whispers backstage. "Careful; careful," says the writer), there, palms inward towards his breast gathering the good news, eyes disappearing in a smile, there waited B. B.

"A coup de theatre," B. B. sang, his voice as tightly resonant as a guitar string. A slow sad song: "Every day I have the blues." Slightly pudgy, he moves sparingly; hands are used for rhetorical purposes, the commas and periods off each lyric. "Evra, evra day I got the blues"; and everything fell into place like one of Mondrian's geometrical designs. But B. B. is much larger than this. On the stage, this bleak, chilling night, he *exists*, in actual being, as no character of the imagination can possibly exist. Stereotypes have to fall—the watcher only chills the heat of B. B.'s life into cold ink.

Underground radio (from Toronto, where B. B. will appear at Massey Hall February 14) had coughed up some information: B. B. King was boss, *the* man of the blues. Otis Redding? Junior Wells? Mere disciples! B. B. with Lucille, his guitar, was one of the wellsprings of the blues; his history had been the blues' history, his suffering their suffering. To some he had risen as Martin Luther King's foil. When the preacher improvised at the end of a sermon, "Let freedom ring..." the singer would cuddle and caress Lucille, coazing her for one note more, one note higher. "I have a dream," Martin Luther would exhort, "that someday..." And on stage at the Regal in Chicago, or in Montgomery Elks Club, Southern Pride Lodge, the other King, B. B., would give them that day—in one racking, cathartic, NOW. Saturday night, and Sunday morning, the secular and the sacred had been in dichotomies in the Negro's life. And the two Kings had come to life. And the two Kings had to come to stand at either pole; the one dying into history, the other living out of it.

"I'm sorry I'm so late," he explains, the band was playing softly behind. "But I was slowed down at the border." People are relaxing. Skillfully they have been warmed, enticed into B. B.'s atmosphere. (Later he says: "If you're the least bit willing, a good hypnotist can put you under in no time.") He goes on: "But here we are anyway... and, if you let us, we'll give you the blues."

The blues. To the northern white, this is the music of sorrow, sadness, and despair. And jazz and blues writers keep re-creating this attitude. Like a self-torturing Prometheus, says Eric Larrabee, the blues delve "inward in sorrow and sinfulness." "The blues," says Leonard Feather, "... sprang from troubled minds ... reflected anxiety, depression." And to Paul Oliver, when singing the blues: "the Negro gives form to the blues of his experience."

"The blues," says B. B. flatly, "aren't sad. They're about experiences, places I've been to, the women, the jobs, everything about my life." All about him is in a swirl; Elmore Morris, his entr'acte singer for the last eleven years, preens himself before a mirror; the band sits quietly puffing away on expensive thin cigars, listening to Schubert on B. B.'s tape-cassette. "Everything about my life," he goes on, "has taken a long time. It's been hard, and slow." From the Mississippi Delta to the pages of *Time*, and the *New York Times*.

Born Riley B. King in Itta Bena, Mississippi, B. B. King had to quit school after Grade 9. In the trembling heat and the wild, wide-open fields he used to pick cotton, eventually being allowed to drive tractors. "You ever seen those planes, the Blue Angels, that fly in formation? We used to plough that way. Eight tractors churning up dirt in formation." How many times had he told this story before? The story of being drafted, then deferred, because he was needed to plough; of singing in churches, in a gospel quartet; of going on a bus to Jackson, Oxford, or Hattiesburg to play blues on the street corners, to listen to other bluesmen?

"After the war, I went to Memphis and lived with Bukka White, my cousin." From there came a chance at a brief spot on WDIA, advertising Pepticon tonic and playing tunes that by 1949 were selling on the Chitlin' Circuit. Songs like "Three O'Clock Blues," "Rock Me Baby," "You Know I Love You." It almost stopped there. "I worked so hard, man. Whoooooo! In 1958, I did 342 one-nighters, but things weren't looking good. I felt sad because of all the years I had put into it. I was forgotten, by the press, by the mass of people. But I was playing to a black audience... and they didn't have much money."

"How can we make a movement to preserve ourselves," wrote Proust, "... in the need of having our sufferings appeased by whatever has made us suffer?" The insularity of this Southern "Chitlin' Circuit" is frightening. Some never leave, but play to the same people, the same way, every year. And in the early '60s the rhythm and revolution of the Top 40 stations pushed the heads of those emerging blues singers underground even further. B. B.'s records were selling for $1.99 in supermarkets and "we shall overcome" had become a middle-class sentiment. "Just being a blues singer was hard," he says. "You know the role, illiterate, wife-slugging bums." But some were listening. Suddenly one day, a new English group, the Rolling Stones, were playing Muddy Waters and Bukka White. And the Beatles were on to Chuck Berry. But not to B. B. King. A second revolution was needed. Pop music was still skittering in old directions, bubbling gaily along the surface. "White bluesman like Paul Butterfield I always will be grateful to. They've opened doors, and, more important, they've always acknowledged where they got their songs from."

Doors were open, but not enough. It was almost as if the purveyors of pop felt that the emerging blues would sing rock's requiem. But when the revolution came, it was from Chicago, and Detroit and New York, from the scathing cultural implosion of the Negro ghettos, from the arrival on the scene of the young rhythm 'n' blues blacks, their music diamond-hard, electrifying, and loud, much too loud to be ignored.

B. B. leans back and thinks of this. Bluesman Buddy Guy has come backstage, but sits quietly by, his suit crumpled after a long ride from Toronto, his hands nervous after the impromptu session onstage with King. For the first time, B. B.'s quiet; he doesn't talk about the time his second wife left him, her memory now sublimated into his songs; or his grandchildren, or the money he owes.

This is deep stuff, the blues. But almost overnight, six months ago, it seemed, there was B. B. King. Although he's no relation to Albert King, another known blues guitarist, B. B. was suddenly known, recognized, respected. In the same breath as John Coltrane, Jimmy Smith, or Ray Charles, people were talking about him, incredible. "Yet... well, I know one thing," he says. "If it wasn't for the younger cats like Buddy here, B. B. wouldn't be known." As close as he can come, Buddy blushes: "Listen. If it wasn't for B. B., we younger guys"—Buddy's thirty—"wouldn't be here."

And B. B. ponders some more, searching for another answer to a twenty-year-long "overnight" success! "The years I've spent." Flickerings of memory churn. Remembering. "I travel about eighty thousand miles a year, and in the last twenty-one years, I've had only two months' holidays. There have been days off, sure, but only twice have I ever had a vacation. It's the hard work that's made it for me. That, and never letting anything worry me. You've got to stay on top of the blues, and never, never get submerged in them. Hotel and motel rooms are my home, I do my business out of this (patting an expensive attaché case). But I listen a lot to everything—classical, rock, and jazz. I'm reading the Schillinger book so that I can arrange my own material... [this work being one of the more abstruse works on mathematical concepts in music]... and I keep learning. A lot of people claim that the modern guitarists came from me. Well, that might just be. But it's all part of one process; I picked up things from Lonnie Johnson, T-Bone Walker and Elmore James."

These with singers like Sammy McCrary of the old Fairfield Four, and Blind Lemon Jefferson, Bumble Bee Smith, Leroy Carr, Tommy McClennan, Tampa Red, Gene Autry, and Peetie Wheatstraw all have found niches in B. B.'s style. And the French guitarist, Django Reinhardt. "And little Charlie Christian, too. But Django's the man who stole my soul." These men form much of his own twenty-thousand record collection.

"I started collecting when I was a deejay down south. But then we didn't have the distinctions we have now. Then, rock, the blues and what you now call rhythm 'n' blues was all 'race music.' When I started playing, we were into everything. I once had a big band—I hope to get another—and was great! That big sound. In a small group, especially like this band, who have been with me a long time, you can play something that is almost jazz. But with more sidemen, it's got to be stricter and straighter. The twelve-bar blues."

Now, there is no let-up, no sign of tiredness. "I'll be forty-four next September. And have been playing the guitar since I was fourteen—"

"Hey, Sonny says you is only forty-two," Cato, his driver, and valet cuts in.

B. B. looks up: "Well, Sonny's being kind, he musta slept a year or so. And I own an apartment building back home. But I've gotta keep travelling."

Abruptly he stands up. Intermission's over, and B. B. has to struggle into a new suit. Hair sleeked down with Ultra Sheen, he smiles benevolently on all, as everybody seems to move in concentric circles around him.

There will be a party after, but there's this chick in Detroit... onstage, this will all be forgotten. "Now... ladies and gentlemen, B. B. KING! He doesn't have the down-and-out grittiness of Muddy Waters, or Buddy Guy's virtuosity, but he goes past all that.

"Ah bought you a ten-dollar dinner,

You said, 'Thanks for the snack.'

I let you live in my penthouse

You said it was just a shack.

I gave you seven children"

(And B. B.'s hand goes *plop* on his hip. He wiggles slightly from the waist:)

"An' now you wanna give 'em back."

And it shakes you up, out of the cozy suet of your life. You think about it on the way to Toronto, in Buddy Guy's bus. Sometime later that night B. B. will go past on his way to Detroit. The city lights of Kingston at night are receding, like these words, each containing its own world. And remembering B. B. telling the crowd, at the end, as perspiration dropped to their applause: "I'll be back. I'll be here—don't fret now."

MUDDY WATERS

1971
TORONTO TELEGRAM

WHEN BLUESMAN MUDDY WATERS first came to town a couple of years ago, it was somehow a point in your favour if you knew that his real name was McKinley Morganfield. That's all that was really necessary. His style then—as it is now, at the Colonial where he'll be all this week—was tough, menacing, almost forbidding: His slithery guitar-playing and gruff singing generated a sultry atmosphere, like the calm heat before a hurricane. And maybe you didn't like him. But you had to hear him.

"Hey, now don't you worry about that!" Muddy said last night. "I've been doin' these blues for almost thirty-five years now. I've been doing them pretty much the same."

Watching his little band warm up the crowd for him to come on, he sighted down the length of his cigar: "The only problem I've got is with my crutches. Had an accident that broke my hip last October. Guy swerved into me, killed himself, his girlfriend, and my driver. And liked to have killed me, too." So now, Muddy has to hobble up on stage to play it tough. He sits in a chair perched precariously close to the edge of the stage. With a high forehead, he seems to be glowering all the time, a looming, black figure, hunched up over his guitar, only barely noticing the taut, punchy sounds the quintet behind him is making.

Somehow all of this makes him irresistible. And the band only helps the impression. Paul Oscher on harmonica—the only white kid in the band—can be superb without taking off his sunglasses. And with drummer Willie Smith and bassist Sonny Wilber laying down a rock-hard foundation Oscher, with pianist Pine Top and Pee Wee Madison on guitar, can create a performing group as good as any in the blues.

Waters is one of these too-rare performers who can build fine bands around him and develop each performer as a soloist. The only hope for the opposition is to imitate him. And, when in 1962 the only "opposition" in pop music to the blues were the emerging English rock bands, that's exactly what happened. In fact, the Rolling Stones took their name from the title of an early Muddy Waters album. By 1968, after having borrowed songs, titles, techniques, and slang from Muddy Waters, the so-called white blues musicians started to admit their debt. That year, he appeared at all the chic rock clubs in New York City, establishing where his sound had come from in the first place—from the Mississippi Delta country by way of Chicago, where he'd sung to the Mississippians who had migrated there for something better and didn't really find it. After that year, Waters, now in his fifties, began to work all the harder. The pace was telling. His sound started getting lax, bottom-heavy, and boring.

But good things can happen in reverse. And by the time the "blues boom" in pop music was over, when the heavy, urbanized rhythms were replaced by softer country music and musicians like The Band, the pressure seemed to lift from the blues performers themselves. And last night Waters's band was as free and swinging as it has ever been. From Waters's "Hootchie Cootchie Man," to his "Got My Mojo Working," the music was nicely sour, primitive, out of tune, honest, and brimming with good times.

FIFTIES FOOTSTEPS

FATS DOMINO

MAY 1967
GLOBE AND MAIL

AFTER TWENTY YEARS OF nightclub appearances, TV shows, and movies and no fewer than nineteen gold records, the only thing corpulent about Antoine "Fats" Domino, who winds up a week at the Embassy tonight, is his wallet. In the mirrored telephone booth the club calls a dressing room, surrounded by his wardrobe manager, road manager, waiters, New York agent, and members of his band, Domino this week discussed his recent demise as an adolescent musical idol.

"I haven't changed much in the past years; people have tried to change my style, but I can't sing like anyone else, I'm too much me. One time every singer was following me, but things have changed. The Beatles, and new interest in rhythm and blues have come along. But even they have not bothered me much."

Fats Domino reached his peak popularity between 1952 and 1958 when pop music was at its comic-strip, honking, self-pitying best. But with payola, Dick Clark's *American Bandstand* and the adolescent inanities of Fabian and Frankie Avalon, rock 'n' roll pushed itself to self-annihilation. Since nothing exceeds like excess, only two singers of that era—Bo Diddley and Ray Charles—have managed to retain some of their popularity. And while Domino is in some ways like both of them (all three are Negro, and all three have a style born of jazz), he has remained where he was, imbedded in the denouement of New Orleans' hybrid hot jazz, and so in that background.

His nine-piece New Orleans Band (brass, reeds, guitar, bass and drums) produces a boisterous, raw sound in which the beat takes over precedence over subtlety. Having travelled with the singer for several years (the tenor sax man has been with Domino for twenty years), the group's approach to a set is casual to the point of extroverted sloppiness. Domino's piano-playing is deceptively simple. With the fastest right hand this side of Horowitz's practice studio, he elaborates a filagree of notes over the left hand's repetitious boogie-woogie bass. Each song follows another at a breathless pace; he manages to squeeze into each set about twenty numbers, most of which are his own. And at the beginning of each set, the Embassy would turn into a vast tap-, clap-, shout-, and sing-along. Everyone knew the tunes, for they represented a synopsis of pop music history in the fifties. As one patron breathed into my ear, "The Beatles and the other groups sound good until you're eighteen; when you're out working you don't like that childish stuff."

Childish stuff? Domino was in Toronto several times during the mid-fifties to headline rock 'n' roll extravaganzas at—where else—Maple Leaf Gardens. Then, it was his soft, husky voice that turned on the sideburned, blue-jeaned teenagers. And this week, ten years later, they came back in droves to the Embassy like so many pot-bellied ghosts to haunt what was left of their adolescence.

Although he hasn't released many records in the past few years—his last hit was "Whole Lot of Lovin'" in the early sixties—Domino has amassed nineteen gold records. Yet from his first recording, "The Fat Man" (1949) to "Goin' to the River" (1953), "I'm Walkin'" (1957), or “I’m Going to Be a Wheel Some Day” (1958) it wasn’t the singer who progressed but recording techniques.

A hybrid of jazz, blues, ragtime and rock, Domino’s music is a remnant of the type played in the old Storyville section of New Orleans where ragtime piano playing was commonplace before the turn of the century. But he epitomizes that age when rock ’n’ roll was simple, and unpretentious, when Rodgers and Hammerstein, not Lennon and McCartney, were sung, when rock ’n’ roll was a cute teenage toy, with none of the air of impotent and static rage it has today.

Fats Domino is getting old. At thirty-nine, with eight children, he is a superannuated pop hero; his records are not selling well and the kids are no longer screaming at and for him. But when he was performing at the Embassy this week, nobody walked out on him.

JERRY LEE LEWIS

OCTOBER 1967
GLOBE AND MAIL

AFTER SIX YEARS' ABSENCE, rockabilly pianist Jerry Lee Lewis is performing in Toronto for two weeks at the Embassy. Perhaps performing isn't the correct word. You don't listen to Lewis; you experience him. Most of his songs—"Just Because," "Great Balls of Fire"—are technical fireworks displays in which musical logic is burned in effigy. A holdover from the Elvis Presley era, he has all Presley's fury and too little of his sound. Too often he slobbered upon the audience an exhibitionism so debauched that an admiration for shamelessness was inspired.

Yet throughout a likeable personality was evident. If his piano pounding is any measure, Lewis is not unlike the typical movie villain of the 1940s: roaring, bellowing, ebullient, suddenly depressed, then overly loud, overbearing, suddenly demure, only to bellow out a song once more. Such was his gamut. With his younger sister, Linda Gail Lewis, whose nasal backwater voice made even the electric guitars sound pleasant by comparison, Lewis caused the sound of rock 'n' roll to sound silly.

For if you consider Bob Dylan to be the Dostoevsky of popular music and the Beatles the James Joyce, then Lewis is its Edward Lear; incomprehensible, apparently slightly mad, yet likeable beneath all the insanity.

JAMES BROWN

NOVEMBER 1967
GLOBE AND MAIL

A FEW SHOUTED IN DISGUST, "Hey, man, you can't sing!" Some left. But the majority of the four thousand persons stayed to ogle the Maple Leaf Gardens' stage last night as rhythm 'n' blues singer James Brown filled the atmosphere with his own brand of musical aphrodisiac.

Brown was many things at once: irreverent, savage, assured, audacious, and constantly filled with a whirlwind vitality. Never profound, his singing was often outrageous in conception and maniacal in performance. But any lack of invention in the music or in the range of mood was obliterated by Brown's dynamic sense of showmanship. In the din created by his fourteen-piece band, the Fabulous Flames, his shouted lyrics were as incomprehensible as vaudevillian double-talk. It was like listening in on a conversation at the next table which one could almost hear, but not quite decipher. Not being able to hear, much less think correctly, one's attention became riveted to the contorting figure of Brown. This, I suspect, was exactly what he planned.

If beneath his sleazy, fat-cat smile there was the mind of an artist, it was well hidden. Brown was a showman first; a musician a distant second. He concluded every song by pulling out all the vocal and choreographic stops in his arsenal. He screamed, groaned, and bounced rhythmically across the stage. With assorted bumps and grinds in between, he leapt over and around the microphone with a speed that would have made the Bolshoi Ballet envious. All of which, when he was finished, left listeners limp, emotionally drained, and sighing a mixture of relief and satisfaction. His appearances on stage were calculated to increase the emotional level of the evening. Each entrance, after the stints of his revue (singers Bobby Byrd and Vicki Anderson) introduced a more frantic performance from the star.

It was a combination of empathy and disgust, compounded with curiosity and genuine interest, that created his popularity. Brown was a figure of extremes; but one shade dominated, and, it seemed, lay at the core of his communicative power—emotionalism. This feature of his act has become a sore thumb among blues lovers. It is an element in every bluesman's singing; but in Brown's case it was annoyingly in the foreground. And the vital sense of proportion between the emotion and the meaning in his music was replaced by a raucous instrumental and verbal effusiveness.

The current popular Detroit sound of the Supremes is soft-spoken, refined, and polished by comparison. But Brown represented the blues in the raw. The only relief he offered was a wholesome bawdiness and humorous self-mockery. Whereas white rockers sing of alienation, Brown's constant subject was the armed truce between the sexes. In its gospel fervour, its emphasis on action, disrobing, and pleading, his singing was mainly directed to women.

But this was to be expected. In pop music there is nothing so rare as the normal. Brown's method is always bizarre, heightened and spotlighted by his emotions, driven by the intensity of the blues. And the fact that the mere mention of the name James Brown will produce smiles and nervous twitches on musicians is no surprise. As he did last night, Brown brings a strange type of madness to a kind of music made stodgy by others' seriousness.

RONNIE HAWKINS

OCTOBER 1970
TORONTO TELEGRAM

RONNIE HAWKINS IS A singer so earthy, so raucous, so hilarious in every action, that his show at Le Coq d'Or that started a two-week run last night passed through being merely fun, through being funny, through being fantastic and everything else, and became an invitation to wonder where he's been all these years. The answer to this is simple: He's been living near Streetsville, languishing in exile after his last Toronto performance, again at Le Coq d'Or in May 1969 after he and the club's young manager, Bill Bulucon, had a falling out. Perhaps he'd be there still. But there's a certain pull Yonge Street has for Rompin' Ronnie—its giddy ribaldry matches his own—and it is inevitable he should return. And return he did. With style.

For a Hawkins show is less of a musical performance than a free-for-all. And before he was through last night, he'd blown almost all the fuses for his equipment; he'd invited various girls from the audience to dance go-go on stage; had led his latest band, the Fayetteville University Collegiate Clan, through a series of old rock hits; and he'd introduced a truly fantastic new girl singer, B. J. Cook. It was, as he said, and not altogether seriously, "One of the weirdest Monday nights in history. Man, oh, man we have gone through just a little bit of everything."

Yes sir. It was just like the good old days when Ronnie, riding on a wave of hit records like "Forty Days" and "Bo Diddley" back in the early 1960s, would breeze into town all shiny and slick. Back then, things were slightly different. He wasn't wearing the fringes, and leather, and the extra thirty pounds he had on last night. But these changes were minimal. His backup bands have always been good—remember it was Ronnie's old group, then called the Hawks, who later became The Band.

"But, man, to get the group I've got now," he said, "I auditioned thousands of kids, just thousands." To get the band he's got now, he had to drop his last group, now called Crowbar, and go out west to find just the light, country-oriented touch he wanted. And pianist David Foster, organist Dwayne Ford, drummer Brian Hilton, bassist Steve Pugsley, and guitarist Hugh Brockie fill the bill ideally. And in getting the new group, he ended up with a new girl singer, B. J. Cook. Now "twenty-eight going on twenty-three," she's had a long trip to get to Hawkins. She played with several hometown bands in Victoria, and even put a month in with Spanky and Our Gang. But now, all that's behind, and, as she says, "Ronnie's the key to everything."

In the past, Ronnie's been the key to a lot of things. When John and Yoko Lennon arrived in Toronto last December to promote their abortive Peace Festival, they were Ronnie's guests on his farm. And as they would plan a worldwide series of events, he'd still be answering the phone as "the world's oldest rock 'n' roll star."

Then, of course, there's the members of Hawkins's old groups who've gone out and staked a name for themselves. A couple of members of the late Janis Joplin's backing group are examples, as are King Biscuit Boy, Tobi Lark, Jay Smith, and Fred Carter Jr. Ronnie's own career in the last year or so, on the other hand, has had its ups and downs. For a while, after an article in *Rolling Stone* resulted in a recording contract with Atlantic Records, Hawkins's career seemed to be on the up. But the album that resulted from this partnership was a bit too subdued for him and, not to help matters any, it wasn't promoted enough.

But after last night, it's becoming more and more apparent that even with Atlantic renewing his option for one more year, even with the new album coming out shortly, Ronnie's not a part of the current rock world. For Ronnie's half creator of his own myth. He sprints across old rock 'n' roll turf—doing old things like Chuck Berry's "Maybellene" and new things that sound old, like Delaney & Bonnie's "I Don't Want to Discuss It." And all this is sung with a half-regenerating velocity. His milieu is not the rock emporiums like the Fillmore East, but little clubs like Le Coq d'Or. His satisfaction comes, I suspect, less from singing to a crowd, than singing with a crowd.

He's an anachronism—but one we need desperately. He does things for sheer zeal of doing them. He understands rock to its very core and, because of this, he understands our reactions to it to the very core. Things, you see, can be simple, "We're going to take a short break," he said sometime late last night. "And we're going to learn a few more tunes. So keep drinkin'. And don't go away—we need the business."

BO DIDDLEY

NOVEMBER 1970
TORONTO TELEGRAM

NORMALLY, you probably wouldn't notice Ellas McDaniel on the street. He is getting thicker about the waist as he approaches middle age. The thick-rimmed glasses he wears make him look rather bookish. And all in all, he wears his sense of cool well. But on the stage at Le Coq d'Or, where he's better known and remembered as Bo Diddley, it's an entirely different story. Up there, Bo smiles his sleepy fat-cat smile; shakes his hips just so; giggles at his woman, Cookie, beside him; and then lets loose a reverberating *thwack* on his electric guitar.

Bo Diddley is an original. In the past fifteen or so years he's been cutting records which every young guitar player worth his A-string has copied. His style, with its strong repetitive rhythms, one-chord songs that may last twenty minutes, blends with his ability to make very little go a long way. And compared to other black guitarists whose music comes from the blues, Bo Diddley is an anomaly. "It is recognized that singers like Chuck Berry, Fats Domino, and

Bo Diddley can be called blues singers," writes Charles Keil, in his book *The Urban Blues*, "but they are really showmen first and bluesmen second. Their appeal rests primarily on novelty songs, catchy lyrics, and visual appeal."

In the early fifties, before rock was anything more than what Frank Sinatra called "the martial music for every long-haired delinquent," Bo Diddley had already achieved some small measure of fame. Bo Diddley was playing all the major blues clubs—like the Apollo in New York City—before white DJs like Alan Freed started playing black music for the larger—that is, white—audience. And take one look at his past LPs and see how readily he caught the nearest way. It was *Bo Diddley's a Twister*, in the middle of the twist craze; and *Surfin' with Bo Diddley*, and *Bo Diddley's Beach Party* during the California-included surfin' sand craze; and it was the Super Super Blues Band when the English rock groups had suddenly made the blues respectable again. So, while it looked like old home night at Le Coq d'Or, with Ronnie Hawkins dropping in to urge Bo on, it wasn't surprising that Bo Diddley was involved in something new.

For, gone is the punchy little rhythm 'n' blues band that used to back him up, and in its place is an all-white quartet, with psychedelia on their souls and all the latest tricks in their fingers. When the music was getting a bit thin and it was getting late, Diddley and Cookie started into a song. "Shut Up Woman," that woke the nerve endings up. It was a mean little nagging song, with the man and woman exchanging insults; and it built, dramatically as well as musically into the best thing of the evening.

LITTLE RICHARD

JANUARY 1971
TORONTO TELEGRAM

"I'M THE KING," he would yell, "the king." And, indeed, Little Richard (Penniman) is probably the only rock musician who is what he says he is. His voice zooming to a screaming high falsetto at the end of a song, has been instantly recognizable since the mid-fifties. It is a sound that is neither black nor white, but which stamps his songs with a feverish, erotic energy.

Richard took the Beatles on tour with him once, and each of them started to reiterate his mannerisms. Jimi Hendrix played with him before the late guitarist went to England and made his break. It was Richard's ego that suppressed Hendrix—the same ego that caused Richard to duel with Dick Cavett's ego, telling the TV host to "shut up." But behind all this has been Richard's awareness that without him, rock wouldn't be the same.

And now, suffering from cancer of the intestines, he's making sure that rock won't forget him. He's on a tour that might bring him to the Fillmore Market (at Jarvis and Front) this Friday night. In between his live appearances, he's writing songs and recording with various groups to spread the word—the word, in this case, being a fiery amalgam of rock and religion. (He retired from rock for four years in the early 1960s to study theology.) Richard's already completed an LP with Jefferson Airplane, called *Bludgeon Of The Blue Coats*, to be released in the U.S. in four weeks, and one with Mylon, called *He's Not Just a Soldier*, to be released on Cotillion.

Just before his appearance in London last Saturday, he finished a record with James Gang called "But I Try," to be released on Dunhill; and shortly he'll be starting one with John Fogerty of CCR—another group that's successfully copied much in his style—to be called *Little Richard and Creedence Clearwater Revival.* More significantly, his own new LP, *Cast a Long Shadow*, will be coming out on Epic. Soon he'll be going out to England to do both sides of a single with Mick Jagger and will go into the studio with Paul McCartney with ten songs he's written expressly for the ex-Beatle. And, hopefully, April will bring to TV *The Little Richard Show*.

"All the albums," he says, "should be out the same time—eight releases at one time. All the groups invited us to record. To get the music down, you understand. Little Richard will be a living legend when they're all out. We don't get old like everybody else. There ain't no bags under our eyes, no extra fat, or anythin'. We are still goin' on—and we'll still be remembered. Remember. Richard's a showman. He just comes that way from being a black singer from Georgia, one of the most beautiful singers of his time—a real beauty."

CHUCK BERRY

JUNE 1969
TORONTO TELEGRAM

TO CHUCK BERRY, it all must seem rather ironic; having been one of the first voices heard in rock, even before Elvis, mass popularity avoided him until rock went a full circle. First the Beatles unabashedly copied his style, then there was the blues revival. And Berry found himself caught up in his own revival—last week he was a major catalyst at the Toronto Pop Festival, causing the flagging crowd to suddenly bellow itself into life, and last night at the Rock Pile he created the same effect in miniature. Perhaps because of the cancellation of scheduled Dr. John, the Night Tripper (because of throat ailment) only 600 kids showed up. But that was enough. And Berry played upon them like they were extensions of his guitar. The steady thump-thump repetition of his twelve-bar blues patterns hypnotized. Above this, spilling out recklessly came the boogie-woogie rhythm of his voice.

The effect was that of a pneumatic drill caught in the iron cage of the beat. And there he was, greasy slicked-back hair, tapered clothes, a style right out of the fifties and all. Nothing could have been more simple, nothing could have been more direct. "My songs are simple," he says, "unchanging, because the important thing is to get through to the audience." And like a middleweight eyeing a strange sparring partner, Berry sized them up. One, two, "Hey!" he shouts. Everybody responds—but not enough. Again, and again, he prods them, exorcising their inhibitions. "Heyyyy!" And the exchange is on. He quickly slips in and out of one song then another. So basic are their similarities, that you barely notice the shifts. "Olé!"—this is not the traditional tone of the blues, with its loneliness underscored with a sensation of pain. No, Berry's style, lean and biting, is ebullient, sometimes extravagant, almost orgiastic in its affirmation.

Articulate, and intelligent, Berry early in his career caught the mood of the white American teenager. As a black bluesman, he travelled the Chitlin' Circuit, that endless series of endless bars stuck deep in the South. His influences, he claims, were from jazz and blues, Charlie Christian as well as T-Bone Walker and Carl Hogan.

But his strident, unaccented voice sounds curiously white. In contrast to Norman Mailer's "white Negro," Berry is almost rock's first black Caucasian. His music isn't particularly black or white or anything. Its subject matter, "Sweet Little Sixteen," "School Days," is that of any kids living in the sixties. What he offers, then, is something cross-racial: pure excitement. Excitement, eight-to-the-bar, six songs to the hour, and no Sundays, please.

FOLK

RAMBLIN' JACK ELLIOTT

JANUARY 1967
GLOBE AND MAIL

FOLK MUSIC FOR THE average audience is too often like the emasculated and gimmicked variety—the double entendres, vocal whoops, and guttural growls being toned down to make it acceptable beside Mantovani and Muzak. But folk singing, as done by Ramblin' Jack Elliott, has that undiluted earthiness which shows that it is as much a way of life as a form of music. Elliott, who opened last night at the Penny Farthing, sang with a backwater nasality that derives from the same sources that produced Woody Guthrie's style. "I lived four years with Woody," he said, "and I used to imitate him heavily... but now I'm off on something of my own."

His low-key humour, off-key guitar playing, and often no-key singing was rarely taken seriously by anybody, including the singer. With his dry, husky voice, Elliott would dissolve the vocal flurry of bluesy coloratura figures, but then come back to end the song with a chorus of rhythmic, head-back singing. The slurred, swallowed, often broken lines, the sardonic humour, the talking blues such as "Talking Fisherman," were much the same as Guthrie used; and often Elliott sounded like an elder Bob Dylan, a former Guthrie-ite. Yet in Elliott's style there was none of the electronically amplified, plugged-in primitivism; and where Dylan's songs abound in anti-social anguish, Elliott's are full of freshly husked corn.

"Oh, I know Dylan, all right ... you know, he even imitated me for a while. But I really like the new things he's doing. I really like this folk rock thing, in fact the Lovin' Spoonful and the Beatles are my favourite groups. Right now I'm doing other people's material, but I've got a few things of my own that I'm going to try out." For the next two weeks Elliott will yodel through country and western songs and gasp through an old harmonica, but do very little talking: "I didn't come to preach ... just to pick the guitar."

ODETTA

MARCH 1967
GLOBE AND MAIL

TRAINED TO BE a second Marian Anderson, but influenced by such older folksingers as Lead Belly (the late Huddy Ledbetter), Odetta is too much her own person to emulate merely either. Not a folksinger, but a singer of folk songs, lullabies, and spirituals, she's trapped artistically somewhere between the Top 40 and Schumann Lieder. "I haven't studied formally for years," she says, "but I still have some technique. It's not of the sheer bravura variety, but lies more in the realm of dramatics."

At the age of nineteen, after a typical high school education, an abbreviated college career, and several years of formal voice lessons, Odetta started singing folk music in the Los Angeles area. She has been singing her own brand of folk-cum-blues-cum-jazz for the past seventeen years. "I find the medium of folk music closer to the people. Jazz and classical music are too abstract as far as our lives go. I don't mean that I'm a folk-singing protestor; I think many of those types of songs underestimate our intelligence." Her fuzzy-soft, childlike voice belies the power of her singing in the same way that the subtle sexuality of her smile overshadows the intensity of her purpose as a performer.

Like most popular singers, whatever their style, Odetta is striving through her singing to communicate with people. To communicate, the Beatles concoct their electronic potpourris and Bob Dylan fights his lonely poetic war with himself. Odetta tries to connect with simple powerful singing. "I'm sort of a prophet and a teacher; my singing involves more teaching than entertaining. A good song must consist of more than interest, artfulness, and force. In any one of my programs, I'm striving for a state of concern or love. It's not always the result that counts, but the striving toward it."

Gradually she pans to move into other fields. For example, she plans to do Gian Carlo Menotti's *The Medium*, and some straight dramatic acting, and in July she begins work on a production of *Finian's Rainbow* with Petula Clark and Fred Astaire. Yet for all her personal and artistic freedom, Odetta remains conscious of her race and nationality. "I'm sure not a turn-the-other-cheeker," she says, "I can't see, from all the information the government has given me, why my people should be fighting in Vietnam. In my eyes, this is the first war between the races—between the whites and the coloured people. This is why I want to educate. In the United States there are two groups that have to be taught—the blacks and the whites. And while mass media can help put my songs on hit parades as they did Joan Baez; it can also help me to get across what I want to say. When you are interested in things, you assume a responsibility for them."

To open her two-week Toronto stay, Odetta walked to the stage from the Riverboat's anteroom (née kitchen) last night like the first-string preacher at a revival meeting. With a colour-splashed print robe draped over her five-feet-eight frame, her presence and her voice would have been no less noticeable in a concert hall. And, with the band clunking along obediently behind her, she proceeded to fill the room with raw, open-throated, air-siren-intense sound. For all its potency, her voice was able to slither among the notes to recreate the aura of the blues.

For while many folk artists, such as Dylan, Ochs and others, delight or dismay by their murkily symbolic poetry, Odetta's innovations come through in her performance. It's not what she does, but how it is done that makes each Odetta performance fresh. And last night was no exception. Her children's song, with its primitive drum-pounding, sounded like a psychedelic vision of Disneyland; the blues, "Black Woman," became a low moan as she suspended her chant-like voice over the pulsating bass.

Not all of her material was equally successful. "Two Minutes from Yesterday," a new pop ballad by Robert Jason had depressing overtones of vintage Elvis Presley. Yet throughout, her singing went beyond the hard-times type of emotionalism of many singers in the folk and blues idiom.

Whether singing protests or blatantly bawdy love ballads, Odetta adapted to each individual song's meaning. And as Dietrich Fischer-Dieskau comprehends Schumann or Hugo Wolf Lieder, and thus can sing them with their spirit intact, Odetta gets to the heart of the blues. Although most folksingers are personalities, few are described as musicians. Odetta is one of the exceptions. "When I sing folk and the blues," she said yesterday, "I can achieve that sense of freedom that I can't anywhere else. And I'm constantly fascinated that classical singers like what I'm doing."

ARLO GUTHRIE

APRIL 1967
GLOBE AND MAIL

THOUGH MANY MAJOR FOLKSINGERS blatantly follow in Woody Guthrie's wake, copying his mannerisms, the Midwestern flatness of his voice and his type of songwriting, his son, Arlo, who opened a two-week stay at the Riverboat last night, has managed to avoid the more obvious aspects of his heredity.

Nineteen-year-old Arlo is a more urbanized artist; and although he has none of the urbanized, laboured hipness, he is still a contemporary artist. His act is not so much a collection of songs, but a continuous stream of nervous comments on his background. In "Alice's Restaurant," a thirty-minute talking blues that at times sounded like *Finnegans Wake* set to music, the younger Guthrie rambled on from the current buffalo crisis (there isn't any) to draft-dodging in four-part harmony.

With such eclectic material, Arlo has still managed to define his personality. With his father lying ill and silent at Brooklyn State Hospital, Arlo still managed to carry on the un-amplified, non-psychedelic, humane genre of the art. It is impossible to hear Arlo Guthrie without realizing the crises in popular music he represents. But when Woody Guthrie—the back-forty bard who has been likened to many U.S. poets from Stephen Vincent Benét to Carl Sandburg—could sing songs which were stingingly relevant to his time, with Arlo Guthrie they would become quaint artifacts of Americana like vintage Ethel Merman records.

Folk songs can no more stand being fossilized than can jazz. Not that this type of music must be a contemporary collage of rhythm, riots and revolution, but if folk is to have any operative as opposed to promotional significance, it must constantly build on the old, must be in as constant a state of flux as Heraclitus's river. Ramblin' Jack Elliott, with first-hand authority and personality, almost succeeded in emulating the elder Guthrie; but compared to Bob Dylan, who used Guthrie's style to develop his own, Elliott will always remain unnoticed.

Arlo Guthrie is well aware of his position. "While I don't feel that I should do one of my dad's songs just because I'm his kid," he said, "yet there is no reason why I shouldn't do it. If it's a good song, I sing it."

MARIPOSA FOLK FESTIVAL

JULY 1967
GLOBE AND MAIL

IN NORTH AMERICA there have been, traditionally, three radical elements in society—youth, the Negro, and the intellectual. What happens, then, when representatives of these groups are crowded into the two hundred acres near this lake under the aegis of the seventh Mariposa Folk Festival? Very little. Some hapless hippies tried to disturb the quiet atmosphere, but their iconoclastic buttons, beards, bands, and behaviour failed to turn the folk music fans on or the ninety police officers off. "Everything's been so quiet," said one officer, "that they've been calling me 'Sir.'"

For artistic director Estelle Klein and the festival committee it was a triumph of content over style, of message over medium. With only a passing nod to modern pop music, the festival emphasized traditional approaches to folk music in both idea and performances. For the performers, who had been betrayed by Bob Dylan (he went folk-rock) and bewildered by the Beatles (who went folk-strange), Mariposa was an opportunity to reveal something of the backgrounds and traditions of the art. For the audience, it was an escape from a jukebox day and Yorkville night. For both, Mariposa was a chance to study the breadth and depth of traditional folk music styles. It provoked few outbursts from other artists or audiences, but it was the closest Toronto will come to folk authenticity in a long time.

But sitting in monk-like reverence, the audiences watched most of the five concerts, workshops, seminars, and films with the detached sensitivity of a group of sociologists watching aboriginal tribal dances. "It's been too academic," singer Tom Rush remarked, "it's really not a very festive festival." This was not the performers' faults. Traditional folk music has come to be regarded as a relic of another era. In the new pop music, the listener is to be totally involved, all his senses are immersed in the frenetic interplay of sight and sound. To quote McLuhan, "In the new music, the ear favours no point of view. We are enveloped by sound. It forms a seamless web around us." At discotheques, the eye is as important as the ear; but traditionally folk music requires one only to listen.

While there was this emphasis on the older styles, each of the three major evening concerts had something for everybody—even for those with no taste at all: From Southern rural bluegrass (The Lilly Brothers and Herb Hooven) to northern urban Negro blues (Buddy Guy's Chicago Blues Band), music from the time of the holy rollers (The Staple Singers) to the rock 'n' rollers (Kensington Market), from the pretentious folk-rock prattlings of O. D. Bodkins (Elyse Weinberg) to the soft, supple soprano of Joni Mitchell.

And after an artistically uneven Friday night concert, Saturday night's performances were well paced. Sippie Wallace (a blues singer who first recorded in the 1920s and whom folk music has discovered much the same way jazz rediscovered Earl Hines, brought more vitality to her gospel and blues singing that did many singers one-third her age. Like a number of other blues artists (Blind Roy Fuller or Brother Son Bonds), she was able to keep the two types apart. Gordon Lowe showed more sensitivity at adapting (notably in Leonard Cohen's

"Suzanne") than as an originator; the Pennywhistlers, a greater instinct for complex rhythms (as in Macedonian, Bulgarian, and Russian songs) than half the Toronto Symphony; and twenty-year-old David Rea, more critical aptitude for his guitar playing than his singing.

Following him, the Travellers, Joni Mitchell, and Kensington Market were a brief catalogue of what folk music was, is and will be. And although Richie Havens's incendiary guitar playing and his broken, lisping singing took the audience on a chilling night walk in a Rorschachian landscape of ideas, the climax of the evening came with the arrival of Buddy Guy's Chicago Blues Band.

Sunday's concert, the first in the festival's seven-year history, was like the other two. The common denominator for all the performers was a unique and specialized approach. The result: a diversified but consistently musical program. After the vibrancy of English traditional singer Louisa Killen's voice, Leonard Cohen's sounded emasculated. But like the early Bob Dylan, Cohen's technical inadequacy on the guitar and his penchant for stereotyped chord changes took little away from his lyrics. Novelist (*Beautiful Losers*), poet (*The Spice-Box of Earth*, *Flowers for Hitler*), his imagery is often flagrantly sexual though always in taste.

Buffy Sainte-Marie, the acknowledged star of the festival, was equal to her billing. Dressed in a flowing orange-and-yellow robe, she appeared on the stage like an Indian Ophelia. Her rich contralto was emotionally strong but always in full control. Her songs had a ring of joyfulness that they have not had before. This is perhaps understandable: she announced her impending marriage.

JULY 1972
TORONTO STAR

BOB DYLAN, RARELY SEEN in the past five years, hugged Gordon Lightfoot, before escaping fans running after him. Neil Young led four thousand in a singalong as Joni Mitchell looked on. It all happened on the twelth annual Mariposa Folk Festival, on Toronto Island, which ended last night. What had started Friday in typical low-key Mariposa fashion almost ended Saturday amid sudden, driving rain squalls that forced the promoters to turn off the performers' electrical systems. It finally finished yesterday, however, with the unexpected and virtually unnoticed appearance of what one fan described as "more folk superstars than have ever been together at one place at one time for any one reason."

Central to this was the slight figure of Bob Dylan who, in jeans, white shirt and wearing a red bandana and rimless spectacles, wandered unrecognized with his wife, Sara, through the crowd of fourteen thousand. In the still-wet fields away from the six performing areas, Dylan was given a bottle of beer by a passerby. Then, circling, he stood briefly in a crowd, watching some fiddlers before moving to another area to listen to old blues pianist Roosevelt Sykes and blues guitarist Bukka White. "We've been here for Mariposa's three days," he said. "We even got rained out like everyone else on Saturday. But this looks like a really nice festival. I've been to Mariposa several times in the past; but this year it reminds me of the way it was ten years ago. I won't be playing, though. I've been doing other things."

So were most of the thirty-three thousand who attended the three-day presentation of 151 different concerts and craft displays by more than two hundred singers, dancers, musicians, and craftsmen, and who had been lulled by Mariposa's starless star system and quiet meandering pace. The attendance was about eight thousand higher than last year, when the festival lost $7,000.00. According to festival spokesman Dick Flohil, a profit can be expected this year, though he couldn't say how much. Organized to both protect performers' anonymity and to disseminate as much "authentic" folk music as possible, Mariposa stopped its practice of ending each day with a major concert after gate-crashing took place in 1970.

It started Saturday when singer Murray McLauchlan cut short his otherwise engrossing concert to introduce Joni Mitchell, who immediately started singing. Her sure and steadily rhythmic guitar work, and her high-pitched, keening voice for songs like "Both Sides Now" and "Woodstock" soon drew fans from other performing areas. This process was repeated yesterday when singer Bruce Cockburn, after providing the best concert of his career, introduced Neil Young.

Shortly afterward, Gordon Lightfoot sat down on a picnic bench and started singing without a microphone, accompanied by several guitarists in the audience of 150. "The whole thing was accidental," Lightfoot explained. "I was just sitting there when someone handed me a guitar." Lightfoot, who was suffering from a disease called Bell's palsy which partially paralyzed his mouth when he was in Toronto three months ago, said that he is now almost completely cured.

What the festival organizers had feared started to happen when two dozen fans all but chased Young into the performers' compound, and then another dozen or so recognized Dylan, and started to follow him. Dylan, too, retreated to the fenced-off performers' area, and started talking to Lightfoot when it appeared that a crowd might jump the fence. Within fifteen minutes he was hustled off the island in a harbour police boat, leaving at least one fan crying.

POP/COUNTRY/JAZZ

GLEN CAMPBELL

AUGUST 1969
TORONTO TELEGRAM

UNTIL A BETTER ONE comes along, Glen Campbell will remain TV's answer to the Barbie doll. There's something irrepressibly cuddly about him, like someone's clockwork toy with its machinery running smoothly. It all seems too smooth. The not-too-long, not-too-short hair, the "aw-shucks" grin.

After watching his TV show all last season, a bottle of milk seems somehow vulgar by comparison. But before a near capacity crowd at the CNE Grandstand show Saturday and Sunday evenings there he was:

"Ladieeees and . . ." But the announcer needn't have gone any further. "Ladieeees." And in a spectacle of the spirit rarely seen outside the wrestling matches, they rushed the stage, falling in the rain, jamming elbows into each other's camera lenses, pushing, trying to get a shot of . . . HIM! "Ladieeees . . . Glen Campbell!" And on stage he stopped, half bewildered, half bemused by it all. Somehow he seemed lost on the carnivorous stage; his high tenor seemingly out of thin air. Spotlights played off him catching his suit (Brooks Brothers out of *Bonanza*) like a moth in a flame. And for a moment he seemed frightfully frail and perishable.

But soon the lush orchestrations and the equally lush sentiments poured over the crowd like thick syrup. Songs where there's love without passion ("Time"); sadness without despair ("Dreams of the Everyday Housewife"); blues without soul ("Sittin' On The Dock of the Bay"); travelling without pain ("Galveston"). And the music came from all around you through the excellent speaker system. Yet somehow its omnipresence in the air seemed much easier to believe than the realization that it was coming from the slight figure on stage. For Glen Campbell has been drawn into the wake of a great middle-class reaction to the hip, and the cool, in short, to rock. So what if he is surprisingly like the confectionary dreams of every Hollywood hack?

So what if he is the externalized version of America's dream of the cowboy-as-folk-hero? Hatred of middle-class heroes, since Johnny Mathis, is an old story. For the children of rock 'n' roll this response is as natural as buying the next Beatles album. It's inevitable. Two years ago it was Herb Alpert and before that Ray Conniff. But lately this hatred has taken on a new chic. If you like Glen Campbell you're probably from the Midwest somewhere and voted Republican and support the Chicago police, right? Glen Campbell isn't merely Glen Campbell. He's the symbol for the great unknown factor in the U.S., the attitudes of the middle class. And that, baby, is a lot more frightening than the Doors' Jim Morrison pulling down his pants in front of a lot of Miami kids. At least we know why Morrison did it.

But there's a flaw here. Campbell is talented. "You know," he said earlier, "that's all I really care about. I don't think in terms of image. There are certain songs I like doing, songs that have some meaning for me. Beyond that there are no other considerations. Playing in clubs. Then you had to do everything—jazz, rock, heck, I first started imitating, I mean singing Frank Sinatra songs." By 1961, Campbell was a studio musician. He backed up almost everybody from Jimmy

Dean to the Beach Boys. His first record, "Turn Around, Look at Me" was recorded for a small label, but soon attracted Capitol Records' attention who signed him. Then came a Joey Bishop show on which Tommy Smothers saw him. The rest is history. Yet, there's that lingering TV image of him on your mind whenever you watch him. There, as on the grandstand's stage, his talent is spread out two-dimensionally. There's no sense of distance; of a back or a front. It's all there, laid out flat. And it all begins to run too smoothly. You miss the rough edges, the mistakes that happen when something really artistic takes place. People jostle each other as if they were crowding a TV screen. "Ohhh … look at him!" a girl next to me said. "Do you want to meet him after?" "Oh heavens no. Just look at him, though …"

JOHNNY CASH

NOVEMBER 1969
TORONTO TELEGRAM

JOHNNY CASH is the pop hero without metaphor. "I think folks go back to my music," he says, "to find the basic thing, the grassroots." And there's probably less there than meets the ear; his stories are tales of death, love, murder, and other verities, his lyrics aren't throttled by any symbolic apparatus. He just sounds—and most likely is—tough, a bit crude, direct, and unambiguous as a bullet. And he's at Maple Leaf Gardens November 10.

Cash's spiralling to everyone's surface awareness is the blend of a curious set of trends. Of a country whose last two political leaders have found it better to be Right, than merely right; of attitude that's tired of systems, and looks for situations. But wait: All this for gravel-voice Cash? "Why not?" his manager, Saul Holiff asked. "After all, the Americans are always looking for a hero—and fortunately for them, John's honest. But oh, how they've tried to make him fit! People up in New York keep trying to find these arty types with 'messages' and things.

"More specifically, the progress was like this: The *Johnny Cash at Folsom Prison* LP was a big hit. Then came that documentary on NET *[Playhouse]* called *Cash*, the one that was later released as a movie. Suddenly the pseudo-intellectual in New York thought that John had a message or something. Well, after the NET thing was well reviewed, there was a deluge of articles. But the market came before his TV show. I have to keep telling ABC that. People were well aware of him before that. For example, we went into Detroit for two shows on May 4 before the network show started and sold out. It's just that people aren't ashamed any longer to like music that isn't deep." Maybe so; but depth will always be in the ear of the digger.

More country performers, from Buck Owens to John Hartford to Jerry Lee Lewis to Glen Campbell have become national performers. And pop stars, Bob Dylan, and the Byrds, Paul McCartney, and others are approaching a more countrified style. But for most, their "country" music is cast in nostalgia. And in many ways, the pop-cum-western singers are more country than their originals. Outside of Nashville's Grand Ole Opry, there's usually a parked Jaguar or two. Inside one of the more well-known bar-and-grills, you can hear chatter about the latest thing in psychoanalysis. But exactly! Cash with his simple songs hit stride before it became the nasal stridency of much modern country music. Musically, perhaps spiritually as well, he's closer to Tex Ritter than Ferlin Husky, yet closer to Bob Dylan than either.

He could be the son of those people Walker Evans and James Agee chronicled during the depression of their *Let Us Now Praise Famous Men*. Born thirty-seven years ago in a three-room shack in Kingsland, Arkansas, Cash learned to plow, pick cotton, and all those other not-so-neat things the one of seven poor children learned. After a four-year stint in the army, where he learned to play the guitar out of sheer boredom, he formed a trio with Luther Perkins and Marshall Grant. And the route upward started. The pace was furious—and telling. Over four hundred original songs resulted, nineteen albums, three gold records, over two hundred concerts a year, night after night in small motels en route to another motel and another concert and … Cash was caught on amphetamines, almost one hundred Dexedrines a day. He got over that, slowing his pace a bit. Last March he married June Carter, one of the famous Carter family. Then came the boom. "And that was it," says Keith Hampshire from CKFH. "Cash made it because of the TV show and a funny record—"A Boy Named Sue." Yeah; that's it folks. And maybe the older young people think he's some kind of folk hero."

But to those directly involved, Cash's climb is not all surprising. Says CFGM general manager Dave Wright, "on a country music station like ours, he's always been a star. I feel that progressive rock is something people over twenty-five can't really identify with. Actually a song like Cash's is a two-and-a-half-minute soap opera. And its problems are real, and understandable to everyone."

NEIL DIAMOND

MARCH 1970
TORONTO TELEGRAM

LIKE THOSE GREAT modern inventions, the hula hoop, enzyme detergents, or high-octane gas, singer Neil Diamond represents a triumph of the supply meeting the demand. And his demand looks like it may never diminish. For his songs are the product of his own inventiveness. He's their best salesman. And like any good adman, he knows the source of their demand intuitively. In fact, Diamond's recent successes are rather phenomenal. Unknown as a performer four years ago, with some success as a songwriter before that, there's an excellent chance that he will head the summer replacement for *The Glen Campbell Goodtime Hour*.

At his show last night in the Automotive Building on the CNE grounds, the 3,500 kids raised one collective gasp when Diamond finally appeared. There was nothing cool, or modishly detached about them—although this attitude seems almost to be a prerequisite for listening to modern pop. Giggling, jiggling, and totally involved, they sighed when he sang and eyed him as he moved. And, in one way, their reaction defined what he was all about: for Neil Diamond might be the last true romantic hero left in pop music.

You would never know to look at him that the Beatles, psychedelia, or the hippies had ever happened. Diamond's style is that of the fifties. His songs are neat and compact, embodying no more than one emotion at a time. And lean and tough-looking, he was that special kind of aware, existential cool that seems to have been formed out of Elvis Presley's shadow. All of which Neil Diamond is perfectly aware: "Four years ago, I went into a recording studio for the first time to cut one of my own songs. I wasn't worried about success; I just wanted to hear myself on radio. I had a fantasy that one day I'd see some pretty girl listening to one of my songs and she'd see me and try to seduce me." Now, rock singers haven't had to *worry* about girls seducing them since Elvis had his hair cut to go into the army. But the girls at the concert—many of them in their middle teens—didn't seem to know that or even care. And Diamond played upon this, controlling emotions the way you can click a light switch.

At twenty-seven, his reputation exists on his abilities as a songwriter. He penned two of the Monkees' hits ("I'm a Believer;" "A Little Bit Me, a Little Bit You"). But when he sings them, a new dimension is added. With his trio romping along behind him (Carol Hunter on guitar, Randy Sterling on bass and Eddie Rubin on drums), Diamond's voice stands out in bold relief. And last night even an atrocious sound system couldn't curtail his effect; a wide-ranging voice with a dark tone and an edge that reverberated throughout the hollows of the huge building.

For Diamond has presence, a style that all but jumps off the stage and grabs attention. In songs like "Solitary Man," or "Holly Holy," or "Sweet Caroline," there are no complexities to juggle. Nothing's terribly involved; while everything's involving. The response is direct and emotional. And intentional. "After a while," he says, "I gave up trying to write for what all the people might want. I found that I was writing for myself. I mean, I couldn't really get too worried about what the hip, or underground people wanted. I had to write the way I thought best. And as long as people like me…"

After his show, girls were still milling around. The reason they were there is probably the reason Diamond will stay where he is. "Neil?" asked one.

"Yeah?" he said.

"Nothing. Just saying 'Neil'…"

DIONNE WARWICK

JUNE 1970
TORONTO TELEGRAM

THE ROLE OF POP music has changed, and along with it, the pop musician. It's been squeezed between two basic necessities—to gain sumptuous financial returns, and, at the same time, to appear as popular expression. And no one has handled this apparent imbalance better than singer Dionne Warwick, who'll appear at the O'Keefe Centre, tomorrow.

Frank Sinatra once called it 'the martial music of every sideburned delinquent on earth." But pop music now floats very near the cultural mainstream. Its only delinquencies are in taste; about the only real radical action its people indulge in are corporate mergers. In Dionne Warwick's voice there's a mixture of high life and common attitudes. The style in her singing is the style of pop today, a smooth blending of jazz, rock, gospel, and rhythm 'n' blues. It doesn't sound particularly black, white, or particularly anything.

Her songs, starting with "Don't Make Me Over" in 1962, sound like love-talk in a vacuum. Things like "I Say a Little Prayer"; "Trains and Boats and Planes"; or "The Windows of the World," all latter hits, have a surface calmness that only barely implies the emotion that's underneath. But it is in this implication where her strength lies. It's like a movie closeup of Julie Christie's face, or the silence that falls between talkers in a radio interview show; it tells a lot more than it says, it gives details that can sketch in an entire story. "Music is music wherever you sing it," she once said. "If you are enough of a craftsman, it won't hamper your contact with an audience. Above all, you've got to get inside a song, to learn what it means to you, and what you mean to it."

Rarely can the singer make a song; nowadays, it's usually the other way around. And much of Dionne Warwick's success has been due to the success of writers Burt Bacharach's and Hal David's songs. Bacharach one day found her mouthing doo-wap-bee-doo background lyrics in a recording session and asked her to record on her own for Scepter Records. Before that, she'd been studying music education at Hartt School of music, at the University of Hartford, in Connecticut. It gave her a talent, a steely sureness to it which showed up one day several years ago when taping a CBC TV show *The Rock Scene: Like It Is*. The band hired for the occasion with an addition of some string players from the Toronto Symphony, couldn't play her arrangements. And the conductor couldn't conduct them. So she stepped out and: "Okay, this is the way it goes..."

Her connection with the Bacharach-David team, while growing more and more successful, grew more and more odd at the same time. After all, here was a young black singer doing straight pop tunes, by two white writers, while all around her grew the biggest explosion in black music and black singers since the 1930s. But, as she said, "Emotionally, I can't sing the blues. At least, not as a blues singer might. I've always tried to find a song that I like, regardless of its so-called category. I really can't classify my style."

Of the three emerging black female singers in the sixties, her career took the straightest route. Diana Ross came from rhythm 'n' blues, and only later did she mould her material into a nightclub act. Aretha Franklin started in gospel, had her singing straitjacket by some early Columbia recordings, then, in a sense, went back to where she started; to gospel-oriented rhythm 'n' blues. But Dionne started with Burt Bacharach material. In a sense, it's shaped her career ever since.

Marlene Dietrich was so impressed by her recording of "Anyone Who Had a Heart" that she personally introduced her at the Olympia Theatre in December 1963. Of course, there were the TV appearances, from the *The Ed Sullivan Show* to *The Jerry Lewis Show*. But she did things on a broader scope. She appeared at the Sanremo Festival, and, in 1968, at the Newport Jazz Festival. Her first movie, *Slaves*, with Stephen Boyd and Ossie Davis, premiered in Baltimore this year in May. Things kept changing around her, while her style stayed relatively the same; cool, direct, urbane, and telling. And right at the centre of pop music today.

ANNE MURRAY

JULY 1970
TORONTO TELEGRAM

"EXCEPT FOR ME, I don't think anyone really knows what kind of singer I am," Anne Murray sighs. At first, it doesn't seem much of a problem for the Nova Scotia–based singer, considering she's just signed an exclusive contract with the CBC for some TV shows, and is just finishing out a hitch with CTV. "Nobody seems to know exactly what kind of singer I am," she says. "When I was in Vancouver on one of my tours, they pegged me as a country singer. And I couldn't believe it. I didn't even like country music until a couple of years ago. It's always like that. When Capitol Records in Los Angeles heard the first LP I made for them in Canada, *This Way Is My Way*, they said it was too diverse. And they wanted me to go into a certain bag. To develop a certain image, you know. And in the Maritimes, they think I'm a . . . a, well, a . . . I guess I don't know what they think in the Maritimes."

The Maritimes aren't alone. Anne Murray's voice is a deep and knowing contralto, yet she looks like an apple-polishing schoolmarm, all clean and neat, and with an air of sheer wholesomeness so thick you'd swear she rented it for special occasions. It's a problem, and one compounded in a couple of ways. First of all, her background seems to have been scripted by those health education handbooks on How to Succeed. Now twenty-five, she was born in Springhill, Nova Scotia ("a very nice place"), majored in phys. ed. at the University of New Brunswick, and just exudes health with her short, blonde hair; honest, direct eyes; and a pleasant, but not-too-obvious figure.

And her professional background is safe and secure enough to have been wrapped in Saran Wrap. "Oh, I'd always been singing," she explains, "and one day in 1964 I decided to audition for *Singalong Jubilee*. But I didn't make it, until two years later the producer Bill Langstroth called me up and asked me to audition once again. Although my pride was sort of hurt, I came down and they accepted me. "I didn't really know if I was going into show business at that time, so I kept teaching high school and wondering. Funny thing, though, I started getting a lot of calls, so I decided to do the *Let's Go* show out of Halifax and went on the club and concert tours a singer needs to do to polish his act." She signed with Arc Records and did one LP for them. Then she transferred to Capitol Records, did another two LPs and became a part of their push to fill in the gaps created when the Canadian Radio-Television Commission decreed that there should be more "Canadian content" played on the airwaves.

And this brings up the second problem. "I guess I'm considered a square," she says, "and that's a drag. Being too straight these days isn't easy, you know. There are no pockmarks on my face. And I even had a very happy childhood. I figure to make it, I'll have to do something incredibly rotten. To improve my image, you know."

It won't happen next year, though. While she's at present trying to locate an agent to help her direct her budding career, she's been booked for a series of Canadian TV shows. To be exact, she'll be appearing six times on the *Nashville North* series on CTV, ten more times for *Singalong Jubilee* and eight times for *The Tommy Hunter Show*, both on the CBC.

"The point is, that for next year after I've moved to Toronto this September, I've got to get some agent who'll promote me as I am. Now, what that is, I'm not really sure, but there are certain things I know I'm not. For example, I'll never become something like a sex symbol, you know, with a wig and a tight dress and all that. Besides, I think that would be virtually impossible. I guess I'll always be square as far as my public image goes. Yet, it might work out okay in the end. I mean, my public is pretty diversified. And this I think is what matters most. I hope so. You can get caught up in this image-making thing. I've seen so many good performers who've been lost because of it. What I'd like to do most of all is just stay around the Maritimes, where everybody is happy. In Toronto, all everybody does is talk about the depression going on in the Maritimes. But what a joke that is. Sure, the people make little, but they spend little. And somehow, they all seem happy. So that's what I'd like to do. But every day I will turn on my radio, and fear that I'm going to hear some girl singer with a deep voice like mine, and figure that's it for me, that somebody's got to where I'm going first. God, how square can you be?"

NOVEMBER 1970
TORONTO TELEGRAM

"ISN'T THAT ...?" asked the woman, peering through the cocktail lounge's gloom.

"I think so," said her friend. "Isn't that nice?"

"No, no that can't be her," said the other, crossly. "*That* one's got a drink."

"No!"

Yes. And not only was Anne Murray drinking, and smoking, but she was getting pretty tired of this purer-than-snow, Annie

Applecheeks image that has followed her success both on records and on TV like an albatross. "I'm beginning to hate this wishy-washy image with the polished cheeks and all," she said. "Once I wish someone would write that I had a joint in one hand and a bottle in the other. But the image business works the other way, too. It's great that I could never become a sexpot. I'm just not like that. When I open at the Royal York (next Monday evening) I'm glad I won't be coming on stage with big breasts and slink. 'Cause I couldn't do that."

"There she is again," said her manager Bill Langstroth. "Miss... World... Health!"

The only problem about all of this, is that Anne Murray is a lot more complex than most of her interviewers seem to think, and her image is a lot simpler than she seems to think. The details of her sudden success have followed such a straight, recognizable line, that it all seems to have been scripted by some Hollywood hack writer struggling with a B-movie plot.

Now twenty-five, born in Springhill, Nova Scotia, she first majored in physical education at the University of New Brunswick, and it wasn't until 1966, with her debut in *Singalong Jubilee*, that she started thinking of singing professionally. She later signed with Arc Records, did an LP for them, then transferred to Capitol Records, where her Gene MacLellan–penned single, "Snowbird," became a million seller. "Snowbird" became the key to everything. The CBC signed her to an "exclusive" two-year contract, but this extends only to her appearances in Canada. Recently she signed with William Morris Agency, probably the most influential talent agency in the world, and under the personal supervisions of William Morrison's Nick Sevano, has already started on her U.S. exposure, which includes a four-year contract with the Glen Campbell show, which means at least four appearances a year plus the possibility of her own show as a summer replacement for Campbell's.

She still has coming up three more guest appearances on CTV's *Nashville North*, which she taped before her CBC contract; she has done and will be doing a CBC special; is expected to appear on both *Singalong Jubilee* and *The Tommy Hunter Show*, and headlines the Wednesday segment of CBC Radio's *After Noon*. Meanwhile, she's trying to get another LP out as fast as she can, because Capitol has already set a February release date.

Strangely enough, she seems a lot cooler about it all; than various writers who suddenly discovered they had a real, live star on their hands. Thus, on one hand, she's described pretty much the way the Royal York's press release explains her. "Anne Murray is probably very much like the first girl you ever loved. She has a simple but pretty face, a smile that comes easily, and eyes that can see through all the masks that you wear." On the other hand, there are those who see her career not necessarily as rags to riches, but more like schoolmarm to vamp. In fact, one writer quoted her in an interview as saying that there were "real" people in Hollywood, "not like the phonies in Toronto."

And that, as they say, hurt. "It's so easy to come out sounding like a rat," she explained. I mean, when people read that I had called people at the CBC phony, everyone got upset. People started writing to my father, worrying about it. And what made things worse, is that I never said that. If anything, the CBC has been very, very good to me. It's all very strange. It seems all the people who have told me to 'stay pure' are the ones dumping on me the more things I do. But the whole thing is that I've been here when all of this has been happening. I've stayed in Halifax. I may fly down to Hollywood to do a TV show—but I get out of there as soon as I can. But I think this whole idea of 'going Hollywood' is changing now. For instance, I've noticed how people react to Glen Campbell—and he appeals to basically the same audience as I do. He's the kind of guy you can walk up to and slap on the back. It's someone like Dean Martin they seem in awe of—but he's probably the last of the Big Time Stars. If people wouldn't keep hounding me about this success thing, I wouldn't get near the preconceived idea that would be 'going Hollywood.'

"I've always felt proud of being Canadian. But mainly I'm proud of being a Maritimer. The Maritimes is where I learned everything I know. Of course, people in the Maritimes feel a certain inferiority compared to the rest of Canada—but that's just like the kind of inferiority Canada seems to feel when being compared to the States. Of course, I'm getting terribly busy now. But I don't mind that. I just want people to like me. I care about people who like me—who have seen the truth about me. Now, if I don't like somebody, I usually say so. Maybe that's a problem. But I usually will do anything anyone asks me to. Maybe, because of these demands that may keep me too busy, I'll have to curtail my career somewhat. Right now, I'm just thinking of the Royal York. I'm scared to death of the Royal York. It's so big, and I suppose the audience is geared to another type of performer than myself. But people don't really get to know you from a TV performance. They're cheated until they see you live.

"But that's what the people are going to see—me. Now, if someone came to me and said that I'd have to change the kind of clothes I wear to become famous, well, I'd say to them they could." And for a glorious moment, Anne Murray, with a drink still in front of her, almost told those people exactly what they could do.

LIZA MINNELLI (2020)

SO, THERE SHE IS barely halfway through her show and her eyelashes fall off: you know, the black, brittle eyelashes that make classic Liza Minnelli look like Bambi well done on a rotisserie? It's opening night Saturday on the road somewhere and oh, sweet Jesus, no! She has what look to be two couture caterpillars crawling on her face.

"I so wanted to be chic for this beautiful new hall," she mumbles as her two male dancers hover anxiously. They're paid to move at her whim, terrified to stop lest gravity catch up with them. The hall in question is Roy Thomson Hall in Toronto, named after a media baron who had little love for acts such as this one.

The lashes won't be moved. She sighs, peeling the "little suckers" off her flesh. Deeper sigh. Oh, the troubles she's seen. Does this happen to Cher? Raquel Welch, who's not exactly smooth, has never had to stand, sweaty and hot, fixing her face in front of a smart, deep-pocketed crowd who've paid $150 a seat. You can bet on that.

Did this ever happen to Judy Garland? No, of course not. Garland's daughter is no longer Garland's little girl. The year is 1982 and thirty-six-year-old Liza is on her third marriage—on the past

Saturday night, she sang "Maybe This Time" to her husband, Mark Gero, as a third anniversary present—and she has finally crystallized a style of her own.

Or, rather, she has an anti-style. Call it klutzy class, an emergent Donald Trump kind of thing. She's brilliant at it. At moments, her show sparkles with everything bright. Maybe too bright. This supernova of a woman is seemingly everywhere, while going nowhere.

It's all very athletic, marching its physicality like a high school championship team parade through hometown. Most every costume change is done on stage, from black tights to those Kit Kat Klub decadent frills looking like they're from a George Grosz etching.

She's backed by a twelve-piece band, yet the night really features the actress in her, not the singer. And it centres on two key pieces from two key movies in her career: *New York, New York* and *Cabaret*. They're like bookends for everything else, ending the first and second halves of her two-hour concert, respectively.

Along the way, she makes enormous demands on our sympathy. She also demands a blind eye to her many tricks. She gulps down a drink of water, where else but centre stage so everyone can feel her raw thirst. The moment reminds my companion of her own young daughter, showing off.

This, of course, was exactly the point: Liza, allowing an apparent flash of insight into her personality-in-the-raw. Unabashedly, Liza is forever the kid showing off, the plucky showbiz babe throwing caution and illusion to the wind—carefully, then not so carefully.

All this is overdone and overbearing and, at times, even her breathlessness becomes so much pure hot air. But when it works—and this is trimmer, much better focused than things she's done a few years earlier—it works in a world of its own.

She remains, in one way, the ultimate fan; her act is not really show business, but an act of praise to show business. If nothing else, you can revel in her sheer enjoyment of what she does.

But then again, maybe there is a parallel. In fight terms, she's a puncher, a brawler, and a fighter. She's not a boxer. She gets along not by finesse but through an arsenal of power. She's not going to feint and hit you where you aren't looking. Instead, she's going to make you wait for that knockout punch; she's going to tell you it's coming and *wham*! You may be ready for it, but she's going to floor you anyway.

Her act's first half sets up the first knockout punch, the strutting, kicking, nothing but climactic "New York, New York." En route, the steps are less triumphant although the first hour includes a lovely moment or two, including a rather subdued (for her) "How Long Has This Been Going On?" It also shows her at her worst in "Liza with a Z," a mindless piece of music wrapped around a logo for an idea for a perfume called, you guessed it, Z.

But as the medley of New York songs begins, everyone knows where it's leading. This is heavyweight stuff. This is Frank Sinatra territory. We know the punch is coming. And there she is, bent in half with her head up and her eyes on the crowd, winding up for the punch—winding up literally. Her right fist is rotating like a windmill as she goes for that first high note.

Pow! And, in case that didn't finish you off and the bit from *Cabaret* wasn't enough to end the second half, her encore is a reprise of "New York, New York." Complete with the head down, wind up and punch bit.

John Simon, the critic from *New York Magazine*, once criticized Liza's appearance, suggesting that her nose resembled a ski run and her lip, a pendulum. Simon was on the right track but for all the wrong reasons. He scented failed glamour. Liza, ski-run nose and all, is all about the glorious struggle to gain glamour.

"I pick the roles I do," she once said, "because I believe that no matter how crummy a thing is, there are people who come through. The interesting time is when they stumble but get up."

Like her.

CANNONBALL ADDERLEY

NOVEMBER 1970
TORONTO TELEGRAM

ONE OF THE SMALLER yet more durable mysteries in music these past few years is an understanding of just what is jazz and just what is rock, if indeed there is any difference. Take the Cannonball Adderley Quintet—excuse me, the "Amazing Cannonball Adderley Quintet,"—now at the Colonial for a week. Not too many years ago, saxophonist Adderley had achieved not a small reputation as a jazz improviser of considerable merit. But something happened along the way. He started wearing strange duds: beads, striped pants, and all. And his music went through some unaccustomed changes—it seemed more simple, more "melodic," a little more like rock 'n' roll. Stranger yet, his quintet had a couple of hit records. And for a jazz group these days, that's not only strange, but positively eerie. With brother Nat singing the occasional blues tune, and pianist Joe Zawinul coaxing some strange floating effects from an electric celesta, their whole performance is indeed a rocking romp.

But is it jazz? And if not, does it matter? One of the biggest pieces of nonsense to come along recently is the so-called jazz rock group; with bands like Chicago, or Blood, Sweat & Tears being used as the prime examples. On the other side of the coin, certain jazzmen like Miles Davis or Tony Williams, have been accused (at least by righteous members of the jazz community) of "going rock." But in all the infighting, the main point has been missed: rock and jazz growing from the same set of musical roots, are merely different expressions of the same thing. Now, the cultural contexts may differ—with rock being primarily a white music, while jazz, at least the best jazz, is black. But the difference between the two is one of degree, and intent, not of expression and content. Rock seems more interested in form and volume, where jazz's interests lie with content and improvisation. And when Cannonball's quintet starts blowing those simply bluesy bass-emphasized lines, you're watching a fine old jazzman opting for popularity. And if his sound is too simple, or simple-minded for the jazz fan, it's at least 90 percent better than anything most rock musicians are sweating and straining over these days.

MILES DAVIS

DECEMBER 1970
TORONTO TELEGRAM

ALMOST A YEAR AGO, Miles Davis glared at an interviewer and said, "I could put together the greatest rock 'n' roll band you ever saw..." And for his concert last night at Massey Hall, that's exactly what he did.

In the middle of an evening that stretched almost three hours, in fact, in the middle of a piece that itself lasted an hour, the sullen, cool trumpeter who had become since the early fifties the epitome of the public image for a jazzman, rocked as no one has ever rocked before. But what Miles did with his group—bassist Mike Henderson, organist Keith Jarrett, sax Gary Bartz, drummer Jack DeJohnette and Airto [Moreira], a young Brazillian percussionist—went way beyond any ordinary definition of rock.

Like an abstract painting, this music defined itself as it was made. Certain ideas recurred; an octave-leap pattern became a theme. Davis would quote from an early bop solo and think to finish the whole evening with the corniest jazz lick of them all. Bartz and Jarrett would exchange rhythm 'n' blues lines. And Henderson and DeJohnette would lay down a tub-thumping beat. And when it all ended around midnight, the whole concert having started just after 8:30 p.m., they had changed our ears around, reordering all our preconceived notions of just what popular music was.

Once, in a *Playboy* interview, Miles said: "I'm too vain to play anything really bad musically. If ever I feel I am getting to the point where I'm playing it safe, I'll stop." So far, Davis, now forty-four, has never played it safe. His apparent onstage arrogance was well known. His temper had become famous, as had his demands on his musicians. Yet, from the start, he seemed musically limited, urging a bright, burnished tone out of his horn, but not including in any pyrotechnics. However, as trumpeter Art Farmer said of him: "When you're not technically a virtuoso, you have to be saying something. You've got no place to hide." So, like last night, Miles did things as tersely and emphatically as possible. As everyone wailed around him, he'd approach centre stage, as impeccably dressed as ever, raise his trumpet high above his head to signal the start of a new section, and blow a few gruff notes.

Compared to other jazzmen, Miles has always done well, both in terms of publicity and financially. But it was with his second-last LP, *Bitches Brew*, that he really hit the mass markets. And his latest LP, *Miles Davis at Fillmore*, has been hustled out by Columbia Records to catch the growing interest. The idea of "jazz-rock" has been percolating for a couple of years, since groups like Blood, Sweat, & Tears, Chicago, the Nice, and Soft Machine had started selling records. Even jazz musicians like Cannonball Adderley seemed converted to a blend of elaborate solos and simpler forms. But for Miles Davis to do it seemed, a few years ago, as unlikely as it was before 1952, for Stravinsky to use twelve-tone technique. Listeners, however, didn't seem to remember how deeply Miles involved himself in Spanish popular music, things like flamenco patterns and the deeply personal cante jondo for his *Sketches of Spain* LP of almost ten years ago.

There has been a consistency to his music since the start. He's always kept it simple, preferring a minimum of chords. "I think there is a return in jazz," he said a while ago, "to put emphasis on melodic rather than harmonic variation ... too much modern jazz has become thick with chords." And nothing could be more harmonically simple, and in need of melodic invention than rock 'n' roll. Enter Miles Davis. He is no longer introverted, as his solos showed last night. His musical range goes from the most primitive of sounds—dry scratches and a wail in a trumpeter's night—to the most obvious, good old kid stuff—rock 'n' roll.

JOSEPHINE BAKER

1970
TORONTO TELEGRAM

"I LIKE TO SHOCK PEOPLE," jazz singer Josephine Baker said quietly in her hotel room last night. "When I'm on stage, I dance and sing. Yet, mostly, I frighten people. I will fall down, and they will wonder whether I will ever get up again. No one ever knows what I'm going to do." But no one has ever known. At over sixty and looking almost half that age, Josephine Baker's career has spanned two continents and seven decades, yet she opens an exhausting two-week stint tonight at the Royal York's Imperial Room—her first appearance in Toronto since 1964. She first performed when she was twelve in local clubs and rent-parties in the black ghettos of hometown St. Louis, yet in the Paris of the 1920s she had become a star of the Folies Bergère. A French citizen since 1937, and famed for her flamboyance, she danced nude for the café society and walked her leopards down the Champs-Élysées, yet with the German invasion of France in 1940 she worked with the resistance, for which she received the Legion of Honor decoration.

Now she's raising twelve adopted children of various races in the villa Princess Grace and Prince Rainier of Monaco helped find for her at Roquebrune-Cap-Martin in Monaco and working on a four-volume autobiography. "There's just so much to remember," she said, sitting barefoot on the floor. "One book will be about the children—they range in age between seven and nineteen. Another will be about my career, you know. I knew Louis Armstrong and Sidney Bechet when I did chorus work on Broadway in New York City, and then Ernest Hemingway and Maurice Chevalier in Paris. But they all were just friends then, and not famous. Another book will be about my seven years with the resistance. For that was a time when no one had any money, and when we all thought that we were all working together for a better future. And the last book will be a collection of photographs and letters: I've collected newspaper articles about me since 1925. I even have some that supposedly recorded my death in 1940.

"There will also be many of the letters I have received. There's one from General de Gaulle and another from President John Kennedy, just before his assassination, about a civil right march I was going to go on. But as I've worked on all these books, I keep remembering on how little things have changed. And it's the young people who keep changing things. Like myself and my friends in the 1920s, young people have always wanted freedom. This is something that's always been the same. So, in a sense there's no new music: music like rock 'n' roll has always been here. And while I might have shocked people running nude around the Champs-Élysées, you can see the same thing happening now with nude dancing and girls' minidresses. I didn't do anything just to be shocking, though, I did things to be free. With my twelve children to support, I'm broke right now. But with my freedom, I'm rich in so many other ways."

Being broke is not a new situation for Miss Baker. At the height of her fame in Paris, she was billed as the "Dark Star," and created a minor sensation dancing on a mirror naked except for a curtain of bananas. With her theme song, "Two Loves Have I," a standard in nightclubs, she bought a villa outside Paris and filled it with works by Picasso and the Dada group of painters. She made her film debut in 1934 playing the title role in *Zou Zou*. She completed two others, *La Sirène des Tropiques* and *Princesse Tam-Tam* and was at work on her fourth, *Fausse Alerte*, when war broke out. In between her club dates she also appeared in the operetta, *La Créole*, which had been specifically adopted for her from Jacques Offenbach's music.

She announced her retirement in 1956, only to be lured back to the stage at the Olympia, in Paris, to star in the 1959 production of *Paris Mes Amours*, a musical loosely based on her own career which she eventually took on world tour in 1960. But, by 1963, she faced eviction from the fifteenth-century Château des Milandes she had bought near Périgueux in southwest France. Household debts had reached $368,000, while the chateau itself only realized $57,000 on the auction block.

So, Josephine Baker was back performing again. "The way my life is right now, "she explained, "I haven't even thought of movies or records. What I do is piecework—each one of my club appearances is one piece of everything I do and it's a piece I fit together to create something larger. It is a bit like making a quilt blanket. As you add more and more pretty, soon it all comes out as something. Besides, I'm more free that way."

SINGER-SONGWRITERS

GORDON LIGHTFOOT

JANUARY 1967
GLOBE AND MAIL

IF HIS OPENING-NIGHT PERFORMANCE at the Riverboat is any indication, Gordon Lightfoot remains something of a paradox. Some came last night to hear him as an entertainer, while others—listening intently to each word—appreciated him as a folk artist, purveying something beyond music.

Many of his songs are concerned with the ossifying city existence, yet he sings them with a country-and-western edge to his voice; and to deepen the confusion, he is a folksinger who has a hit-parade record that laments a gigolo-jilted go-go girl. With bassist John Stockfish and lead guitarist Red Shea playing discreetly in the background, Lightfoot's essential quality—that of a fine singer—came well into relief. Electronically amplified folk-rock too often assaults the listener to force him to experience what there is to be said, but Lightfoot's performance last night compelled, rather than cudgeled you to listen. He has assimilated his apparently dissident materials into a style that is listenable, memorable, and, judging by his success this year, saleable.

Lightfoot is the writer of most his material, yet there remains a carefully maintained equilibrium between Lightfoot the singer and Lightfoot the composer. Several of his songs have become pop standards in the hands of other performers. "For Lovin' Me" was a hit for Peter, Paul and Mary in North America, Australia, and in Europe; and Marty Robbins's single of "Ribbon of Darkness" became number one on the country-and-western hit parade. Few artists, however, perform Lightfoot songs as well as Lightfoot.

APRIL 1967
GLOBE AND MAIL

GORDON LIGHTFOOT'S CONCERT LAST night at Massey Hall was a crucial one. After the most successful year of his career, with its multiple coffee-house appearances and several futile forays into the hit parade jungles, his style of songs was due for a change. But most of the material he used was the same country-and-Lightfoot parade of Canadiana.

Singing his own material—a Canadian Charles Aznavour in blue jeans—he showed himself to be a competent lyricist, an individualistic performer, and an unusually gifted melodist. Everything he sang, every guitar chord that fell predictably into place, was so well controlled that it lapsed into a folky-showbiz surface hipness. Yet with a few more songs such as the Indian-raga-influenced "The Way I Feel," or "Softly," where Red Shea's guitar and John Stockfish's bass wove a careful progression of semi-jazz chords around the melody, a new, less stereotyped Lightfoot style might appear.

With his carefully planned ad-libs interspersed between the songs, he sang for almost two and a half hours, never descending into the off-key bleating of many equally hard-pressed folksingers. But although the voice held out, interest didn't. Lightfoot is in danger of becoming one of the sacred Canadian cows. But if something doesn't happen soon, he is merely being fattened for extinction.

JULY 1967
GLOBE AND MAIL

GORDON LIGHTFOOT, TORONTO'S FOLK laureate, faces two dilemmas. With last night's Riverboat opening representing his third appearance in the city during the past year, he is beginning to suffer an acute case of overexposure. And the confrontation between Lightfoot's rural training and imagination with his new urban environment has reduced his musical development to a state of suspended animation, neither hick nor hop. Backed by bassist John Stockfish and lead guitarist Red Shea, Lightfoot's lusty singing proved that his vocal chords, like his imagination—he has added thirteen new songs to his repertoire—are as strong as ever. But it's not volume, but variety that he lacks.

If being hip is having the sophistication of a wise primitive in a giant, organized jungle, Lightfoot prefers to stand removed from current trends. His songs contain neither the romantic anarchism of Tom Paxton, nor the moral nihilism of Bob Dylan. Instead of looking for some measure of humanity in the face of the sterility of modern life, Lightfoot still is searching for a latter-day Walden.

Caught between the Top 40 and the back forty, Lightfoot rationalized it thus: "I'm doing music I believe in, and if the hit parade accepts it, that's all the better. The trend to accept my style of music will never come around, so I'll have to sell myself as an individual. I would like to get a hit, but the Top 40 is not an easy business—you have to juice up your material—but that's not the important thing. It's still the music that counts to me."

While most pop music lyrics are like yeast to an idea-packed society fermenting already, Lightfoot's songs reach back to the same simplified, naturalistic, and unadventurous language as other Canadian writers such as W. O. Mitchell and Farley Mowat. The words register quick stabs of picturesque detail, sense impressions, and the musical reactions of a rural disenchanted singer.

MARCH 1969
TORONTO TELEGRAM

THE PROCESS HAS BEEN LONG, tiresome, sometimes tedious. But an end of some sort was reached last Saturday night in Massey Hall. The moment was imperceptible in its passing. But it was there; and Gordon Lightfoot seemed to realize exactly what Gordon Lightfoot was about. In the past, the focus on Lightfoot has been fuzzy—for most of his critics (including me), and, I suspect, himself. His songs were still-life watercolours, skillfully etched along his fine melody lines. But their relation to the roaring, demanding, joking, pushing offstage Lightfoot was puzzling. In front of footlights, his self-consciousness would diminish the force. Then, everything seemed too easy to take. The subjects of his songs, and their creation, were safely removed from us in time and place. And there were always the reminders, the gosh-shucks suddenly thrown in to remind us of everything's artificiality, that nothing really serious was happening, and not to worry.

And we didn't. That is, until last Saturday night. Then, Lightfoot's performance took on a strange intensity; of the singer's clambering through the metre of his songs, hand over hand, singing at and with a world he never made and was only beginning to understand. "How old are you?" he asks himself. And answers: "Never old enough."

The occasion, one of four evenings (the last being tonight) where almost every place in the 2,650-seat hall has been sold out, was being taped by United Artists for a live album. But the resulting LP will catch only the surface of the concert. The buoyant interplay between Red Shea's guitar, and the soft contoured lines of Rick Haynes, who now replaces John Stockfish; the colour, the lights, Lightfoot's peach-and-brown-suede-with-frills outfit; the singer's enthusiasm at being back at the hall after touring England and the States; and that tension thrust at the mic during each song—all somehow beyond the most delicate of recording techniques.

And new songs will be pressed into wax; those that should be like the "Affair on 8th Avenue"; and those that shouldn't, the "Ballad" (not Battle, as some have described it) of Yarmouth Castle." Perhaps Lightfoot will receive another gold record to add to the two he received yesterday afternoon. Maybe there will be more accolades: the thirty-year-old Lightfoot did this; his singing did that; his writing continues to grow in stature, etc. These will fit everything into meaningless compartments.

And nothing could be more misleading. For Lightfoot was simply and abundantly alive; the rarest of phenomena, an act of constant revitalization. Lightfoot didn't indulge in the business of sweeping bravura gestures. His range still remains limited, a perceptive glance here, now a near-perfect melody like in "Canadian Railroad Trilogy." But within these confines there had come a rhythm and contour that grew quite powerful; powerful through its irregularity. The more relaxed he became, the more Lightfoot let slip through. And sometimes a song or an attitude or a line of patter was sparked—the brief glint of extra imagination and personal perception coming out.

Suddenly there was something peeking through the transparency of performance. Something quirky, a bad joke, an awful pun, satire, as in "Divorce Country Style," turned in upon itself and its singer. There was a rangy, thrusting kind of nervous vitality that bound the concert together. He put his arms around his two accompanists and bounded across the stage away from his audience. There was a curious sense of toughness muted by tenderness—like an old Humphrey Bogart movie.

REVIEW: *SIT DOWN YOUNG STRANGER*
APRIL 1970
TORONTO TELEGRAM

A NEW GORDON LIGHTFOOT album for Toronto is a lot like a new Beatles album for the world. It's somewhat of an event. It sums up old trends; gives new directions. And it somehow changes people as it passes through gathering sales. But the new Lightfoot LP, *Sit Down Young Stranger*, should have the same effect as if the Beatles started playing zithers. Not only are there differences between this and older material enough; differences seem final. What has made a live Lightfoot performance great, is that any one of his songs could reach out and unify an audience in a shared response.

The one sad thing about his career was that the one medium that would have increased his capacity to reach larger audiences, the LP, usually prevented him from doing so. As beautiful as the songs might be, something on his older albums always seemed crabbed and cramped. Either the release was mistimed, or the promotion misdirected.

But some curious things started to happen. In his one major interview in recent years, Bob Dylan explained his new musical direction in terms of trying to capture Lightfoot's sound. Then, Lightfoot's songs started to change. His lyrics became urbanized, more involved with an inner wilderness. His melodies took on new, sophisticated turns. Changes were the order of the year, and he switched record companies—from United Artists to Warner Bros., which controls Reprise. And Reprise washed away some of Lightfoot's lovable barnacles.

Sit Down Young Stranger is glossier than anything he's done before. It's a more "perfect" album; the melodies with their almost Mozartean grace, the lyrics and the orchestrations, are all held in strange suspension that's almost too silent to be real. Produced by Joe Wissert and Lenny Waronker, the cuts add various artists to basic Lightfoot sidemen, Red Shea and Rick Haynes. The string arrangements on the first song, "Minstrel of the Dawn," were done by songwriter singer Randy Newman. And Newman doesn't let them intrude into the lyrics' quiet sadness.

"Me and Bobby McGee" (by Kris Kristofferson and Fred Foster) is the only non-Lightfoot song on the LP. With Ray Cooper's bottleneck guitar-playing twisting around the square melody, the tune takes on its own charm, folksy, sly or poignant in turn. "Approaching Lavender" is possibly the weakest thing on the LP. Everything about it is indefinite. And nothing in terms of suspense or deliberate ambiguity is added because of this. "Saturday Clothes" offers the strange possibility that Lightfoot's been listening to too much Burt Bacharach. Only John Sebastian's autoharp playing brings it all back home to any degree.

The next three cuts, "Cobwebs & Dust" (almost a children's rhyme, with Van Dyke Parks on harmonium), "Poor Little Allison" (with a ridiculous strong arrangement by Nick DeCaro), and "Sit Down Young Stranger" (the first cut side two) all recall earlier Lightfoot material. "If You Could Read My Mind" brings up another incredible possibility: that Gord Lightfoot decided to out-write Jim Webb using Webb's own idiom. The song's so strong, however, I suspect that even when Glen Campbell starts to do it, it will hold up under the strain. Both "Baby It's Allright," and "Your Love's Return" skirt that dangerous ground between the banal and the low-key. And last comes "The Pony Man." Like many of the other songs on this LP, in fact, like much of the rest of Lightfoot's material, its simplicity is deceptive. Yet, as it passes over the grooves, something strange happens: All the little everyday things gather together, producing something so basic that the only response possible has to be shared.

MARCH 1973
TORONTO STAR

LAST NIGHT AT THE first of his five concerts at Massey Hall, Gordon Lightfoot brought off what a few artists manage only a few times in their lives. He united his audience into a shared response to his music. Everyone in the packed hall—each of the concerts until Sunday night are sold out—seemed as much a part of the music as did Lightfoot or his guitarist Terry Clements or bassist Rick Haynes. The two-hour concert had a communal feeling to it with Lightfoot, in patched jeans, navy blue sweater, and sneakers, being just as surprised as his audience when something worked well.

Backstage, after his encore, he was presented three gold records by WEA Records for his three most recent albums, *Sit Down Young Stranger*, *Summer Side of Life*, and *Old Dan's Records*, each of which has sold over one hundred thousand copies. But the real surprise came early on when he decided to sing a new song written only Tuesday night. It was called "Carefree Highway," but before he would sing it, he dragged out a music stand so that he could see the lyrics and melody line.

To some degree, Lightfoot's casualness was to be expected. Now thirty-four, he first appeared at Massey Hall when he was eight years old. And having appeared there as a solo performer five years previously, last night was, as he mentioned, "sort of homecoming." But it was more than that. He varied his material from one of his first hit records, "Early Morning Rain," to one of his more recent, "If You Could Read My Mind," which sold over 850,000 copies in the U.S., as if to point out not any radical change in his music, but in how constant it has been. Thus, his most recent songs didn't sound particularly new, just as his earliest pieces never sounded that old. Both seemed a part of the same process and were as perfect in their way as any Schubert work.

Similarly, Lightfoot constructed his two-hour show much along the lines he has drawn every year. And he did it shrewdly, building each song in perfect proportions with all its surfaces gleaming. Bassist Haynes occasionally upset his balance with some overly loud runs, while guitarist Clements never contributed as much as he should have. But the results were what was expected. Both Lightfoot and the audience seemed to recognize that not only the occasion but the music was becoming part of a tradition they both had created.

REVIEW: *SUMMERTIME DREAM*
JUNE 1976
TORONTO STAR

LIGHTFOOT'S MUSICAL GROWTH RESULTS in an excellent disc. There seems to be a time lag between what people think Gordon Lightfoot's doing and what he thinks he's doing. And now, with the release of his latest album, *Summertime Dream*, it would appear that even his record company has been left behind. Several months ago, before the album was complete, Lightfoot intended to call it *Race Among the Ruins*, a name taken from one of the songs. But in the interim, he either changed his mind about the name or was persuaded to change it. Yet while *Summertime Dream* is a sweetly evocative enough name, it completely misses the album's tone. The album is not only among the best he has ever released; it's also among the most important.

His work over the past year has grown in stages, the most recent being a period when he consciously worked at producing pop songs such as "Sundown." It was as if Lightfoot, always a strong melodist, had learned to fill out his previously spare songs with a more complex texture, adding an extra dimension to his work. *Summertime Dream*, however, is an important departure from this format. It's an extension of his pop work in a way, but it represents something new in his thinking. For this album, he seems to have worked with the texture itself, writing not just songs, but miniature tone poems. This is the first time, in fact, that he's produced an album which must be heard as a whole, that has several layers of meaning (both musical and verbal) happening at once. It's a sophisticated work but one, because of Lightfoot's discipline and love of melody, that seems simple on the surface.

"The Wreck of the Edmund Fitzgerald" is one example. Ostensibly the song is part of the singer's ballad tradition. But where in the past he would merely have strung out the tale along a line of identical verses and choruses, here he evolves the story in a way that allows the music to bring increasing tension from beginning to end. The song grows with it. There are plenty of potential hits on the album, the title song and "Spanish Moss" among them. But the LP offers much, much more than these.

NOVEMBER 1977
TORONTO STAR

TAKING TIME OUT TO get personal on Gordon Lightfoot's birthday. I have a photograph of Gordon Lightfoot and Bob Dylan taken at a Mariposa Folk Festival a few years ago. They're smiling, arm in arm. Not unexpectedly, they don't seem completely comfortable. Over the years and after countless glances at that picture, I've come to realize it's not Dylan who's creating the tension. It's Lightfoot who's uncomfortable with the implied fraternity, and it's Dylan who seems only too happy to have his picture taken.

It's Gordon Lightfoot's thirty-ninth birthday today, and by his own account, the twentieth anniversary of what he describes as "just doing what I do," or what we used to call folk singing. "Actually, I've been singing professionally since I was ten," he said on the phone from Los Angeles where he's finishing an album. "But I started for real at places like the old Village Corner, and before that even, the Orchard Park Tavern when I was nineteen. I was a dancer on the CBC's *Country Hoedown*. It was twenty years ago that I officially gave up my daytime jobs—I was working at office jobs back then—and started out in the clubs."

A generation grew up listening to Gordon Lightfoot in the clubs, places like Steele's Tavern and later at the Riverboat (although not many of us remember the gig he had as a drummer seventeen years ago in Ben McPeek's revue at the King Edward Hotel, *Up Tempo 60*). In fact, before he actually left the club circuit ten years ago to do concerts in places like Massey Hall, more than a few members of this generation had grown away from him.

It wasn't difficult to understand why. The magazine articles and CBC specials saluted the man for his reverence for the Canadian landscape; we revelled in the city sounds from the cityscape. Dylan had gone electric a long time before our ears were filled with rock 'n' roll. We even started calling him "Gordie." Or even "good old Gordie," with the emphasis on the "old." Lightfoot said on the phone that while he noticed his effect on musicians like Jimmy Buffett, his own "basic beliefs about life haven't changed much." And that's what used to bother me about him. When everything else was shifting, when any idea seemed possible, he stood like one of those darn trees he kept writing about, unchanged and unchanging.

While Dylan was writing songs with all the immediacy of graffiti, Lightfoot was using imagery complete with references to minstrels and knights. But that was my problem, not his, and oddly enough, it was not a song but another picture that made me come to understand his struggles and the achievements that came from them. These pictures are the ones I've in my mind after seeing a CBC documentary several years ago. On the program, Lightfoot explained how he wrote, that he often got up in the middle of the night when an idea came to him and he went to his little work desk where he could write it down. He talked about how hard he had to work at writing. A few days ago, he said that writing came easier to him now that he knows "what mistakes not to make." Yet his songs, however spontaneously they seem in performance, show signs of labour. And they seem more honest, more personal because of it.

I've come to respect him more than I do many other singers, not for what he's earned (and by many accounts, he's very well off), but for what he's had to pay. There's one former marriage and twenty years on the road all for, as he says, "thirteen original albums which, I guess you could say, is my achievement."

AUGUST 1980
TORONTO STAR

IT'S A GRAND HOUSE in the old Rosedale style, offering power more than elegance and designed for all the proper comforts. Just off the front door is the master den, woody, informal, with its walls lined with trophies and mementos. What industrial baron used to plot his profits here? What deals have been wheeled? And why is Gordon Lightfoot, the current owner of the mementos, trophies, den, and house, looking so worried? No reason, really. He's planning to change his life, that's all. And by the time he makes it to the CNE Grandstand stage Monday night to begin his tribute-cum-benefit for Canada's Olympic athletes, he will likely know whether the metamorphosis has begun—whether he'll be appearing in the next Bruce Dern movie, *The Last Desperado*, which starts shooting October 6, and whether behind this desk, scratching his beard, it'll be G. Lightfoot, movie star.

Movie star. He's forty-one, rich, terminally restless and in the middle of what seems to be a never-ending tour, this is one taking him through some American sun belt cities and into Harrah's, at Reno, Nevada, for a week starting October 2.

The point is, he doesn't need this new problem which, just as certain as snow in winter, he'll fret over. He doesn't need it financially, as one look around the halls will confirm. He doesn't really need it to spruce up his public image. Like the better banks, the public Lightfoot—that minor drinking charge of two summers ago aside—has remained a symbol of certainty, a sage emotional investment, sure to retain its value. Among these trophies are his awards, *Playboy* Polls he's won and the plaques from admiring groups wishing to show their appreciation. On the floor are a pile of albums, all his own, each one of which has sold at least one hundred thousand copies across the country, most having sold much more.

So why the movie, then? Peer pressure? Is it because Levon Helm and Robbie Robertson, both rock performers he knows, have had screen success over the past year and Ronnie Hawkins is in the upcoming Michael Cimino western? He glowers and fusses with the scraggy fringe of a beard that he's growing for the role. "We've had three other parts offered this year," he offers. "I've been getting movie offers like they're going out of style. We had two other offers in the last five months. We had an offer to do a movie with Steve McQueen and an offer to do one with Burt Reynolds—and that's the second one I've been offered with Burt Reynolds.

"Now, this one I might be doing now will be the Bruce Dern movie coming after his current one, *Middle Age Crazy*. It'll be a modern-day story called *The Last Desperado* and they've tapped me to play the part of the U.S. marshal, a sort of Marlboro man. I've already done the screen test and now I have to try and memorize the lines. I mean, Bruce Dern has a say in this situation because he might prefer to have a professional actor do it because it's that kind of part. So, what I've been doing is really learning these lines and do the best I can. They're also giving me an acting coach for three days to help me out."

He leans back on his seat as if he's decided to relax. Then thinking better of it, he shifts forward again, resting on his elbows. Bev, his sister and manager, listens intently. "If I don't get that part, I'm still going ahead with the movies. I'll have a cameo role as a farmer and I'm recording the song that'll be used in the picture." As per usual, he has more than one base covered. But he's going more and more public these days. And the more he does, the more he confounds his critics who've suggested he's far too conservative for his own good. Before Carroll Baker, the Good Brothers, Liona Boyd, or Harry Chapin appear on the tribute Monday night, there'll be Lightfoot, completely alone on the very stage he has long maintained he wouldn't play because it was too big. (His first Olympic team benefit four years ago was at the smaller-scaled Maple Leaf Gardens.)

Then again, he agreed to sing on the last Juno Awards show, thus contradicting his longtime embargo on television. Cautious by nature—his songs aren't well crafted by accident—he has nevertheless decided to take some career risks. He's even given up sailing, once his one true passion outside of music. "It was eating up so much time that it really started to get in the way of things," he explains.

In fact, he might have accepted one of Burt Reynolds's earlier offers "except I was going through a personal crisis in my relationship with my girl and I didn't feel like doing it. Now things have resolved (they've split up) and I feel like doing it. I want to do what I think is important, I volunteered to do the last benefit, for this one, they asked me. Originally, I got the ideas of these benefits from a show done in Montreal for the American team. And as I was sitting there watching it, I said, 'Why doesn't somebody in Canada do something to support the Olympic team?' Because I had heard the Olympic team was in rags for 1976. It needs money now for the upcoming Pan-American games. We're going to raise $200,000, eventually, for this team. Some of the athletes will be there at the concert, too.

I might do this in 1984. I might make this a regular event."

But the movie career? "Yeah, well," he says. "This part I'm doing, is for real. I mean I could make a second career out of this. I could do supporting roles for the next ten, fifteen years."

JONI MITCHELL

FEBRUARY 1967
GLOBE AND MAIL

THE ANTI-BLUES, THE FOLKSY, sunny, all's-well, happy half-vision of life seeped through all of Joni Mitchell's songs last night like golden corn syrup, as she opened a two-week engagement at the Riverboat. With all the innocence of a helpless high school cheerleader, she raised her voice, for all its breathier uncertainty, into Joan Baez–like silver-lamé soprano—only to be drowned by her guitar chords. And all the skillfully manipulated images of her lyrics (she writes all her own material) would disappear like a washed-out Monet print.

It is unusual in this total-environment McLuhanistic age to run across message folk songs, but Miss Mitchell's songs (at least what I could hear of them) retained a personal message. "I read very little," she said, "and if my songs have been influenced in any way, it is only from what I've read in high school." And although her songs are at cultural crosscurrents with the Irving Berlin–[Alan Jay] Lerner and [Ruth] Lowe–Richard Rodgers regime, neither have they the

Brechtian bitterness of Bob Dylan's writing. Nor do they go off on psychedelic side tracks as have the Beatles. In the "Wizard of Is" she sang of "the happy ending stories that you hear," and in an introduction to "Just Like Me," she complained that "there was something missing" in all the protest songs that were being written.

While avoiding the saccharine sentimental sophistication of many of the non-rock popular songs, hers were still too flowery and fanciful. And in this case, the medium compounded the message. "I've known people who've interpreted my songs differently than I have. But although my songs are all my own, they're like most modern music, they borrow everything... why, I've even got a blues or two." But for Joni Mitchell, the blues of a well-bred, well-heeled, well-informed ex-Saskatoon female folksinger.

JULY 1967
GLOBE AND MAIL

IN POP MUSIC, there's a new feeling in the air. The disillusioning, depressing songs of the Bob Dylan era are being replaced by ones characterized by a hippie hedonism. The new beat credo is love (on a social as well as personal level), personal freedom is the new necessary condition, altruism its expression, and mind-expansiveness its inspiration. And in this search for a latter-day Utopia, Joni Mitchell, appearing at the Riverboat until August 6, has a new relevance as a singer. Images of tranquility, of children, naturalistic elements, and day-to-day living comprise her poetry; fluid, breathless melodies over original experimental harmonies fill out her music, and a gentle feminism colours her performance.

As she herself puts it, "I spent months knocking on record company doors, but suddenly music is accepting so much more. There is now an accepted female point of view. And my problem now is that I have to decide on an image that I have to fill."

Yet unlike other female singer-writers, for example, Janis Ian in rock 'n' roll, or Judy Collins in folk, there is little emotional complexity or ambiguity about realism in Joni Mitchell's singing. Racism, riots, or revolutions (personal or political) are never mentioned; she even sings a pastel blues. "Protest always seemed ironic to me," she says, "for who do you reach? Those who like your songs agree with you; those who don't won't listen." Perhaps, but while in the most modern songs the attitude is unsentimental, she sings of a "funny day looking for laughter—and finding it there."

The frantic escapism of the Beats of the fifties has been replaced by the wilful self-indulgence of the self-styled flower children. The dark, death-orientated literature of Kerouac's generation is no longer read; and in its place J. R. R. Tolkien's hobbits and Hermann Hesse's escapism (as in *Siddhartha*, where a young boy leaves his Buddhist parents in search of truth and himself) are now in vogue. The hippies are beginning to see themselves as holy barbarians, living lives of inverted sainthood. Drugs are no longer used to escape an old reality, but are employed in an attempt to find a new one. But the fads of the capricious hippie culture, now loving, now messianic, now vengeful, vary as radically as their hair styles. And Joni Mitchell's music, once too sweet, sad, and sexless, seems to sum up what is going on now, and has them drooling like Pavlov's dogs, for more.

NOVEMBER 1967
GLOBE AND MAIL

IN FOLK AND POP MUSIC, creativity has become the latest con game, the newest cant. Record producers rarely offer opportunities to new artists who lack "original material." Joni Mitchell's folk songs last night at the Riverboat were not only original, but distinctive. Their long-breathed melodies, personal imagery, and complex guitar accompaniment were a treat for the ear. In her hands, complexity was reduced to simple, deceptively naive statements. She seemed, like Alice, to have been asking the question, "Who am I, where am I?" then answering with a song. And, as in "Chelsea Morning," all reality was reduced to a childlike state of innocence.

But last night she added something new. The experience gained since her previous Toronto appearances added a more sombre and sobering side to Miss Mitchell's singing. Her voice was more darkly coloured. Many of the lyrics had become more starkly simple. One basic idea could escalate into a song of explosive proportions. All of which is to say that her songs and singing displayed a hard-won maturity that made them seem less fragile and more lasting.

This wider range in mood made the older, quieter songs all the more impressive. And the quiescent and introspective Miss Mitchell had greater impact than most folksingers when they're yelling. She seemed to admit a line rather than sing it. She worked these tranquil songs without fuss. But the importance of her style still lay in its quietness; in its peaceful expansion of microscopically observed details. In the space of the four or so minutes allowed for each song, she sketched in enough material for a short story. Her music and lyrics showed greater discipline. In one song she sang, "Tomorrow he will come to me and speak his sorrow constantly" to a pensive, drone-like accompaniment that underlined the song's despondent mood.

Technically, she was as secure as ever. But it was in the wide range of emotions that she made the most meaningful contact with the audience. For, despite critics and the jeers of hippiedom's avant-garde, Miss Mitchell has retained her highly personal style. Not a servant to reality, she moulded it for her own uses. She didn't make meaningless protests, nor mumble psychedelic nonsense. She just sang to bring happiness.

REVIEW: *BLUE*
JUNE 1971
TORONTO TELEGRAM

"OH, I AM A LONELY PAINTER, I live in a box of paints," sings Joni Mitchell somewhere near the end of her fourth and most recent LP, *Blue*. But the description applies not only to the singer, but the songs. Because her music has been introspective much of the time, and because her approach is highly personal all of the time, the ten songs of *Blue* will undoubtedly be used by fans as a chart to find what course her mind has set. But even for the most obvious of singers, this can be hazardous; and trying to sort out Joni's elliptical songs can be confusing at the best of times.

This is not to say there's anything particularly obtuse about this LP. If anything, it's her best to date. The melodies are less operatic and diffuse, the accompaniment more varied, and her voice has a richer, less keening sound. Every song seems focused, and concisely conceived. As with the songs she first tentatively tried out in the Riverboat years before she moved to California's Laurel Canyon, those in *Blue* rely on visual imagery. She still paints in her spare time. In "All I Want," there are roads she travels down; in "Little Green," her images of crocuses and northern lights go back to her Saskatchewan youth; and there's always some pretty men to help her when "them lonesome blues collide." Her music registers easily in visual terms. While many of her images have remained constant, what she painted on her first three LPs in light colours, now appear in darker tones. Their airiness has been replaced by something more substantial.

All of which makes it easier for me to understand her work. At the Riverboat, when she was just starting to sing and I was just starting to write, we would argue about each song. To me, they seemed too impressionistic, too flighty... too feminine. To her, they were "only what I see and feel—me experiences."

"Since I moved to California," she said some time later, "I know my life has changed. How it has changed my music? I guess it's too early to tell."

That was about a year ago. But this LP gives clues to what's happened in the interim. She's begun to rely more on other musicians for accompaniment—in this case, Steve Stills on guitar and bass, James Taylor on guitar, Sneeky Pete [Kleinow] on steel guitar, and Russ Kunkel on drums. The California experience can be seen elsewhere. That particular mellow mood often heard on records by Crosby, Stills, Nash & Young has seeped into tunes like "All I Want," and "Carey." And in one song, "California," she celebrates her home: "California, I'm coming home/Oh, make me feel good rock 'n' roll band/I'm your biggest fan."

What used to bother me, the ethereal, supine quality to most of her work, to everything she did, is gone.

AUGUST 1979
TORONTO STAR

ELLIOT ROBERTS IS THE very model of the successful rock manager; soft-spoken, as tough as a twenty-page contract, and actually fond of the music. His clients include Devo and Neil Young, but right now they're forgotten with the other worries he has on his mind. For here, in the concrete dressing room of the Blossom Music Center, the sensuously sculpted open-air theatre on a hillside twenty miles south of the city, Joni Mitchell has decided to take time off from her twenty-five-city tour and talk. And talk and talk. All these years she has shied away from the media; all these years of not needing the media.

Roberts looks ever so slightly alarmed as he stands next to the food trays of fruit and cheese slices.

Mitchell has remained remote, rather than aloof (although *The Village Voice* once panned one of her albums with a headline reading:

"Raised on Snobbery"), out of an instinct for survival. This instinct goes way back. "Joan does not relate well," was a note frequently added to her report card in school. As a child, growing up in Saskatoon, she remembers hanging out, not with her schoolmates, but "downtown, with the Ukrainians and the Indians: they were more emotionally honest, and they were better dancers." And when, in recent years, the press started panning her albums—first with *The Hissing of Summer Lawns*, then *Hejira*, and most emphatically, *Don Juan's Reckless Daughter*—she was hurt by the reaction, feeling that she had finally made an artistic breakthrough no one apparently completely understood. The final blow seemed to come several years ago when *Rolling Stone* magazine ran a lengthy gossipy piece on her, outlining her affairs with Graham Nash of Crosby, Stills & Nash, and others. She even quit touring, fearing that it would "threaten" her writing, that she'd end up, like so many others, writing about a rock star on the road, a narrow perspective on life at even the best of times. Yet, I suspect, it was her writing that brought her back out on the road and meeting the press.

Working with [Charles] Mingus was proof of her artistic instincts and inclinations. At one time, she says, she would have been happy to have been considered to be as good as Peter, Paul and Mary. But she was always after bigger artistic game. And now it's in the bag. And she's happy about that, proud of it.

But still, Roberts worries.

For a while, though, what she's saying is okay. She remembers working with Mingus, the volatile jazz bassist and composer whose music she set for her current album, *Mingus*. "There weren't many conflicts between us," she says. "Maybe because I was a woman. He liked women. He was such a flirt." And she becomes brightly enthusiastic about her band, which includes bassist Jaco Pastorius and guitarist Pat Metheny along with percussionist Don Alias, saxophonist Michael Brecker, and keyboard player Lyle Mays. It's a band that can truly embrace her music, with its fluid rhythms and liquid melodies.

Ah, yes. Everything free and easy here, as she begins to reminisce about her appearance on Bob Dylan's Rolling Thunder Revue (which was in Toronto four years ago), the last time she appeared in public...

She was all nerves and vision back then: Skinny Joni Anderson from Saskatoon, who idolized James Dean, tried art school in Calgary—she now does many of her own album covers and a collection of her work will be appearing in the forthcoming book, *Starart*—and who left Chuck Mitchell, her then husband of eight months with this memory: "She always had a strong visceral sense of what to do."

But now it seems, much of what she has wanted to do, she's done: she's where she wanted to go. She's a handsome woman; her broad shoulders, tapered, well-muscled hands, and deep tan give the impression of a strong calm. She's relaxed. She has also gained weight, not much, but just enough to make you notice her body and her physicality. She now moves on stage, throwing her hips into the beat, letting her shoulders relax into the flow of the sound.

In one of her albums, *The Hissing of Summer Lawns*, she mentions the turn-of-the-century French painter, Henri Rousseau, whose works are a fantastic collation of exotic scenes and bold primary colours. Her fascination with Rousseau has not stopped; her concerts are a jungle of colours. The Persuasions, the acapella male quintet, open the show, reaching way back into gospel music for their bittersweet harmonies. Their singing comes from the gut, but it is no more visceral than hers, starting with the rolling version of "Big Yellow Taxi," a subdued "Court and Spark," and next, "Coyote."

Her concert spans about forty years of music, with her Mingus collaborations—"Goodbye Pork Pie Hat" and "The Dry Cleaner from Des Moines"—being both literally and figuratively the centrepieces.

The music's as lush and as softly textured as tropical jungle. What she has accomplished with pieces such as "Furry Sings the Blues," "Raised on Robbery," or even "Why Do Fools Fall in Love," sung without instruments, but with the Persuasions, and finally, "Woodstock," is bring the colour she so loves to use in her painting and forces into her verbal imagery directly into her music. You can almost see what she's playing. There are grumbling, almost maniacal solos by Pastorius—the dark tones for her picture; saxophonist Michael Brecker hoots and honks out old rhythm 'n' blues riffs—slashes of red; Metheny spins out a glistening solo with notes darting like swifts around a belfry.

Backstage, she tells another story about her work with Charles Mingus—about how, during one rehearsal, she sang a certain note and he attempted to correct her. "He said I sang the note 'square,' that I should do something differently with it. We got along well. I overrode his decision a couple of times, and he insisted on a thing or two. But this time I thought I was right. 'Charles,' I told him, 'that note may have been square in your time, but it has been so long since it was done, it's hip again.'" She pauses: "Working with him was a radiant experience," she adds. "Everything was such a high.

"When I was just a little kid—before all the pop thing came along—I listened mostly to jazz. I have more bebop melodies in my head than anything else. I'm thirty-five now, so it's natural for me to have listened to jazz."

But did she listen to any singers of thirty or forty years ago, Anita O'Day, perhaps? she was asked. "She was white, right?" says Mitchell. "No, I don't know her—maybe it's the whiteness in my voice you hear. I can't help but sound white. Although now"—and here she shrugs—"there's something about black people I feel very close to. I know that sounds weird, because I'm a WASP and all. But, well, I don't have much respect for technology, although I drive a car and work in a twenty-four-track recording studio, and I have a tremendous respect for those people who are not that many generations removed from something really basic.

"I've not been given a lot of liberty with my music," she says. "It wasn't until this year that I got hip about radio formats—you know, music for ten- to twenty-five-year-old males and all that. My position, right now, is like a president's in office. People out there will say, 'Okay, you've had your ride, now it's someone else's turn.' But I feel I still have my best work left ahead of me. I always make my music to please me, not to please someone else. I like to think that if it does please me, it will please someone else, too. This thinking has served me well, so far.

"Like these benefits you're asked to do. I've been asked to do the anti-nuclear concerts at (New York's) Madison Square Garden (next month, along with Jackson Browne, Bruce Springsteen, John Holt, and James Taylor), but I don't know. I'm more of a pro-type person than a negative one. I'm against nuclear energy as such, but I think, while you're against something, you have to come up with some feasible alternatives. I prefer to stay out of things like that.

"The kind of political things I like to take part in are the ones where there are immediate problems with immediate remedies. I did the James Bay benefit (in Montreal several years ago) because there were a lot of people who would be displaced immediately, and there would be immediate problems. I just don't want to go off half baked on anything, not even if half of me is for it. I don't want to be naively radical.

"In the sixties, if you didn't do benefits, you were made to feel that something was wrong. But I think I saw through that. Even when I was living under my parents' roof, I saw through the self-righteousness of do-gooders.

"I suffered some ego bruises during the Rolling Thunder thing. It was something that could do you a lot of harm as well as a lot of good. The experience was rewarding in one way, in that it taught me about handling superstars on the road together—something I'm aware of with my band, now. Mostly, with Rolling Thunder, I wrote a lot."

She paused again, and looked over at Roberts, nodding that they should go. As it turned out, he hadn't anything really to worry about. It was just Joni Mitchell talking.

NEIL YOUNG

JANUARY 1971
TORONTO TELEGRAM

LAST NIGHT WAS A night full of strange surprises. First of all, there was Neil Young, probably the most introverted singer ever to play Massey Hall, receiving one of the most flamboyant ovations I've ever heard. Then there was the audience's reaction, which seemed almost a direct contradiction to what went on in the concert itself. For Neil's performance (his second of the evening) rolled by like one vast, lazy silence punctuated only by his intense songs.

Yet there were still other aspects of the concert that upset one's normal expectations. As warm and earthbound as his songs were. Neil managed to look a little frail and wraithlike with his black hair falling over his face and almost concealing intense eyes and set jaw. (Although this wan appearance may be explained, in part, by the fact that this tour bringing him to Toronto has been long and tiring, and he's had to wear braces to support a weak back.) Even the deluge of applause seemed a bit strange, if not ironic, by the end. For less than two years ago, Neil had drifted back into town, had performed at the Riverboat to modest audiences, and had then drifted out again, with no one really missing him.

So, as excellent in every detail as his performance was, if it wasn't for Neil's reluctance to play the superstar revisiting, last night would have been a homecoming of epic proportions. Everything was cool and detached instead. Sitting alone on stage, flanked on one side by his guitars and on the other by an ebony concert grand, he seemed splendidly isolated. He announced his intentions simply: "I'm going to sing most new songs ... I've written so many new songs that I don't know what else to do with them except sing 'em." And while many of these new songs were composed during the current tour, they all seemed like further extensions of the material he recorded a while ago for his current best-selling LP, *After the Gold Rush*.

There were new songs about his ranch and his life in California, and old sentiments that were his favourites; on finding love, on loneliness, on losing and being lost. Most of the songs were subdued, and many were the closest thing a rock 'n' roller could get to what country musicians call "hurtin' mush." But all brimmed with nostalgia:

"Now, I'm goin' back to Canada
On a journey to the past..."

The past has a remarkable pull on Neil Young's songs. Many of their initial impulses started when, in the spring of 1966, he and another Canadian, bassist Bruce Palmer, ran into two singing guitarists, Steve Stills and Richie Furay in Los Angeles. They decided to form a group, added a drummer Dewey Martin, and named themselves Buffalo Springfield. Initially they toured with the Byrds and the Beach Boys; but it wasn't until their third single, "For What It's Worth," written by Stills, that they achieved national recognition. But by the time their third LP, *Last Time Around*, had come out, they had disbanded—with Stills and Young eventually forming part of Crosby, Stills, Nash & Young, while Richie Furay and another ex-Springfield, Jim Messina, formed the country-rock group Poco.

It was between groups when Neil performed at the Riverboat.

And, leaning back against one of the booths one night, he sounded tired and dejected: "I just can't take the rock the way groups have to live it now. There are just too many hassles, so I'd rather go alone." And, in a way, he has. Although they produced one bestselling LP, *Déjà Vu*, Crosby, Stills, Nash & Young seemed to be less of a group than a corporate enterprise. Yet, through everything they did (and this is particularly noticeable when he joined them after their first LP had been recorded) Neil Young's influence could be felt.

Meanwhile, he was recording on his own with his group, Crazy Horse. And as pop started to veer away from the romanticized excitement of the later sixties to the desire for a more personal music from groups like the Beatles and Led Zeppelin, to solo artists like Rod Stewart, James Taylor, Joni Mitchell, Dave Mason, Elton John, and the individual Beatles, Neil Young emerged with record after record of solid songs.

It's something he's selective about. "I want to play for you a song I wrote for *The Johnny Cash Show*," he said late in the evening. "It's a song you're not likely to hear again. Once every six months I hold a meeting with all my songs to see which ones will get recorded. Well, this is one that wasn't even invited to the meeting..." Generally, however, his songs couldn't be tossed aside so lightly. Each one—even some older things like "Don't Let It Bring You Down" and "Down by the River"—seemed like a personal impulse made public.

And that was the strangest of all the evening's surprises. As part of the audience, you felt you were seeing more of Neil Young than you should—that each tune was a little bit of his own life strung out on the high wire of his own nerves.

REVIEW: *AFTER THE GOLD RUSH*
OCTOBER 1970, TORONTO TELEGRAM

NEIL YOUNG IS NOT the easiest person to pin down. In fact, there are probably several Neil Youngs, each glaring at one another and wondering what to do. There's Neil Young, pop star, former founding member of Buffalo Springfield, and later the last name on Crosby, Stills, Nash & Young's billing. Then there's Neil Young, son of Scott Young, the *Toronto Telegram* sports editor, long, angular, and looking like he'd be perpetually late to hockey practice. And finally, there's the Neil Young who put out his latest album, called *After the Gold Rush*, that's been getting some airplay around town recently, but is only serving to confuse matters all the more.

To date, his career has been divided into three uneven stages. Before they were through, Buffalo Springfield had achieved such a tight, homogenous, blend it was difficult to establish just who in the group contributed what to which song. Then there was a brief period, when Neil swore off groups—vehemently—and did several solo gigs. It was at the Riverboat one night where he said: "I can't imagine... no, I will never play in a rock 'n' roll group again. There are just too many hassles."

But a few months later, he was in a rock 'n' roll group again, and one that has to be the most hassle of all. Crosby, Stills, etc. from the start have been a strange blend of personalities, and musical styles. As a much-proclaimed supergroup, they've contributed relatively little to pop culture and just a bit more to pop music. But that's Crosby, Stills, etc. as a group. Individually, each one has contributed a small body of lasting songs. And no one has done more in this regard, I think, than Neil Young; and especially with *After the Gold Rush*, which, for all its outward plainness (the cover art is in basic black, with Neil frowning in some sort of basic fury) contains several minor classics. "Most of these songs," he says, "were inspired by the Dean Stockwell–Herb Bermann screenplay *After the Gold Rush*. More than this, however, each one seems like a snapshot of some imagined picture."

Neil deals in images much the way the electric Bob Dylan did; that is, surrealistically, with a trace of acid, and a touch of anger. Lyrically, nothing seems settled—as if the singer has just too many thoughts to ever be able to collect them into some nice, neat ordering. Melodically, however, this LP is stunning at times. In a song like "Southern Man," the doldrum fury in the words is marched by an instant beat, and a gently falling bass line. Suddenly the pattern will stop (a favorite device of his) and his pause will further intensify the unsettled nature of the song.

Structurally, the following tune, "Till The Morning Comes" is quite similar. Yet, the overall effect is totally different. "Till The Morning Comes" is short (one minute, seventeen seconds), fascinating, and memorable the way no other tune on the album is memorable. A lot of things on this LP don't work, of course. But, like many of pop's best albums, you can sense an overriding concept behind everything. This unity is achieved musically, (with Steve Stills adding some deft guitar strokes here and there; and pianist Nils Lofgren remaining pleasantly heavy-handed throughout) and, to a lesser degree, lyrically.

But what ties everything together is something that can only be described as being part of Neil Young. And, if nothing else, *After the Gold Rush* shows us that this Neil Young at least has everything put together in the right way.

MURRAY MCLAUCHLAN

1970
TORONTO TELEGRAM

THE REMARKABLE THING ABOUT Murray McLauchlan is that he's still around to talk to, and about. Few other young folksingers—he's twenty-two—have courted both professional and personal disaster so completely or so often. In fact, his activities this following week seem like a comeback in a career that's been like one constant comeback: Over the weekend, starting tonight, he'll be appearing with Lighthouse at the St. Lawrence Centre; and starting next Tuesday night, he'll be a week at the Riverboat.

So, right now things appear a bit frantic; and they are made to seem even more so because of his first LP he's getting ready, and the possibilities of being managed by Albert Grossman's office. But, as he practises in his apartment with his bassist, Dennis Pendrith, everything outside seems hermetically sealed off. "Oh," he says, breaking the quiet, "I haven't really been ready for the kind of acceptance you've been talking about. Up till now, I'd say I was basically competent, but not particularly inspired."

In a strange way, Murray's apartments have been an accurate reflection of whatever situation he was in. The first one had only two rooms, "but we couldn't even use the kitchen because it was too cold." And later, when he was considering giving up his solo act and forming a band, and things weren't going well, they moved into a Queen Street place where he almost had a nervous breakdown because everyone thought the place was haunted. But their present place has a cluttered homey feel to it—as if they are intending to stay a long time. When the band didn't work out, and they had moved, rather desperately to New York City for three months to find something else, they returned and moved in here. The refrigerator is painted an off-purple, an old barrel sits in a corner, and the one kitchen window looks out on the red-brick side of a shop on the north end of Kensington Market.

He says: "The reason we went to New York was simple. We were starving to death, and I was having a nervous breakdown 'cause we had no money. Because I had given up on my single gig, nothing was happening, and work stopped coming in. We first went to Connecticut to see if there was any final possibility of the band starting, but there wasn't, so we went on to New York. We were dropped off in front of Albert Grossman's office (he manages Bob Dylan, among others) with only $12 and our suitcases tied with ropes. Well, there I sold my song catalogue (two of Murray's songs, for example, were recorded by Tom Rush on his latest LP, and Bruce Cockburn on his first album included another) and received a fat cheque. We then moved into the famous Albert Hotel, with its famous cockroaches that you have to hit six times before they die. But eventually we had to leave. New York was ruining my health. And I wasn't equipped to deal with a city of such savagery. Their whole East Village scene is frightening, man—thirteen-year-old kids walking around in the winter in bare feet, starving. Besides, Toronto's such a fine place. I always like to see one citadel of WASP-dom left."

Murray McLauchlan is a deceptive character in many ways. He seems to view everything ironically—as if it all couldn't be happening to him, but it still does. Outwardly, he looks like a psychedelic cowpoke, in jeans with a belt having a huge buckle, and his hair puffed out of his head as if he were in shock. But, after a while, you begin to suspect, that if he had been born ten years earlier, he would become a trucker's helper. Lean, tough, and slick with a greasy ducktail. He first arrived on the scene, six years ago, by walking into one of the old Yorkville folk clubs, the Left Bank, and saying he had a guitar and that he'd like to sing.

He did, and somebody from another now-defunct place, the Village Corner club, heard him, and he performed there. Then others heard him, and "eventually I graduated to the big time and sang on *Let's Sing Out*." But nothing kept happening for the general advancements of his career with amazing redundancy. "I guess," he says, "that I've always been allergic to hype. And I always have been. The thing that always amazes me about audience-type performers is that they seem to forget that their success depends on people digging them. That's the important thing." And starting tonight, this will apply to Murray McLauchlan more than ever before.

BRUCE COCKBURN

SEPTEMBER 1970
TORONTO TELEGRAM

NO ONE REALLY KNOWS when a young singer starts to make it, when suddenly everything he does finds a following. There are no signs, usually, no great belches of publicity, and no undue fuss made. It just happens. And at last night's opening of a week's stay at the Riverboat, Bruce Cockburn made it.

Six months ago, when he last played at the Riverboat, only four people showed up—Cockburn, his manager Bernie Finkelstein, his producer, and myself. Last night the place had a crowd usually reserved for a Gordie Lightfoot appearance. It was just that kind of night where everything falls into place. Cockburn's guitar work had never been more secure, his piano playing never more robust. His old songs had gained interest in their aging; while the newer things showed him working in new areas. And his voice, usually a frail, wispy tenor that sounds like he's singing down a tube, had gained some body, and its intonations had gained some accuracy.

But why last night? Coming originally from Ottawa, Cockburn's been around Toronto for the past three years. His first ventures into pop music were through some experimental rock bands, which, unfortunately, were much more interested in experimenting than rocking. So nobody gave a second thought to him. In fact, rarely was even the first thought given to this slight, gentle, and private person.

Going solo, he made several appearances at the Mariposa Folk Festival and appeared at various local clubs. Gradually he built up a repertoire of songs, most of them his own. And, just as gradually, he built up a small, hard-core following. Then he signed with Bernie Finkelstein's True North record label, and with ex-rock guitarist Gene Martynec producing, released his first album six months ago. The reaction to the LP was amazing. And as he toured Canada and did the occasional TV show, like *Nashville North*, he was firmly established. Even the second generation—Joni Mitchell, or David Rea—had developed a distinctive style and distinctive success. But the third generation was by and large a mystery. And Cockburn didn't help clarify things: his music required a different set of ears, ones not accustomed to the dense, verbal imagery of Dylan, or the countryside twang of other folksingers.

For Cockburn—as his songs showed last night—is definitely a city boy. His material throngs with city sights, sounds, and insights. Something like "Happy Good Morning Blues" mixes at least three languages, English, French, and a bit of German, into a mix of Beatle-like chords, blues intonations, and strong western picking. In a tune like "Thoughts on a Rainy Afternoon," a dreary landscape becomes more interesting as "my alley becomes my cathedral." In "Dirty Red Comes of Age," what appears to be a sustained sexual shaggy dog story turns out, in the end, to be merely a play on words. "Musical Friends," at the piano, is a pleasantly bouncy piece of fluff, not meaning much, but not pretending to mean more. While "High Priestess" (based on the third card in the tarot deck) uses a breathlessly long model melody spun out over a creepy drone effect on the guitar.

The variety never seems to end. But perhaps that's the best, if not the only way to tell that moment when a singer has made it, that there is no looking back.

TIM HARDIN

FEBRUARY 1970
TORONTO TELEGRAM

IT USUALLY WORKS OUT that the less identifiable something in pop is, the greater are its chances of making it. Not for Tim Hardin. His style and songs have created a legion of imitators, but somehow have left him elusive—and allusive—as ever. His work is tense and tender and coiled with tension like a switchblade about to snap open. Alone at the Riverboat this week, he's still in fine form. In his words, he's still the "shining black sheep boy." A short figure, he cradles his guitar close, and leans aggressively into each song. At one moment, there's something provocative about him; he doesn't seem to be asking for response, but rather daring it to come. Then, depending on the time, his volatile moods, the temperature in the room, or whatever, he'll suddenly withdraw and practically disappear behind the lyrics of his song.

Hardin had once achieved an almost legendary, insular sort of reputation. Other folksingers knew him as did some jazzmen, but that was it. Reports came back that he was one of the best white-blues singers. Others said, no, that wasn't it at all. Tim Hardin was a folksinger. As he said last year, "I really can't give a definition. Jazz people listen to me and call it jazz. So, what can I say?" Before his first album came out in late 1966, (apparently it was two years in the making) people have started to record him. Then Bobby Darin recorded "If I Were a Carpenter"—even to the point of mimicking Hardin's fleeting vocal style—and Hardin was dragged, unwillingly I suppose, into the limelight by association.

The course of Hardin's development can only be charted from his albums. The first one is one of pop's classic LPs. The second moved over some gentle ground with songs like "The Lady Came from Baltimore." The third was a reissue of some earlier blues tapes never intended for release. In trying to pinpoint just exactly what Hardin was all about, several comparisons were made—with Donovan (whose airy fairy-isms make Hardin seem like Rasputin by comparison), and with Dylan (who magnifies the impersonal into a shining series of images, while Hardin reduces the personal to its essential meaning).

"When Bob Dylan did *John Wesley Harding*" (from whom Hardin is descended), writes Lillian Roxon in her *Rock Encyclopedia*, "there was a lot of talk about the new calm, the new simplicity of rock. Hardin has never been anything else." But the only comparison I can think of is with Sidney Bechet, serene jazz clarinetist from New Orleans. Both were able to make a basically unsentimental type of music come close to being romantic. There's a sense of intimacy in both musics. Hardin embellishes a melodic line—like in, say, his "Tribute to Hank Williams," or "Lenny's Tune," for Lenny Bruce—with series after series of inventive variations. But this ability only comes from a greater one: Hardin's mastery of time, of rhythm, of rhythms within a rhythm. His accompaniments on guitar and (less and less these days) on piano are spare and simple. But they sound just right, as if nothing else could possibly be done at that particular moment. And, perhaps, this is Hardin's greatest contribution to popular music. He knows what not to do, and when to do it. By reducing his music to its simplest components, he somehow manages to heighten his appeal.

JANIS IAN

JUNE 1971
TORONTO TELEGRAM

THERE ARE, BASICALLY, two attitudes toward girl singers, mutually exclusive, and divided into what might be called the old and new style. The former is the smoky voice from a plunging neckline playing cabarets and dark saloons and dropping hints with every note. The latter is the recent phenomenon, with a delicate soul who makes impressionistic little LPs, full of deep personal anguish. She's called a lady, knows Zen, and lives by her zodiac. Then there's Janis Ian. At fifteen, she recorded a nagging little protest song called "Society's Child," which later became a single. Overnight, Janis became the Voice of Dissatisfied Youth. She was quoted. She delivered the message. And in various publicity photos, she could be seen skulking around New York, looking angry.

You could no more imagine Janis Ian winding up in a nightclub singing old Barbra Streisand hits than becoming one of those limpid folksingers. And four years later, with a new LP out, and new career started that will bring her to the Riverboat tonight, she's emerged as a rather unique performer. "Being thought of as a committed person," she said, "got to be tiring. I got tired of people who wanted me to do things for them all the time. I was committed the way anyone at fifteen is. I thought of everything in terms of black and white. It got to be too much. I stopped singing for two years. I sat around the house, did a lot of reading, and tried to find out more about myself. Perhaps, in the long run, I had a hit when I was so young. That way, when I took time off from singing, I had a chance to develop that I might not have had if I was performing."

Raised in various places in the New York–New Jersey area, she went to the prestigious New York High School of Music & Art. When "Society's Child" came out, the rest of her classmates and some of her teachers suddenly realized that this fifteen-year-old kid was making a bundle while they were still struggling. Then she quit school. And soon she quit performing. "It wasn't that the audience was sapping me. It was just that I needed something more than applause. I didn't think I could get up on a stage all alone anymore. For me, singing then was a very lonely thing."

She now lives in Philadelphia. "But as soon as I get enough cash together—I need about $2,000—I'm moving to the island." The island, in this case, is Ross Island near Grand Manan Island in the Bay of Fundy off the coast of New Brunswick. There, she hopes to be able to live for six months and then go out on the road for six months with her small band.

"There is a whole new feeling around in music," she says. "That makes it easier to perform again. There are so many new good chick performers. When I started there was only Judy Collins, Joan Baez, and Buffy Sainte-Marie. But now there's people like Carole King and so many others ... It's really hard for a chick to get a Top 40 hit. Most of the audience is female and they want to hear a man singing to them. Probably the only exception to this is Melanie, who I don't like anyway. I don't think of myself particularly as a girl singer, really. Mainly, I'm a musician. There are enough problems just being a musician. I mean, do you write to get a hit? Or do you write for other musicians? And with that to worry about, being a chick isn't a problem."

JUNE 1971
TORONTO TELEGRAM

"WHEN I WAS TRYING very hard to be Bob Dylan, at about fourteen, I used to write all these very serious songs about men who made guns and stuff. Then I gave up. I couldn't do it. First of all, there already was a Bob Dylan. And being a girl didn't help. I guess it comes to everyone that way."

When Janis Ian starts taking off in one of these zigzag monologues in front of her audiences, no one knows what to expect. Here's this pint-size singer, her hair all fuzzy, sounding like an embryo Elaine May. It's not upsetting exactly; but it's unexpected. When Janis Ian—who opened a week's stint at the Riverboat last night—starts to play piano with her back bassist and drummer, everything falls into place. It all—even the monologue—starts to make sense.

It's not a music easily defined. Part country, part gospel, part folk, it has a special kind of quirkiness that sets it apart from anything you might have heard anyone else do. It mixes toughness and tenderness in equal proportions. It can be bright and breezy one second, and then, with just one chord change, with one new line added, it can have a darker meaning. Take a song, innocently enough titled "New York in the Springtime," for instance. The first line is all sweetness, conjuring up images of Irving Berlin, and Madison Avenue. Then it takes a turn for the nutty when she sings: "Spring . . . when all the pimps come out and play." For those who remember Janis Ian more than four years ago as that nice serious kid who at fifteen recorded the bestselling middle-class protest epic, "Society's Child," this new material might upset a few preconceptions.

If anything, Janis Ian is more than ever before society's child. Her voice is untutored and loud—with all the carrying power of a kid yelling to another two blocks away. And her piano playing is delightfully ham-handed. It's an urgent, percussive style, full of odd little embellishments. Like everything else about her, it sounds original. The sum total of all this is enough to give you the impression of a girl singer, who, if she'd only been a bit bigger (about a foot), hadn't wanted to be Bob Dylan at one time, and hadn't been a girl at any time, would have been the toughest kid on the block.

SIMON & GARFUNKEL

JANUARY 1967
GLOBE AND MAIL

EIGHTEEN HUNDRED TEEN AND POST-TEENAGERS, many pea-jacketed and mini-skirted, were scattered about in Massey Hall last night, listening to two pop-singing heroes. No one was screaming, writhing, or fainting; all were absorbed in a hush of post-puberty intellectualism in the cerebral sound of Simon & Garfunkel.

Paul Simon and Art Garfunkel are the latest additions to the small company (comprised of Bob Dylan, Phil Ochs, John Lennon, and a few others) of folk and rock intellectuals. For Simon & Garfunkel, as well as with the others, the song was as important as the singing, the words as essential as the melody. And last night the songs, all written by Simon, were sung with a quiet deliberation that evoked all the restrained desperation of the lyrics. Each song contributed to the all-encompassing mood of seriousness; each contributed something to Simon's literary shotgun blast at the hate, sterility, and lack of compassion he sees in society. Consequently, his adaption of some incomplete lines from the Beatitudes became a twanging, vibrant, discordant collection of non-sequiturs such as "Blessed is the man whose soul belongs to." Although there was little humour in their performance, the evening didn't become too heavy as they spaced some innocuous turns throughout.

On records, the electronically controlled veneer that the recording studio coats their voices with belies their naturally strong and flexible voices. And in their setting of Orlando di Lasso's *Benedictus*, each line of the sixteenth-century polyphony was clearly delineated. Yet throughout, it was Simon's poetry that tied each song together. The words flowed from the all-too-ordinary melodies in a gush of piercing perceptions. While Bob Dylan's poetry is often grotesque and disjointed, Paul Simon's has a completeness that is easily adaptable to music.

Although Art Garfunkel seemed always to be beyond the pale of the floodlight (as Simon had the solo in most of the songs and was the sole instrumentalist), his lighter voice added a dimension to each melody and lessened the harshness the words gave to them.

Caught somewhere between Tolstoy and Tin Pan Alley, Simon & Garfunkel are helping to create a new classification for adolescents, the teenie-thinker.

REVIEW: *BRIDGE OVER TROUBLED WATER*
FEBRUARY 1970
TORONTO TELEGRAM

UNTIL RECENTLY, SIMON & GARFUNKEL have always seemed like two dead-end kids in drag. Mixing tough and tenderness as mindlessly together as a Hollywood B-movie, their approach to music was sing softly and carry a big schtick. Much of Paul Simon's early poetry read and sounded like term-paper rap. And their voices sounded like those of two street punks turned choir boys. But as they made more money, got older, and started wondering about their relationship together, something changed in their music.

They aren't out to impress anymore. Their latest album, *Bridge Over Troubled Water*, doesn't beg any particular response. You don't have to be hip to like it, or clever, poetic, political, or enlightened in any particular way. It's after much bigger game. From the first and title tune on, the LP wades hip deep in nostalgia and never really gets out. It might turn out to be pop's parallel to Proust. Each song seems to carve off a slice of past common experience. There are overtones of gospel, images of moon-June romance, of old rock 'n' roll concerts, of historical names, almost forgotten, of scraps of conversations only half said and almost forgotten.

And why much of it works, I suspect, is because of what they've been through along the way. In 1967, calling themselves Tom & Jerry, just two Queens, New York, high school kids, they had a hit called "Hey, Schoolgirl." They even played *The Dick Clark Show* and ... but that seemed to be the end of it. In the early-sixties folk boom, they made an album (using their proper names now) called *Wednesday Morning, 3 A.M.* But everybody was recording Dylan songs like they had, and the album disappeared into the nether world where old albums go to die. Once again, this might have been the end of it all. Paul Simon left for England; Garfunkel went back to university.

But one DJ kept playing one cut from the album, "The Sound of Silence"; and a producer for Columbia Records, Tom Wilson, saw that there was something in it. Adding a soft-rock backing to the single, Simon & Garfunkel rerecorded it, and this time it was a hit. Album after album followed; some tunes like "Fakin' It" sounded well; others like "The Dangling Conversation" didn't. But gradually, as they became more sure of themselves, their music took on new breadth. With all its faults, their last album, *Bookends*, was one of the finest to date. And with *Bridge Over Troubled Water*, they expanded further the ideas initiated in *Bookends*.

Starting with "The Boxer," already released as a single, it passes through three exciting numbers. "Baby Driver," "The Only Living Boy in New York," and "Why Don't You Write Me." But next comes a strange and surprisingly effective touch. Over the sounds of a huge crowd cheering, comes Simon & Garfunkel's version of Felice and Boudleaux Bryant's "Bye, Bye, Love"—and done as well as the Everly Brothers did in the fifties. There's more clapping as the song fades out. And more clapping—it just seems to hang in the air—as they fade into "Song for the Asking," a soft voice ballad, deliberately cloying and unconsciously sad.

There's something terribly final about that last cut. And with rumors increasing that Simon & Garfunkel might be breaking up, "Song for the Asking" might be an impossibility in the future.

ART GARFUNKEL

SEPTEMBER 1980
TORONTO STAR

ART GARFUNKEL OPENS his hotel room door a crack. "Yeah?" comes his muffled voice from the other side.

"Interview," I whisper. If he wants to play this scene mysterious, mysterious he'll get.

Thunk.

The door closes and a great mumbling comes from somewhere within the room. Minutes pass. What's going on? I wonder. His third movie role as a manipulative psychiatrist in *Bad Timing* gained him good reviews at the recent Festival of Festivals where it was premiered. So maybe he's still in the role. Maybe he's still reacting to the press brunch he's just finished. Maybe he doesn't like me.

Thunk.

Well would you believe? Here's Art Garfunkel, smiling as prettily as a choirboy and as anxious to please as an under-tipped head waiter. He's thirty-eight but little changed since his days with Paul Simon, who just so happens to be at Maple Leaf Gardens tonight, in town hyping his new movie, *One-Trick Pony*. Before they split up in 1970 after completing their *Bridge Over Troubled Water* album, and after he'd finished his first film role in Mike Nichols's *Catch-22*, they'd become pop music's answer to three college credit courses in New American Lit 101.

They were sensitivity itself, if you can forget the grotty, unsensitive nineteen million records they sold through the sixties. Oh sure, we knew it was Simon who did most of the songwriting. And it was Simon who played guitar. We knew, quite frankly, Simon was the brains behind the entire operation. Still, they were a unit just like Mutt and Jeff or mustard and relish. Simon & Garfunkel wouldn't have been quite the same without the sweet, soaring tenor from this one-time high school teacher, who grew up with Simon in Queens, New York.

The question remained, though, what exactly was Garfunkel's role in all this? Who exactly is he? His post-Simon solo albums have been, he admits, rather ephemeral: Garfunkel without Simon was atmosphere without a planet. And he has remained tight-lipped about his life away from singing or acting. His marriage in 1972 ended with as little publicity as it began. He travelled a lot, heading to and from Europe several times a year. He developed a few hobbies and, at one point, attempted to learn to play the harpsichord. He was a sweet voice, a puff of blond hair and that was that.

Except on film. In both *Catch-22* and *Carnal Knowledge* in 1971, Mike Nichols brought something that was missing in his music alone. It came from his eyes. There was something set, resolute, and troubling in his stare—you can see it in Nicholas Roeg's *Bad Timing*, as well—that would completely contradict his sweet, rather plastic smile. This stare says that what he's thinking has nothing to do with what you think he's thinking. It brings some complexity to the air of naive blandness.

So why did he wait so long—nine years—for only his third movie role? I ask him.

"Well, that depends on how you look at it," he says still smiling. "I wasn't aware I was taking a long time. I mean, what's the proper amount of time? Actually, I received a number of scripts over the years which I turned down. In retrospect, the only one I regret turning down was *Slaughterhouse-Five*. The role of Billy Pilgrim. But admittedly, there has been a certain degree of typecasting involved in what I was offered. Often you're offered something by people who have an advance notion of your acting range—"

Ee-yow. The TV set suddenly blares out and I jump. But not Garfunkel. Cool. Darn if this man isn't cool. Garfunkel remains fixed in position, talking: "And that's what intrigued me about the role I play in *Bad Timing*. It was a role that stretched me as an actor. There were so may layers to the character I was playing, so many layers of mystery. With a director such as Nicholas Roeg, you have to offer yourself up as so much plastic to be moulded. Before I'd go on for a particular shot, I wouldn't know what I was going to do. When I was before the cameras, I'd fall into the present tense. I'd just let it happen. I'd let him take me where I should go."

Ke-rank! What was that? Heavens, even Garfunkel seems to have noticed the racket coming from the television.

"Uh, why then has little of the emotion ever come across on record?"

To which, it seems, there's no answer. "I admit I haven't gotten the feeling on record yet," Garfunkel adds. "And, in truth, I think I've been too smooth in my approach. Because I like powerful music."

Hmmmm. Did he try to help Paul Simon out with *One-Trick Pony*? Aside from a brief appearance in *Annie Hall*, this is, in effect Simon's debut, and Garfunkel has all the experience.

"No," says Garfunkel. "Paul and I are good friends, of course," he adds.

The door goes *thunk* as I close it behind me. Garfunkel's still sitting and smiling and playing with one particular curl out of the mass that make up his hair. The TV set is still on.

PAUL SIMON

JULY 1983
TORONTO STAR

"WE'VE ALWAYS BEEN BETTER friends than partners. We've known each other for a very, very long time and it's been a fairly frictionless friendship. But there have been some rough edges between us when we've worked together. They're still there."

Paul Simon's and Art Garfunkel's reunion for the famous *Concert in Central Park* two years ago came about by accident—a concert Simon planned to give alone, but which turned out to be a sixties revival meeting with five hundred thousand people on hand. "The concert implied a tour," he said. And this, in turn, became a whirlwind worldwide series of concerts with 130,000 turning out to see them in Paris and massive crowds appearing from London to Tokyo. "The tour implied a live album," their first one together in thirteen years, that he's currently hard-pressed to finish.

By now, the accidental reunion has been formalized. They're out on tour together, starting in Akron, Ohio, Tuesday and followed by a CNE stadium concert Thursday. The show comes complete with a 172-foot-wide stage and a 660-square-foot video screen. The tour—and the reunion—ends in Israel in late September with two concerts. Although a huge proportion of the estimated one million fans who will turn out will be looking for nostalgia, Simon maintains the tour isn't, strictly speaking, a reunion.

"When we broke up, we never made an announcement about it," he says. "So, we never did anything that we'd have to change our minds about. That hasn't changed. We've no definite plans beyond what we're doing right now. We aren't going to continue beyond what we've planned now. Nor should anyone expect the Simon & Garfunkel they may remember. We're only doing older material we feel comfortable with. And the songs I've written have made the music of Simon & Garfunkel change shape. What we were—that's gone." He also separates this reunion from the wave of reunions throughout the summer. The others might have been expected, but not theirs. No one should be too surprised there are so many reunions, he points out. "It was part of sixties thinking that as soon as a group got together it started breaking up. It was part of the sixties nature always to change. But as soon as you get older, you disregard the rules you made when you were younger."

But his reunion fills a gap in his life. Several years ago, he told me he wanted to write material for a Broadway show. A few years later, he told me he had shelved Broadway for Hollywood, and the movie *One-Trick Pony*, because he felt more "comfortable with making movies—they work more like making records." But the career move failed to blossom. In 1981, he agreed to do a Central Park concert for the city of New York. In planning that, he thought about adding Garfunkel for a song or two. As the planning took shape, Garfunkel's participation grew to a concert-long partnership.

"But I don't feel by doing this I'm repeating myself," the forty-one-year-old songwriter added. "For one thing, the way we're doing the old songs—with a band—has changed. And we've changed. There's no way we could do them the same way. And we aren't going to do songs I don't want to do. A lot of those early songs"—I mentioned "The Dangling Conversation" and he snapped back that he wasn't going to sing *that*—"sound naive; they're 'young' work. You see, a lot of the work I did when I was very young became very popular, but that doesn't mean it was the best work."

LEONARD COHEN

APRIL 1985
TORONTO STAR

I TRACKED LEONARD COHEN through two recent books and his brand-new album before finding him on a park bench at the Inn on the Park, halfway through a sales pitch for his appearance at Massey Hall on May 11. When Cohen decided a short while ago that it was time to resume his singing career, neither his record company nor his agents exactly fell over themselves making plans for him. It had been five years since he had recorded, and longer since he had toured. It's two decades since he was the famed dark poet of serious sixties sensuality. He has had to make the rounds to let everyone known he's still there. So there he was, looking exactly the way Leonard Cohen should look; thin, just a few solid meals away from gaunt, dressed in black and dark blue, with a gorgeous pair of hand-tooled black boots. His black hair with a touch of silver here and there was slicked back over his head.

His new CBS album, *Various Positions*, was released only a few days ago, yet its melding of romance and religion, sex and epiphany was anticipated in his 1978 collection of poetry, *Death Of a Lady's Man*, from which "The Other Village" comes. "Dance me to your beauty with a burning violin," is the album's opening line. The richness of the music blurs the identity of who exactly is being addressed, the poet's God or his lover. Or are they the same? As it turns out, Cohen himself is not sure. "I've probably achieved the ultimate confusion of woman and God with this album," he says with a halting smile. A tiny vein pulses just beneath his right eye. "But you know, sometimes when you meet a person who is really touched by the spirit, it looks like they're in love. You can't really tell in love with what." Nor is he sure at exactly which point a piece of work becomes a song or a poem. Some of the pieces in *Various Positions* were written around the time he worked on *Book of Mercy*, the collection of psalms published last year.

He has a cello for a voice, full of sad notes and long lines. It sounds rather like the singing voice you hear on record. Recently, *Star* book critic Ken Adachi noted that unlike other poets "who develop vertically," Cohen "seems to have developed laterally," with one bit of work, in whatever medium, emerging from the next. Certainly, he has explored every media available to him—even video. His *I Am a Hotel* continues to win awards internationally. His collaboration with Montrealer Lewis Furey for the movie *Night Magic* will premiere at a special midnight screening at the Cannes Film Festival May 8–20. He has not, he points out, been inactive. Even the preparations for this tour, which has already seen forty-five concerts in Europe, have taken up a considerable amount of time. "Because I haven't toured for some time, of course I was a bit scared of going out onstage," he continued. "I rehearsed a long time with my band."

These days he can anticipate an interviewer's surprise when he talks about being a musician. "I played in a country band when I was sixteen and seventeen and I lived in Nashville for a couple of years," he pointed out. "I was that serious about music. I would go down to listen to the Grand Ole Opry and those singers I still consider today as the finest singers in North America. That kind of music is the most authentic music around. For a while back in the late seventies, I felt very much on the outside (of music). But there's a lot of young groups who are today acknowledging me as an influence. There's Echo and the Bunnymen and groups like the Sisters of Mercy that have named themselves after one of my songs. And there's Joy Division. I feel there is a tradition and that I'm a part of it. This has just happened in the past few years that the young singers and groups have acknowledged me as one of their mentors. Somehow a decision was made by the powers that be that I was not a mainstream singer—that I was a singer or a poet who sets poems to music. So I got that tag and I never got the kind of support from record companies that enabled me to mount a tour across the vast spaces of North America."

But it's not just his musical plottings that have met with resistance. His American publisher, Viking, wouldn't put out *Book of Mercy* and "Random House finally took it," he said. Then again, "I was never sure that was a book meant for the marketplace. Jack McClelland of McClelland & Stewart was happy enough to publish it and Dennis Lee, my editor there, liked the book very much. The other publishers didn't take it because they didn't see it as a book and I'm not so sure I see it as literature, as a book. It's there if anybody needs it or if anybody is in any kind of trouble. If you can use that old-fashioned word, it was 'inspired.' I don't think you can plan to write a book like that unless it's true—unless it really comes from the deep place. I don't want to get into my own dismal, personal predicaments, but there are those times when you feel yourself stopped and silenced and you have to try to penetrate that source of mercy, that source of forgiveness in your own life. That's what those psalms are about—trying to locate that source of mercy that enables you to re-enter the world."

PERFORMANCE ROCK

THE MONKEES

APRIL 1967
GLOBE AND MAIL

THE STARS OF YESTERDAY afternoon's rock 'n' roll blast at Maple Leaf Gardens were not the Monkees, but the 18,200-plus teenagers who packed the place. It didn't seem to matter to them that the Monkees are a pre-packaged, consumer-oriented television fabrication, or that the act is held together by a surreal mixture of slapstick, pseudo-Beatles singing and pictures of the stars projected on a huge screen behind the stage. What mattered was the fact that what was formerly unattainable was now within screaming and throwing distance. After the usual frenzied warmup acts, the Monkees—Peter Tork, Micky Dolenz, Davy Jones, and Mike Nesmith—trundled out on stage in a moment of sheer screaming and popping flashbulbs.

And after an hour of breathing out the adolescent agonies of wanting to be alone, and indulging in Beatles-like histrionics in "Last Train to Clarksville," the four enveloped their audience musically in a wraparound, total gestalt experience of electronic wheep, warps, and whoofers. Rambling all over the stage, their puffs of neo-Rolling

Stone Hair flopped on their heads; and as Davy Jones, in his self-styled Anthony Newley way, began to lean back onto the floor, in a swelling roar of motherly feelings hundreds of girls began to lean, push, jiggle, then run toward the stage. Appearing as a group, then singly, the four managed to hold their performance together in the face of a vast, gaping maw of wailing teenagers that would have made Dick Clark, Fabian, Frankie Avalon and Johnny and the Hurricanes wince—in unison. This was a rite of spring, brought about by throwing thousands of teenagers into a huge, resonant rock 'n' roll emporium with four mythological picaresque folk heroes. There, stuffed into multichrome stretch pants, and in a leather-belted, brass-buckled, polka-dotted blazing obviousness, they had come to forget breadcrumb worries and romances in a two-hour orgy of anticipation. For both performers and audience it was a trip from reality, one which had all the effects of organized religion and alcohol and none of the after-effects.

The Monkees were created to fit into the NBC television series aping the Beatles, to romp through thirty minutes of quick cuts, flashbacks, and cute quips á la Richard Lester, producer of the Beatles movies. They had never met before producers Robert Rafelson and Bert Schneider advertised for "four insane boys, aged seventeen to twenty-one." Their hygienically clean, quaintly irreverent image seemed designed for the Mothers of America, to protect their teenie offspring from the scruffily sexual Rolling Stones and the psychedelic mutterings of the Byrds. But to compare them to the Beatles is to compare Humperdinck to Haydn.

"We're not a group," they've been quoted as saying, "we're an act." While the Beatles are always a musical mile ahead of their fans and fads, the Monkees' calculated, computerized comedy is tuned into whatever the transistorized teenager wants. And as long as their records continue to sell, they can ride above the lobotomized whorl of their popularity. But strip away the sounds of the screaming, clawing girls and the jangling of their all-electric, all-pervasive guitar twangling and all that is left of their tunes is a field of dead pansies. Still, there will always be Monkee music. The girl who is fourteen now and was at the Gardens yesterday afternoon will always be a Beatles fan and as her mother who smiles condescendingly at the afternoon's follies, still gets misty over Frank Sinatra.

The most frightening aspect about the Monkee-type of teen craze, is that somewhere, some lonely, anti-social kid who is about fourteen, is practising furiously to be the next pop guru to resurrect this mesmerizing madness once again. And we don't even know his name.

JEFFERSON AIRPLANE

JULY 1967
GLOBE AND MAIL

SOCIETY'S IMPRESSION THAT TEENAGERS are going to pot would seem to have been dispelled yesterday afternoon when around twenty thousand fringies, beachies, bleachies, and hippies crowded Nathan Phillips Square for what turned out to be the first stand-in in Toronto history. The crowd waited for the biggest benediction from the current high priests of hippiedom, six shaggy San Franciscans called Jefferson Airplane. For if there is one avant-garde god—and that's rock—the Airplane is its current prophet (or profit, if you calculate recent successes). But the experience wasn't primarily musical—it was emotional. Airplane co-pilots Marty Balin, Paul Kantner, Spencer Dryden, Jack Casady, Jorma Kaukonen, and Grace Slick stocked the air with an aphrodisiac, which musically could be called a mixture of blues, rock, and jazz. Performing their own songs, they produced a rough-hewn sound which had the spontaneity of a free-form jazz session. In McLuhanistic terms, it required audience involvement and the crowd responded.

Onlookers draped themselves over the Henry Moore sculpture (The Archer), splashed in the water near the fountains, and ate candy and the apples thrown to them by the group. Both performers and audience were attired as prescribed hippie taste-makers. Flowers, pagan amulets, tiny bells on girls' feet, a general assortment of baubles, bangles, and beards were in abundance, as were bare feet. "That's really in this year," said a girl watching my suspiciously white shirt.

Truly cool, I thought.

"I've never seen such a crowd," said Kaukonen. "Usually they come to look and sometimes to touch. But this group seemed to be getting in the swing of things."

For the Airplane, the swing of things is attained by the corrosive grating of electric guitars and huge loudspeakers blaring out Grace Slick's impassioned voice. The group tries to permit the listener to experience the music rather than just hear it. "The atmosphere we create is just as important as the music," Kaukonen explained, "at the essence of what we do is an attempt to communicate with our listeners." Their mode of communication is music and their concern is with the event and not its meaning—nor with its consequences. For the Airplane sings "of the fantastic joy of making love while under LSD" ("Runnin' Round the World") and in "White Rabbit" celebrates an Alice in Drugland for pre-teen addicts everywhere.

Like many other rock groups, the Airplane members are quiet-spoken, intelligent, musical, and aware of their potency to influence youth. Their aim: to fight the complacency of the Great Society. The too-often result: the establishment of another complacency, this time in the minds of many of their adherents wandering the beachheads of this internal war, the hippie havens from Haight-Ashbury district of San Francisco to Greenwich Village to Toronto's Yorkville.

THE BEATLES

REVIEW: *MAGICAL MYSTERY TOUR*
NOVEMBER 1967
GLOBE AND MAIL

THE BEATLES' LAST ALBUM, *Sgt. Pepper's Lonely Hearts Club Band*, became one of the most talked about offerings in the history of pop music. And while the nabobs of the recording industry appreciated the profits it made for them, they and Beatle fans were soon asking: After this, what else can they do? What can they say? Where can they go? The answer is another zany record by the Liverpool bunch called *Magical Mystery Tour*, plus five other selections.

"AWAY IN THE SKY, beyond the clouds," the notes on the record read, "live 4 or 5 Magicians. By casting WONDERFUL SPELLS the Beatles turn the Most Ordinary Coach Trip into a Magical Mystery Tour. If you let yourself go, the Magicians will take you away to marvellous places." This is no ordinary journey. The album is a preview of a Beatle-produced television show of the same name scheduled to be shown in Britain later this month and in North America early next year.

The bizarre nature of the show has been extended to the album. On the cover, tour guides-cum-sorcerers Lennon, McCartney, Starr, and Harrison are dressed like characters from a nightmare. Inside, twenty-four colour pages—cartoons and still shots taken from the TV production—show a Beatles-in-Wonderland view of the English countryside. Whether the TV show or the album has any value will have little relevance to the record's sales. Its success is assured. Six of the songs released separately over the past months have become hits. And the advance sale for the album has been so large that *Magical Mystery Tour* already has been certified for a gold record award. Before it was released to the public on Wednesday at 11:00 a.m., the record earned more than $1 million in advance sales.

These sales were to be expected. For if the album looks like a slice out of a Richard Lester movie, it sounds like a travelling vaudeville show. It, like *Sgt. Pepper*, is the epitome of studio rock. But rather than being the Beatles' answer to *Sgt. Pepper*, *Magical Mystery Tour* is a bubbling corollary to it. It has little of the other album's acidity or melancholy. And rather than being profound, as many claimed *Sgt. Pepper* was, *Magical Mystery Tour* is merely allusive and elusive. A sense of the unreal, of the mystical, pervades many of its songs. The lyrics touch on the absurd: "I am the egg man, they are the egg men—I am the walrus. Goo Goo Goo Joob." The music is an amalgam of many styles and many cultures, from Vivaldi-like trumpet writing ("Penny Lane") to Indian ragas ("Strawberry Fields Forever"—one of the five other selections).

In it, the Beatles seem to be trying to change things from what they are to what they could be. Their new music, as Paul McCartney explained, is an attempt "to create magic. It's all trying to make things happen so that you don't know why they're happening." This quality, what musicologist Wilfred Mellors described as an "attempt to return to magic, possible as a substitute for belief," gives the second song of the album a flavour of mild hysteria. "The Fool on the Hill" becomes a marvellous little lament, built around one of the longest and most well-constructed melodies that McCartney has written. Streaked with melancholy and compassion, it is, in a mild way, the most disturbing song. Most of the others retain a more joyful inventiveness. "Your Mother Should Know" displays a cleanness of line and arrangement that effectively salutes nostalgia while not indulging in it. And in "I Am the Walrus," lyricist John Lennon had used words with the outrageous authority of a latter-day Lewis Carroll.

Included in the album is the quartet's latest single release, "Hello, Goodbye." At first hearing this seems to be just another wearisome Beatle nonsense song. The title is almost all the lyric content there is; the music sounds cluttered with its dubbed effects of people talking. But, perhaps in spite of itself, the song is much more. For the Beatles' high spirits hold it together and make it all the more cogent. But then comes "Penny Lane." In this the medium and message are in perfect harmony. And the song's effect results from a genuine sense of proportion. As the characters of the song—the fireman, businessman, barber, and flower girl—walk through its shimmering imagery, the music evokes British TV's *Coronation Street.*

The rest of the songs on the album can be considered insignificant. But I must stop for I am falling into the trap the Beatles have laid for any critical approach. I am explaining instead of experiencing and am in danger of letting you forget that *Magical Mystery Tour* is frequently outrageous, always wacky, and constantly a pleasure. For who can deride the magic that works for these magicians? "You see," said George Harrison recently, "we have not really started yet."

COUNTRY JOE AND THE FISH

APRIL 1969
TORONTO TELEGRAM

WHAT'S LEFT OF SAN FRANCISCO'S Summer of Love is slowly disappearing. This was a time, two years ago, when thousands of kids dropped out of the middle of class and dropped into a world of flowers, drugs, love-ins, poster art, and the psychedelic bands. But the hippies have yielded to the political yippies, the love-ins to political rallies. The bands? Most were lost in the commercial shuffle; some disbanding, some disappearing under new names, new guises. But some, like Country Joe and the Fish, still swim in the wake of a year that was.

Inventive, tightly knit, Country Joe's music at the Electric Circus last night had all the feeling of something exciting. It was all there, all right, the under-groundmanship, the audience provocation, the humour, everything. But what a lot of it amounted to was a series of banalities that you might—in a romantic mood—mistake for personal poetry. The 1,200 kids who showed up seemed to listen to the group more out of curiosity than interest. After all, the feeling seemed to go, wasn't this one of the fabled San Francisco bands? Well, it was. But much of the spurious "psychedelic" sound was seen through rose-coloured glasses. So important was it for the hippies as a whole to make it, that their personal groups were carried in the current.

And last night, Country Joe and the Fish seemed to be way beyond their depth. The group played everything up tough and tight—with two ex-members of Big Brother and the Holding Company, bassist Peter Albin and David Getz on drums digging a rock-solid foundation. Yet there was something distant and sentimental about it. As if somewhere along the way to the deeper implications of "psychedelic" music they skidded on some greasy kid stuff. Guitarist Barry Melton's solos were competent, but perfunctory: Mark Kapner on organ meshed with everybody else, but sounded few original notes. In short: all the attitudes were there, but the music wasn't. This problem may not be unique: But for Country Joe it is. Before his last set, he seemed distracted as he talked: With two radio reviewers he talked politics, about "the election insanity being over," about not "getting involved in the dialectic... workings of the underground." What do you think of...? someone would ask. And Country Joe McDonald would quietly shrug an answer. "What do you think of... Ginsberg, Rochdale, Tim Leary, tours, Jackie Gleason and Anita Bryant's Rally for Decency?

And then came a pause. "Right now," he said, "I'm doing things I don't enjoy. I'd like to play soft acoustic music with different people." Gradually he got into a different track. "No one really cares about musicians. I seldom hear my voice because the loudspeakers are set up for others to hear. And the music becomes so loud and so frenzied! It's disgusting. The pressures get to you, now. Early in San Francisco, we thought we were immune, and that San Francisco was the world. But it didn't work because it was impossible... the San Francisco things become too big; it was doomed to become what it wanted to become."

But what? A scene with too many actors in the title role. Bands like Country Joe and the Fish staying together, I suspect, more through personal friendship than musical matters. Their music, once a beautiful idea, now made banal in common property. Musicians with no role left to play, playing with roles.

THE JIMI HENDRIX EXPERIENCE

MAY 1969
TORONTO TELEGRAM

THE JIMI HENDRIX EXPERIENCE has seemed to have come nearer to the burned-out ends of its sexy, smoky days. Passing through customs at Toronto International Airport Saturday evening, the twenty-six-year-old singer was arrested on a charge of illegal possession of narcotics; the following concert at Maple Leaf Gardens caught the mood and became a melancholy reflection on a career. For Hendrix has been rock's enfant terrible: The churning electrically generated guitar chords had a particular deranged fascination; his throaty voice could be hard, derisive, inventive, free, funny, serious, poetic, and abrasive; the effect—which was always total—cumulated into the most corrosive of nightmares.

Most of his songs had the same ponderous, lurching quality. They all seemed fragments of one great piece. As William S. Burroughs attempted in prose, Hendrix tried, in music, "to create a new mythology for the space age." And as always, without a pause for breath, without stopping his jittery dance-of-sex onstage, without ever an apparent stoppage in his inventiveness, Hendrix's act was buoyed up by his tremendous ego, his sheer will to go on. Behind everything he did there seems to be the conviction—or was it the desire for us to be convinced?—of something essential: Jimi Hendrix IS. "I am!" He played. "I am! Look at me. I'm singing!"

But Saturday night his will gave out. The crowd was keyed for his arrival. Hendrix's last appearance in Toronto (at the Coliseum on the Exhibition grounds, March 24, 1968), had been an exhausting event. Now, in Maple Leaf Gardens, Hendrix ambled out, looking like a street corner hustler in purples and greens and scarves and headbands. He solemnly announced a benediction: "We're going to create a whole new world." And suddenly block after block of almost tangible columns of sound built up, music seeming to float on its private cloud.

SEPTEMBER 1970
TORONTO TELEGRAM

ROCK LOST ITS MOST flamboyant personality today when pop singer Jimi Hendrix died from a drug overdose in a London, England, hospital. A spokesman for the hospital said the twenty-seven-year-old guitarist was still alive when admitted but died shortly before noon. Later, his body was taken to a morgue where a coroner's examination will be made. An inquest will be held.

Hendrix had returned to London last Tuesday from a European tour. A spokesman from Hendrix's London agents said: "It's really tragic news. Jimi was one of the greatest figures in show business today. It's a big loss to pop music all over the world." Significantly enough, Hendrix's last trip to Toronto last December 11, was to face charges on possession of drugs during a concert he gave at Maple Leaf Gardens, May 3, 1969. When he was freed of all charges, he said, "It is the best Christmas present Canada has ever given me."

Hendrix, born in Seattle, got his start in pop music as a backup guitarist for various black bands such as Little Richard's. Because he felt he couldn't advance his career far enough in the U.S., Hendrix went to England where he formed a band called the Experience, with drummer Mitch Mitchell and bassist Noel Redding. However, it wasn't until his appearance at the 1967 Monterey International Pop Festival in California that things took off for him. It was at Monterey, too, that much of his distinguishing style was first revealed: his gyrating sexuality, his pyrotechnical guitar work, his onstage flamboyance that often ended with setting his guitar on fire. In the next two years, Hendrix became a dominant force in pop music. In 1969, *Billboard* magazine, for the music industry, named him Musician of the Year.

Hendrix's music could only be described as orgiastic rock. Songs like "Hey Joe," and albums like *Axis, Bold as Love*, not only sold well, but established Hendrix as the inventor of a "new sound." It was music so loud, so inventive, so complex with studio techniques, that by the end of last year, Hendrix couldn't go much further with it. His band broke up; and most interviews with Hendrix were done while he was off tour. Last year, he started experimenting with other musicians like drummer Buddy Miles, getting together LPs along the "supergroup" concept. But it was also reported that Hendrix was exploring his roots and was going back into some older blues material. Hendrix was the second death in pop music in recent weeks. Al Wilson of the Canned Heat died two weeks ago, also, it was reported, because of an overdose of drugs.

JANIS JOPLIN

JUNE 1969
TORONTO TELEGRAM

JANIS JOPLIN IS AN anachronism in a time she helped create. She emerged in San Francisco when the San Franciscan Summer of Love was emerging into the world. She was a blues singer just when pop music underwent a blues revival. She looked cluttered and freaky when freakiness was in fashion. And she became a superstar when the term was just a fiction in a publicist's press release. Super hip, superstar, incredibly super-freaky, Janis was smothered under the avalanche of press copy claiming her to be the reincarnation of Bessie Smith, Bonnie Parker, Ma Perkins, and the all-American earth-momma.

When she pulls into town as part of the Festival Express' two-day fete at the CNE Grandstand, I suspect she'll be greeted that way. The Queen of Hip; the ultimate flower child. The fact that she has a new band (four of its members being Canadian), has developed a new style, and has changed in the five years she's been singing, won't alter it. It'll be Janis! And visions of Haight-Ashbury will dance in our heads.

By the time Janis and the band she started out with, Big Brother and the Holding Company, had made their impression at the Monterey International Pop Festival, had started touring the college campuses, she had become full-fledged pop idol, if not the prototype for the kind. For she was as much a creation of the media as she was of the blues she heard around her home in Port Arthur, Texas. San Francisco in the summer of 1967, and its people, became a sort of journalistic beachhead. And writers stormed in like marines, on a search-and-destroy mission after the elusive, frantic facts. If you were there you couldn't help being hit by some of the flak.

Out of all this a small legend surrounding Janis developed: born in a steamy oil refinery town of some sixty thousand, her father was an assistant superintendent of Texaco Canning Co, her mother, the registrar in the local business college. While the other white kids would sneak out at night to beat blacks up, she listened to old Bessie Smith songs. She blew town pronto. But if she stood out in Port Arthur, she stood out even more in San Francisco.

Janis was the entire Women's Lib to the rest of pop. On stage she wore some wicked clothes, florid velvets, great flouncy shirts with flowers and patterns and things. They flapped as she moved. And she moved a lot, her long hair flailing around her, her pudgy face jammed up close to the hand-held mic. It was all too perfect. She looked like every gun-moll that had ever lived. And she sang crazily, somewhere beyond description, beyond the point where her voice seemed to be breaking, with all the abrasiveness of the whine of a dentist's drill.

So Janis became, unwillingly, the hippest den mother to the most alienated set of kids America had ever seen. "But you know," she says, "I never, never considered myself a hippie. That image thing was all wrong. I always thought of myself as sort of a beatnik. I tried to keep to myself—like a beat. You have to forget a lot of those old hip things that came out of San Francisco. San Francisco is not what it was. I'm not as I was. And things generally aren't as they were. The fact that the whole scene we grew up with happened is important. It happened and we shouldn't forget it. We should keep the good that came from it. But you can't re-create it. You can't go home again, man. The trouble is that when I was there is the Summer of Love and my band was there, we were nobodies. When we got on stage, we were 'The Band,' we were still part of the people. But everything's changed since then. Things are, uh, more political. If anyone wants to go out and change the world, they won't be doing it merely by being beautiful. Right now nothing's really happening in any large way. And this vacuum is affecting a lot of different people in a lot of different ways."

Pop's been coasting for a while. There's an overwhelming sense that the old scene is decaying, of the old underground becoming the new establishment, of all the gold hip symbols, the general hairiness, the token gestures toward transcendent love, peace, and happiness, having been absorbed by the mainstream. Baubles and beads doth not the hippie make any longer. And the pop musician is faced by two basic choices: He either relinquishes his once particularly identifying marks and becomes like Cass Elliot or John Phillips, another entertainer in the broadest, Broadwayish sense; or he dives down, looking for another new underground, where he can develop something individual. The problem's particularly Janis's. As Blood, Sweat & Tears' guitarist Steve Katz says: "Janis Joplin is a good primitive blues singer, but when you're making $10,000 a night, you're not funky anymore—you can't come on hard luck and trouble. She's selling something she no longer is. How can you be a blues superstar. It's such a contradiction in terms."

"Nuts," says Janice. "The old scene, the San Francisco life has passed. It's over. And if you're going to wait around for it to happen again, and worry that it doesn't, you're lost, man. It's like being fifteen, and layin' in bed, and worryin' about dyin'. It's natural, sure. But you can waste the next forty-five years doin' it. The only way we as musicians, can live now, is to be decent to each other. The one thing that doesn't change, is the fact that we must be decent. And you can't criticize us for not getting down with the people. You just can't understand the difficulties there are in waiting to play in a strange town. After a point of travellin' around the country, and you're tired, and hungover, maybe, the whole thing reaches the bizarre.

"Just last week we played in Cincinnati. Well, the concert was cancelled, so I decided that we should play in the park for free. Just in meeting people there comes an uncomfortable point. If you try to talk with only one person, just trying to get to know him, you find you have to talk to forty. And these forty people who are just standing around all of the sudden don't really want to talk with you—they just stare. And stare. And stare. Okay. That's understandable. Everyone's got someone they think is magical. I'd give my eye teeth to talk, to meet with Bob Dylan. You can't get away from the fact of what you are. Think of it: you're on the road, and alone, and you are the hippest person you know; and if you accept all this, you find that your only reward is your music. But why should I cool it and take more time off. I found that I'd rather play music than sleep. You always have to give up something. Look at a housewife. She has to give up a certain amount of her own freedom so she can be secure.

"A musician gives up his happiness, comfort, some consideration, and his friends—you don't get to meet anybody. Well, that's payin' your dues. And all of it just to get high on music. Hmmm. I recently spent one month in Brazil on vacation. Man, it was just the ultimate luxury. I lay there on the beach in my bikini and sippin' good drinks and all. Yet, all I could think of was my band man. My music. Music's my old man. I'd do anything for it. Hell, I've done everything for it. I won't get off the stage until they pull me off with a crook."

OCTOBER 1970
TORONTO TELEGRAM

JANIS JOPLIN ALWAYS SANG as if she wanted to be called, "The late, great..." And now she is.

She was found dead in her Hollywood apartment late Sunday by John Cooke, road manager for her latest group, Janis Joplin Full Tilt Boogie Band. She was twenty-seven. Her body was found wedged between her bed and a nightstand. Sergeant Ed Sanchez of the Hollywood Police Department said she had "numerous" hypodermic needle marks on her left arm. But today her press representative, Myra Friedman, said she would not believe the drug allegation until the coroner's report was in. "Needle marks" said Miss Friedman from New York city. "Janis has bad skin, that's what. I have no reason to believe anything that's being said. It all sounds too sensationalistic. There may have been needle tracks on her arm from ten months ago. But recently she's gotten herself too much together with her new band. When I last spoke to her, her voice sounded completely lucid. And it's my personal belief that some freaky thing has happened... a heart attack, or a cerebral hemorrhage. I don't know why anyone would say anything else."

The problem is that Janis has always been news. Since her blistering performance at the 1967 Monterey International Pop Festival, she has been set apart. Wrote *Cashbox*: "She's kind of a mixture of Lead Belly, a steam engine, Calamity Jane, Bessie Smith, an oil derrick, and rot-gut bourbon funneled into the twentieth century somewhere between El Paso and San Francisco." Actually, it was Port Arthur, Texas, where she was born, learned to drink, started to listen to Big Mama Thornton, who she started to emulate, and from where she ran away at seventeen to San Francisco. It was with the developing San Francisco scene that promoted Janis as much as she could ever promote herself. She emerged with her first group, Big Brother and the Holding Company as the ultimate flower child, braless, in baubles, beads, in what she called her "hooker dress," and instant sexuality.

But I met her first in Buffalo, New York, when she was riding the waves created by her second—and bestselling—album appropriately called *Cheap Thrills*. She sipped capfuls of Courvoisier, eyes beaming, all sex and wisdom. "When people talk about me," she said, "they are always creating an image I didn't know existed." A year later, we talked again, just before she arrived in Toronto to perform at the Festival Express concert at the CNE Grandstand. Already her reputation had increased. She had been arrested in Tampa, Florida, for "obscenity." A TV show, *The Name of the Game*, had done a plot roughly outlining her life, and she was going to sue. By this time she had completed her *I've Got Dem Old Kozmic Blues Again Mama* LP for Columbia and was about to return to Port Arthur to a commencement at her old high school.

And, as she said, "music had become everything. It's my old man. My old scene, in San Francisco, has passed. It's over. It will never happen again. I'm just a rock 'n' roll woman, I have to give up all kinds of comfort, and happiness, and personal considerations, and love, and friends. But look at the housewife—she has to give up a lot of things, too. But I'd rather sing than do anything else. It's all I have left. All the old times are past. And if you're going to wait around for it to happen again, and worry that it doesn't, you're lost, man. It's like being fifteen, and layin' in bed, and worryin' about dyin'. You can't waste your time doin' it."

THE GRATEFUL DEAD

JULY 1969
LANGUID SOUND

THE SAN FRANCISCO SUMMER OF 1967, the "hippie sumer," is just a memory or a press clipping. What was unique there has become commonplace; light shows, big rock emporiums, psychedelia; love beads, bangles, and bards—every city has them now. But from that incredible musical pressure cooker four rock groups emerged. The Jefferson Airplane, through excellent musicianship, came first. Big Brother and the Holding Company because of Janis Joplin. Country Joe and the Fish gathered an underground following through their political activities.

Then there was the Grateful Dead. Bobbing in and out of public view, they seemed always on the point of breaking up. Perhaps last night at the Rock Pile was a temporary reprieve. But there were the Dead, their music streaming over the heads of the eight hundred kids who showed up, like flickering movie images over people in front row seats. And, in their way, they embodied the sounds and "feel" of San Francisco summer. With a sound that owes more to Bach than rock, and more still to third-stream jazz, everything they play is warm and languid.

Compared to their sounds, much of rock is starkly simple. For this reason, the Grateful Dead have become increasingly controversial. Some feel they point to where pop is going (particularly critics in jazz and pop magazines). Others sense that pop has gone and left them (Adam Mitchell, ex-Pauper, says: "They're so loose, so ill-organized.") But last night, things had tightened up. Forms and structures overlapped; one section flowing into another. Styles intermingled; now, some country, now blues, now freeform.

After a long instrumental, lead guitarist Jerry Garcia swung toward the mic: "Trouble ahead; trouble behind," he sang. Suddenly, without a break, everything changed. The bass began to shake the Pepsi machine; huge shudders went through the floor. Loud—LOUDER, the sounds grew, clogging the mics. And what has been free-flowing became rock-hard and definite. The jazzy instrumental yielded to the song which, in turn, gave way to an all-amps-up-full chant. "Walk me out in the morning dew ..." The group moved ahead. People got up to dance; a pale girl in black velvet circled arabesques near me; a boy, naked to the waist, juggled and bobbed, his head inches from the noise-belching equipment on stage.

How much of this was planned? And how much improvisation? Hearing the Dead, these definitions blurred. Their approach to music seems casual, one concerned as much with effect as with artistry. But in pop, the sound and the style have always overlapped. As they carry with them as much of the mystique, as the music, of San Francisco. As performers, they're average; as innovators, they often attempt something too large to handle.

BLIND FAITH

JULY 1969
TORONTO TELEGRAM

ROCK WAS ONCE SO EASY. Kids dug it, but felt guilty. Parents hated it and grew righteous. It might have stopped right there, but Elvis and the Beatles came along. Ah yes, the magic bubble of pop art then engendered an idea: rock was ART, perhaps even great. And when Blind Faith wandered on that stage last night at Varsity Arena, the bubble seemed to swell to its fullest. Their reputations had floated in ahead of them and glistened opaquely through the night. Blind Faith: guitarist Eric Clapton; Ginger Baker on drums; Steve Winwood, organist and guitarist; Ric Grech on bass; an amalgam of musicians from England riding through America corralling superlatives. And, as a secondary consideration, a million bucks.

So much for secondary considerations. Just before playing, the group looked at the audience, like a matador sizing up a bull, excitement mingling with ... fear? For there were kids, nine thousand or so, huddling beneath the huge, looming speakers, watching electronic dials and knobs winking out at the night. Clapton seemed reticent, it seemed as if he were on some electronic pyre and all those kids out there were waiting for some sort of musical immolation. When he and Baker had been with the defunct Cream (with bassist Jack Bruce) it had almost been like that; huge, tortured phrases had been wrenched out of his guitar—it was pop at its most overpowering.

Suddenly: Wham! It had started. A chord was struck, a piece structured. As he sang his own song, "Had To Cry Today," Winwood gulped in air. The crowd shrank back—the first pass had been made. A girl with a *Clapton Is God* sticker yawned. For it was odd; here the musician, who as a soloist has been one of the seminal influences for rock guitarists, stayed in the background. In the next song, Winwood's "Can't Find My Way Home," it was the same. Over the plodding *chug-clug* of the blues chord changes, Clapton added the thinnest of counterpoints. Or in the old Buddy Holly "Well, All Right," Baker's drumming, and Clapton's solos were subdued, controlled ... secondary. On it went. Thinking back, the mind lingered over old Cream performances and all their roughness. With Blind Faith, the blend is smooth. "In any case, I am not really any longer a blues guitarist. I went into Cream a blues guitarist and came out as a rock 'n' roll player." And as he said this, Clapton came closer to the core of Blind Faith than his fans would care.

For that's what they are: one of the few rock and roll bands left in rock. They're drifting away from the avant-garde as much as the Beatles drift to it. Coming from culture's rec rooms, rock originally had no significance beyond itself. The kids loved it; the parents hated it. It was just an experience, not any sort of stereophonic Bayreuth. And last night Ginger Baker's drum solo crescendoed to climax after climax, along with Winwood's gutsy singing and Ric Grech's unobstructive bass lines. All were experiences varying in intensity, but equally significant. For things like "meaning" and "statement" had little to do with Blind Faith's music.

As their sound went faster, it was like speeding along Highway 27, hanging your feet out the car window and digging the thrill of it all.

When everything slowed down, there was something sensual, like the sway of hips at a high school dance. Technically, few groups can touch them. But at heart, Blind Faith's nostalgic. Raunchy, uncluttered, bluesy and jazz... the kids will dig it. Maybe even a few parents will hate it.

LED ZEPPELIN

AUGUST 1969
TORONTO TELEGRAM

AS IF IT WERE going to detach itself and float down Yonge Street, an island formed around the Rock Pile last night, some of them kids waiting three hours. A hot, dark silence prevailed as minutes went by, but no one moved. After all the Rock Pile has been closed six weeks. And the Led Zeppelin were coming.

Inside, a series of disasters loomed. Led Zeppelin, the focal point for all this energy, wouldn't perform until their federal taxes were paid. To manager Rick Taylor, this meant his profit would disappear; which in turn meant the Rock Pile would go bankrupt. Then: "Listen, this is the end," said the group's road manager. "Somebody's taken our distributor cap from the truck. I'm calling the cops."

"Hey. Well, we didn't take it," someone shouted back.

"Lookit. I even saw one of your people do it."

By then the crush of people was pressing the retaining doors. And the temperature, well up in the eighties set everybody on edge. But it all had a sense of style—a corporate battle with beads. Over two thousand kids jammed inside; heat rose correspondingly. Suddenly everything was solved. The group was paid. And toward the door in the back, there was activity as a group of girls, smiling with glazed eyes, jostled for position. Yet even with the heat, the crowds, and the taste of salt in the air, the prelude to Led Zeppelin made sense.

The music rose out of the blues—not copied, but translated into a new medium, earthy, heavy, and oh-so-loud. For all its concessions to artfulness—guitarist Jimmy Page's soaring solos, singer Robert Plant's uncanny ability to evoke a metallic guitar sound with his voice—it seemed completely natural, unaffected, and unforced. They turned Willie Dixon's blues, "You Shook Me" (from the first album), inside out. Page, often reminiscent of guitarist Jeff Beck, was round and fluid, then screaming with the intense EEEEE of a dentist's drill. Drummer John Bonham cut across the rhythmic flow with a couple of double-timing riffs; John Paul Jones kept the bass line steady.

In everything they did—"I Can't Quit You Baby," "Dazed and Confused," "How Many More Times"—there was the same quality. All the jagged edges came through. Perhaps this makes them the spiritual descendants of the Rolling Stones.

While the greater proportion of pop groups have taken early Beatles' ideas to their logical (sometimes, irrational) conclusions, and while others returned directly to the blues, (the place where the Beatles themselves came from), Led Zeppelin maintains the feel of the early Stones. There's an unbridled release of sexuality, and a lack of polish that makes Led Zeppelin seem real. They, like early Stones, return the visceral response to rock. And who knows? Maybe Jimmy Page will be the seventies' reply to the sixties Mick Jagger. It's all there, the gut feeling for their music, a love of its uncouthness, its rages, its noise. As the kids lined up for the next show (another two thousand wilting in the heat), as managers haggled somewhere in an office, Led Zeppelin created an excitement that brought rock right back home.

SEPTEMBER 1971
TORONTO TELEGRAM

LED ZEPPELIN IS A good little rock 'n' roll band whose sound has been overamplified, and appeal overpublicized beyond sane proportions. Like watching a NFB short stretched into a two-and-a-half-hour CinemaScope spectacular, the group is simply too much of too little. Now, there were about sixteen thousand fans at Maple Leaf Gardens last Saturday night for Led Zeppelin's sweaty, muscular, two-hour concert, who would dispute with me about this. If their standing ovations and constant cheering were any indication, Zeppelin's concert was one of the most successful of the past year.

But not only the success, but the reasons behind it were predictable. Zeppelin's current North American tour is one of the most spectacular in their almost-four-year history. About seventeen thousand showed up in Vancouver, and just before the Toronto concert they filled New York City's Madison Square Gardens. The tour was to have coincided with the release of their fourth LP, which, like the first three, is expected to easily sell a million copies when it's released in early October. Yet such mass success has become a norm in pop. In fact, it's the only kind of success pop marketers are willing to recognize.

In Saturday's concert, it meant little that Zeppelin drummer John Bonham's fifteen-minute drum solo in "Moby Dick" was appallingly bereft of ideas; and that Robert Plant's singing was unparalleled in its lack of originality also meant little. The essential fact of the concert remains: the group and the promoters cleaned up. The tedium was the message at this concert. Just as lead guitarist Jimmy Page and bassist John Paul Jones would escalate a few simple lines into something resembling a solo, the group as a whole—notably in "Black Dog," a tune from the new LP—would muddle around with a few fundamental rhythmic patterns giving the impression that all this repetition was planned and not just unavoidable.

The first impression Zeppelin allows is one of toughest,

grittiness—the Real Thing. Plant cavorts sexually enough; Page's guitar work is abrasive enough; and they play at a decibel level somewhere near the threshold of pain. But from start to finish, nothing changes in their act. It's *always* loud, *always* wham-bang, *always* overbearing. It seems not so much predictable, but formularized. Zeppelin's formulas aren't bad just because they are poorly conceived formulas. Hence, we had Plant's announcement that "we're going to sit down" to play some things on acoustic guitar because "after three years we're moving and flowing a bit more." But the tone of the announcement was such that to both performers and audience was made to seem like an apocalyptic moment—as if neither side had been to a folk club nor had heard a quiet song.

Ironically, Zeppelin may have initiated a style of rock that might mean its own downfall. The recent success of both Grand Funk Railroad (coming to Toronto in October) and Black Sabbath may displace Zeppelin from its current popularity, which, only earlier this year resulted in a poll showing them displacing the Beatles as Britain's No. 1 group.

THE BAND

REVIEW: *THE BAND*
OCTOBER 1969
TORONTO TELEGRAM

THE BAND'S NEWEST ALBUM is a record only by necessity. More importantly, I suggest, it's an attempt at musical actuality. It's not a recapturing of anything that's been done before; but with all of the music's rough edges retained, plus "folksiness," it just sounds this way. Last year, The Band set its own standard with the debut album, *Music from Big Pink*. In this, they relied heavily upon their mentor, Bob Dylan. The surface of their songs was gloomy, hard-edged, as if the ideas beneath were creating tensions too strong to handle. But, then again, you often got the same feeling from Dylan himself. But the whole effect of this album is disquieting, a bit uncanny. It's like an old, fading snapshot of someone you recognize but at the same time are dead sure you've never even heard of.

The songs themselves have a quaint charm—like old farm machinery found abandoned in a field with grain growing around it. The composer of most of them, guitarist Jaime Robbie Robertson, blends the old chug-chug energy of jug bands. (Think of old Gus Cannon's Jug Stompers, electrified) with the black-water nasality of the country. Beyond this, it's difficult to break the songs down to their various elements. The Band seemed to play anything and everything that was available—saxes, peck horns, a mandolin, trombone, mouth harp, slide trumpet, etc. Sometimes the result sounds complex and sophisticated—the harmonies of "Whispering Pines" go off in all directions, all of them the right ones. Occasionally there's a definite bluesy feel, with a bass line or two made prominent. In "Up on Cripple Creek," the idiom is folk country; from "Rag Mama Rag," you get the impression of a bunch of country boys who've just hit New Orleans for the first time and won't be beat by anybody, no sir.

Considering the impromptu nature of the recording sessions (done in a house in the Hollywood Hills with Robertson engineering) the balance, the texture, the sense of just-the-right-thing is remarkable. Perhaps what is more remarkable is that this album, along with the Beatles' *Abbey Road*, have helped revive pop music from the doldrums of last year. Now, in any field, works of art that are perfect are hard to find. Perhaps we don't want to find them too often. And perhaps, this record isn't perfect. But as The Band amble leisurely through the country, be sure the way they're going approaches that sense of perfection.

JANUARY 1970
TORONTO TELEGRAM

AFTER EVERYTHING'S BEEN LAID and sung, The Band is still just a band. The only remarkable thing about it is that nothing remarkable seems to happen when they play. Notes click and fall into place like gears meshing. And while most pop goes gaudy and grandiose, they remain concise and compact. But the feeling surrounding their two concerts at Massey Hall last Saturday night was something akin to a once-removed religious experience.

These concerts had all the appurtenances of mythology-in-making. The packed audiences hush for each song, erupting into standing ovations at the conclusion. Just a hint of humour caused laughs. Just a slight bit of cymbal work by Levon Helm and the beat was felt like a shudder. And at times it seemed that the myths surrounding The Band were as much at work here as their music: of Bob Dylan down in Woodstock, New York; of their palmier days with Ronnie Hawkins playing Yonge Street clubs; of their recent *TIME* cover article. This is understandable, maybe. A pop music audience has often dealt with an experience not by trying to understand it, but by trying out attitudes to be adopted to it. While The Band's music is so plain and so surprisingly original, that it demands a one-to-one relationship. You can't dig them just a little.

Their plainness, it turned out, was very elegant. For "Rockin' Chair," Garth Hudson suddenly rounded the set of drums, shoeless and with an accordion. From there, the song gallumped along, with the voices and accordion weaving their lines together. Nothing could have sounded so plain and folksy. Yet nothing could have been suffused with such a sweet nostalgia, with a gentleness approaching gentility. Much of what they did was implied, rather than baldly stated. In "This Wheel's on Fire" Rick Danko's bass line could barely be heard. But it was felt. And the band sounded, slightly top-heavy (as in distinct from others in rock who make their bass line so loud that it sounds bottomless. And should be.). And every so often they would bring out some of their extra instruments—in "The Unfaithful Servant," it's Levon Helm's mandolin and Hudson's soprano sax, mixing in one song, two attitudes. One moment it had a country tinkle, open and faltering; the next, a sleezy urbanity.

Nothing seemed very certain when they were on stage. Their voices seemed to be hanging to a melody by the thinnest of threads. Instrumentally, they *seemed* just good enough to play just enough notes to make a song come off. But this strikes at the bottom of their style. For things are calculated to the degree to make them appear—and sound—uncalculated. Rarely did individuals stand out—like the Budapest String Quartet, The Band's a collection of soloists subordinating themselves into one solo vehicle. Even the emerging leader of the group, guitarist Jaime (Robbie) Robertson, stayed as part of the background. In a sense, however, The Band's music is all background. For "Up on Cripple Creek," Danko, Helm, and Robertson each contributed a simple rhythmic motif. Yet together they gave the song a shifty, a rhythmical feeling, with elements interacting on each other building into an organic whole.

Since the release of their first album, *Music from Big Pink*, The Band have loomed large over a lot of pop. It (and subsequently, they themselves) arrived at a time when rock was becoming so complicated that it only served to point out its critics' simplicity. And in concert, The Band go even further against the rest of pop's grain. They experiment more, their music is lighter, jazzier in texture. Garth Hudson's extended solo for "Chest Fever" touched on an old oompah-oompah silent cinema style of organ playing, some Messiaen, a bit of Bach's *Toccata and Fugue in D minor* and a little Jimmy Smith. It was the only solo effort of the night, but still didn't turn out as the grand virtuoso showpiece, fitting finely with the song that followed.

There were some complaints, however. Too sappily country, not commercial enough, too aloof when they're on stage—all these charges were brought up against The Band by friends with some justification. But one listen to Richard Manuel's wavery voice, and the pea-picker in me rebels. For there are those of us on the underside of society who have little stake in all of the Respectable Culture out there. (Brahms, yes—culture, no.) The Band fills in the gaps for us. They draw discriminately from a culture that spawned Picasso, and from another that gave out Pepsi ads. And they meet us somewhere halfway—where we all are waiting.

REVIEW: *STAGE FRIGHT* (1970)
AUGUST 1970
TORONTO TELEGRAM

***STAGE FRIGHT* IS NOT** only the name for The Band's third and latest album, it is also an accurate description of The Band's collective personality. No group in pop, since they came on the scene two years ago, with the twin reputations of being both Ronnie Hawkins's and Bob Dylan's backup aggregation, has maintained its privacy so completely. Their first album, *Music from Big Pink*, came from nowhere—if you consider the town of Woodstock in upper New York state where they holed up with Dylan while he was in retreat as being "nowhere." Their second LP was long awaited; yet when it arrived, it, too, seemed a complete surprise.

Stage Fright, then, arrives as freshly as the others did. It too is illusive, hiding its lyrics' meanings behind a complex orchestrational web. Its harmonies, too, rely heavily on country and rock 'n' roll motifs. Its mood is also melancholy; with its setting sounding veiled, inaccessible, and somehow remote as if, in the lines from one of the songs, "The W. S. Walcott Medicine Show," the LP was "a dead ringer for something like you ain't never seen." But, like the other LPs, *Stage Fright* shows The Band moving into entirely new areas.

You can't really question which Band LP is the best anymore. Each one has shown the group attempting something new and can only be judged according to how well they bring all this "newness" off. Tunes like "Just Another Whistle Stop," the title song, "Stage Fright," or even the first piece, "Strawberry Wine," seem simpler, more accessible. The chord progressions come clear, with Robbie Robertson's guitar, Richard Manuel's piano, Rick Danko's bass, Garth Hudson's many instruments, and Levon Helm's drumming deliciously heavy-handed. The playing itself seems surer. Every note seems to fall exactly into its place. There's none of the rough-edged looseness of the two previous LPs. The start of "Time to Kill" sounds like it might have come from a band fresh off the Yonge Street bar circuit, and not from The Band that left it all behind years ago.

So much for first impressions. For *Stage Fright* shows The Band much more together, much more at ease with what they're doing, and much more cohesive as a group, as they sing in the middle of "Time to Kill": "Don't know what we got, but it feels like a lot—don't need any more." But the "we" in this case is difficult to spot. Although the band members don't like to be separated, having one member singled out, "Stage Fright" only serves to point up the talents of lead guitarist Jaime Robbie Robertson as a singer, instrumentalist, songwriter, and melodist.

The LP is really Robertson's stage; and as the title tune points out, the LP also shows his fright. It tells the basic story of a ploughboy who, wishing for fame and fortune, ends up with them like an albatross around his neck. Each performance becomes a nightmare, a remembrance of an audience yelling: "Please don't make him stop ... let him start all over again." Robertson either wrote or collaborated on each of the ten songs in the album (running a rather short thirty-three minutes and twenty-two seconds). And the contrast from song to song is remarkable. "All La Glory" is a lullaby, with the singer's voice nestling up to your ear with its low and confidential tone: "Sleeping" on the other hand, could have been written by Hoagy Carmichael as its tranquil melody laid out in neat, honest phrases; "Daniel and the Sacred Harp" shows Dylan's effect to be still with The Band, as the song rambles over allegory and balladry to tell the tale of original sin; and "The Rumor" is a trifle bitter, showing The Band (or Robertson) as its most defiant.

Throughout all this, the group playing is excellent. One wants to say "of course," for fewer groups in pop these days can contrive so much invention, and still maintain the traditional demands of musicians—good intonation, a sense of humour, the ability to surprise, an ability to control their material. Ironically, *Stage Fright* will probably be its own worst enemy. For now The Band will be even more in demand. And they'll just have to keep getting on stage.

THE ROLLING STONES

REVIEW: *LET IT BLEED*
DECEMBER 1969
TORONTO TELEGRAM

WITH THEIR NEWEST ALBUM, *Let It Bleed*, the Rolling Stones have created a perfect balance of sheer energy and musical form. The old blend of narcissism and arrogance spiced with lead singer Mick Jagger's rage, has been altered slightly and transformed a lot. In style and feeling, the LP's a return to the days when the group used to play in local London clubs. In inventiveness, it's beyond anything they've attempted to date. Any more than anything, it's broken down the constant Beatles–Rolling Stones comparison.

Once this was pop music's equivalent to the Stravinsky–Schoenberg polarization. In development, the Stones were always at least one LP behind the Beatles. The Beatles were cute; the Stones, gutsy. But the Beatles were tricky; they used all the devices the modern recording studio offered them. And their records sold. When the Stones tried this, in *Their Satanic Majesties Request* album, the result was disputed. And the record didn't sell. This album, at the same time, explodes another myth—that the Stones were (and are) basically a white soul group.

Now, many blues elements are mixed in here, some bottleneck guitar playing, the basic twelve-bar tonic-dominant blues chordal framework. But in *Let It Bleed*, the Stones have gone as far beyond their "blues origins" as the Beatles have from theirs. And in a different direction. There's a loose, improvisational feel here that could only be achieved through the tightest control possible. In "Love in Vain" (the only non–Mick Jagger–Keith Richards composition) the piece seems to constantly open up, being frontless, backless, and endless at once. But that's only an impression they've built in. Throughout, organic rhythms make the album seem more orgiastic than it is. And few tricks are tried. Two of the songs, "Country Honk" and "You Can't Always Get What You Want," are rewritten from their last singles release. And in the latter, the London Bach Choir gives an ethereal introduction almost parodying Jagger's pronunciation with their "cahn't's" and their "wahnt's." And what emerges is the first record by the Stones that sounds "total" without being repetitive.

More than this, *Let It Bleed* may just be the best pop record of the year—and that is considering two of the best albums ever to appear in pop, both of which came out this year: *The Band* and the Beatles' *Abbey Road*.

THE WHO

REVIEW: *LIVE AT LEEDS*
JUNE 1970
TORONTO TELEGRAM

LISTENING TO A RECORDING of a live performance is like practice-putting on green broadloom. All that added comfort can't quite make up for the original experience. But it's the secret wish of every living rock 'n' roller, it seems, to capture between the grooves that instant excitement conjured up at a rock concert.

So it doesn't really matter that the Beatles produced the best-recorded studio sound in pop. They've still tried to add that extra "live" dimension in their latest album, *Let It Be*. Similarly, it doesn't matter that the Who have a two-record set rock opera under their belts (something only completely realized in a recording studio). They too have finished their "live" LP, *Live at Leeds*. But the difference between the Beatles' album and the Who's is vast and telling. While *Let It Be* sounds rich and compelling at first, it soon wears thin. While *Live at Leeds* sounds one-dimensional at first, it grows as you listen to it, and develops into what is perhaps the finest live rock album done to date.

At Leeds, the Who have an audience of thousands. On *Let It Be*, the Beatles only have themselves. *Live at Leeds* seems to expand in the night air, with each one of Peter Townshend's murky chords sparking off new sounds. *Let It Be* sounds closeted, giving the impression of four British peers chatting over brandy. But there's the question here of exactly what rock 'n' roll is these days. From the early fifties on, it constructed itself along massive lines. It was never subtle or particularly melodic like jazz. It was vital. With power, sheer undiluted power.

From the start, the Who, and particularly their lead guitarist Peter Townshend, have rejected this. The Who was the group which used to smash its instruments on stage. And wore jackets designed like the British flag. And always played louder than it was possible to imagine. "Settle down," Townshend used to say, "and we'll play some rock 'n' roll for you." *Blam, bang*—just like that. And on *Live at Leeds* they've done nothing less.

On this LP there's little that's new with "Summertime Blues," "Shakin' All Over," "My Generation," and "Magic Bus" (really a good copy of an old Bo Diddley song) all forming part of the group's standard repertoire. What makes *Live at Leeds* significant, then, is the way the Who handle these songs. No live album has ever been as carefully recorded—and this includes the early live Beatle recordings, or the Rolling Stones' *Got Live If You Want It!* LP. Instead of being hampered by the acoustical properties of a large stadium area, the Who have utilized them. Every note they play glistens with echo. Not only does the music sound live (as we can hear from the cheering crowd) it "feels" live to the ear, like something crisp and fresh.

In *Let It Be*, the Beatles throw everything at you—from Phil Spector's sloppy orchestrations on "The Long and Winding Road" to George Harrison's lilting "For You Blue"—and leave you juggling with all the pieces. The fact that some of *Let It Be* is "live" seems incidental. And it's only after having seen the movie *Let It Be* do some of the supposed "live" hits come to life.

MAY 1980
TORONTO STAR

FIRST ROGER DALTREY RAN ON, in black leather jacket and jeans. Then came Pete Townshend, also in jeans and jacket, John Entwistle, natty in striped jacket, and then Kenney Jones. And that was that. The Who had arrived on stage at Maple Leaf Gardens last night as casually as a local band playing at the neighbourhood pub. It was just that straight and to the point.

Now, to people unaccustomed to big league rock bands, this may seem to be the only reasonable approach to take. And, of course, it is. Unfortunately, most of these rock bands have collective egos the size of Manitoba and wish to appear on stage as if just descending from the heavens. The Who's ego is in better shape than most.

Of all the major sixties bands, this is the most human—at least, it understands best the human element of a rock concert. Last night wasn't the band at its absolute best; it was better than one show I saw in New York last fall, but not as rounded-out as one recently caught in Denver—but it was still one of the classiest concerts of recent years at the Gardens. Sold out for weeks, it was a night where the blood and sweat, behind the music could be heard as easily as the notes; a night when the music got into the bones, where it could be felt. Backstage, singer Daltrey estimated that last night's—and tonight's—show represented the fifth time the band has been at the Gardens since the mid-sixties when it opened a North American tour for Herman's Hermits.

Outside, scalpers scalped up to $60 a pair for good seats, the police frisked and searched for booze or drugs, and, for the most part, all of this was accepted in good grace. Was everyone trying to ignore the memory of the Cincinnati concert last December when eleven fans were killed trying to get to a Who concert? It seemed so. Although the police seemed to be more in evidence last night, the staff sergeant on hand insisted, tersely, that the staff of forty off-duty police was "the same as it is for any rock concert." In fact, security was everywhere, and it only lapsed once. But that was enough. The band had just finished the overture to *Tommy*, with Townshend flailing out one final majestic chord, when a couple of fans rushed the stage. The guards, though, were elsewhere and suddenly, hundreds of fans rushed the stage. Some clambered up near the band's monitors and on occasion Daltrey would pass out paper cups of water to them.

The Gardens was stiflingly hot and this heat plus the crush of bodies and the band's use of a single red spotlight to cast an atmospheric glow over everything formed a picture of what the night was all about. There is no Who look; no fashion style, no latter-day mod mode. Nor is there really any Who mythology that lives on its own. In truth, Who albums (released infrequently to date) aren't played all that much on rock radio these days. And two members—Entwistle, Jones, and semi-regular keyboard player John Bundrick—are all but anonymous. Quite simply, the Who is a band that must be seen and heard live. It only truly becomes what it is, in concert.

On occasion, though, the band seemed to skim over its material, particularly at the beginning, until it found something interesting to do with Entwistle's blistering version of "My Wife." For the most part, it seemed as if you were hearing new work for the first time. They paired two older pieces; "My Generation" followed directly by "I Can See for Miles." The pacing for both was slightly easier going than in the original, but another piece, "Pinball Wizard," took on an entirely new dimension, one created in part by new drummer Kenney Jones. If Jones can't be deliberately anarchistic as his predecessor, the late Keith Moon, he can add a measure of finesse that broadens out the band's music. Jones has all the power needed, although unlike Moon, who focused it into one frontal attack, Jones distributes it evenly. His transition into the band seemed smooth and complete. But then again, this band survives making the difficult seem simple.

CREEDENCE CLEARWATER REVIVAL

SEPTEMBER 1970
TORONTO TELEGRAM

EVEN IN A SCENE as full of improbables as rock 'n' roll, what happened at Maple Leaf Gardens with Creedence Clearwater Revival Saturday night would have seemed like the impossible. But there it all was. Almost seventeen thousand kids had sat patiently through the two preliminary acts, Wilbert Harrison, and Booker T. & the MG's, only to end up shouting themselves dizzy in Creedence's brain-bath of basic, rocking chords.

The tone of the entire evening was uncannily like that when the Beatles first arrived. Everything on both sides of the stage seemed to gush out spontaneously. By the time Creedence finished their forty-minute set (long by today's supergroup standards), everybody and everything in the building seemed to breathe together. Creedence, you see, is an anachronism in pop today. It's a throwback to when pop music was one outrageously blatant kid-burp in the face of all adult seriousness. Today's pop artist talks of aesthetics and grows fat with recording residuals. His sound is fat and serious, too—a mélange of jazz, blues, folk, and anything else available, with a twist of Lennon added. In short, he can't kid around with it anymore. But Creedence plays with an absolutely mind-crimping simplicity. They're one of the few groups—if not the only group—to gain prestige with their five consecutive gold record awards for singles, four gold albums, and three platinum records (for albums that have sold one million units each, thus earning $5 million each) in both the teenybopper and so-called underground scenes.

But how does this explain the raw excitement surrounding their concert? "The funny thing about all this," said one older (i.e., over 25) observer, "is that a certain percentage of the people here don't really know what this is all about. It's only those who are over twenty-five who know." There was the, by now, commonplace attempt to break into the concert free. Says Stan Obodiac for the Gardens, "What we were disturbed about was that this small group—about twenty-five or thirty—tried to force their way in. They broke several windows, and we had to warn the police. But they were so young!"

Indeed; and everybody acted as if the past five years of rock 'n' roll history had never happened, as if questions of how hip you were didn't matter, and all that was left was that one-on-one relation to the music, that instant empathy with a group you've never met. Consider Creedence's appearance: Leader, chief guitarist, writer, arranger, John Fogerty walked out in a plaid cotton work shirt and actually seemed interested in playing. And throughout the rest of their set, he and his brother Tom who plays rhythm guitar, drummer Doug Clifford, and bassist Stu Cook bantered back and forth across the huge, projecting stage. They reminded you of four Boy Scouts on a day off, with their easygoing style, and bedraggled hair that looked like it had been cut with a bowl.

"The last time we were in Toronto over a year ago we played at the Electric Circus," said John Fogerty. "But the sound that time wasn't very good. We think it's much better this time." But, of course, it wasn't; and the group had difficulties hearing themselves through playback speakers set up on stage. But, of course, it really didn't matter. Having started together almost eleven years ago playing $15-a-night high school parties in the San Francisco area, Creedence has come a long way (and commanding, it's been reported, up to $90,000 a night), but do very little with their music.

Their hit songs they played Saturday night—things like "Proud Mary," their first international hit; "Bad Moon Rising"; "Green River"; "Down on the Corner"; "Fortunate Son"; and "Travelin' Band," this last being a kindly copy of Little Richard Penniman—were, in essence, simple variations on one basic repertoire of chords. But it was the way they played them that counted, without frills, without fuss, or pretentions to anything in particular. They played almost twenty notes for every tick of the heart, earning them roughly $20 per second for every second of the forty minutes they were on stage. The good old days were never as good.

JULY 1971
TORONTO WEEK

BEFORE CREEDENCE CLEARWATER REVIVAL came along, rock 'n' roll had disappeared into a sleepy purple haze. It was 1968, and psychedelia had slowed things down, when, from San Francisco, came reports of this strange little band playing old hits from the fifties, looking like lumberjacks, who didn't take drugs, who ... You get the picture, anyhow. And if things go according to plan, things should become clearer when WGRZ-TV, Ch. 2, broadcasts *In Concert: Creedence Clearwater Revival*, in colour, Thursday, July 22 from 10:00 to 11:00 p.m.

The special centres around a concert Creedence recently did at the Oakland Coliseum where, like most Creedence concerts, it was packed with the widest cross-section of rock fans imaginable: young kids, who had listened to them on Top 40 radio; undergrounders, caught up in the rock nostalgia; and parents, who somehow thought all of this was good clean something-or-other. But, before the concert, the camera crews rummaged around the CCR warehouse (which they call The Factory) trying to show the four, John Fogerty, Doug Clifford, Tom Fogerty, and Stu Cook, informally. And, perhaps, this statement will be more representative: for, if nothing else, Creedence has been one of the least formal bands going.

Let me explain. As rock became increasingly gimmicky, Creedence—led, primarily, by singer-songwriter John Fogerty—has consistently simplified things. In recordings, they avoid fancier studio techniques, getting everything down without overdubbing parts. As rock had sought greater technical feats, Creedence's music is the primitive rock thump first generated when Presley came along. "They call it swamp music," John Fogerty once told me. "But that's not it. Really, it's just old rock—the real rock, hard, and straight."

Just recently, Tom Fogerty has left the group and is in the process of releasing his first solo LP. But before this split, Creedence had been together since the junior high school days, when they played local dance as the Blue Velvets. Shortly after that, they met a super-hotshot manager who tried to revamp their image, call them the Golliwogs, and get their career started. When that didn't work out, they broke up, only to reform a year later, choosing a name inspired by ecological reform: Creedence ... Clearwater.

In a way, the special will seem like a Creedence retrospective. It will showcase old hits: "Born on the Bayou," "Commotion," "Proud Mary," "Down on the Corner," "Bad Moon Rising," etc. And it will allow you to peek into a period of rock that, in the past year or so, has lost some of its energy. With Creedence, the show has a definite focus. It's rock, straight and simple. It's the kind of music, once so unfashionable, that it took ten years, British superstars, and major media coverage to make it respectable enough to allow Creedence to play it the way it's always been.

THE MOTHERS OF INVENTION

NOVEMBER 1970
TORONTO TELEGRAM

WHAT LOOKED MENACING, ugly and mean back in 1966 when the Mothers of Invention came to some sort of national prominence, was comparatively mild and serious at their concert last night in Massey Hall. Back then, a Mothers performance seemed built around the bizarre: what was a pretty weird-looking band to start with was compounded by shrieks, grunts, and some far-flung music coupled with the somewhat overbearing presence of the group's leader and chief guitarist, Frank Zappa. Last night, it was business as usual with Zappa. Occasionally someone from the packed house would yell something out, and Zappa would glare back into the footlights: "Is that an example of Canadian humour?"

In the past four years or so, the personnel has changed. It was only last spring that Zappa announced that he was disbanding so that he could devote more time to film and record production. But, he also wanted to do an extended piece he's been working on, called *200 Motels*, which was to musically detail the vicissitudes of a rock band travelling on the road. Thus, Zappa gave birth to a new set of Mothers—and this one was perhaps the most musically impressive of the lot.

There are a couple of exceptions to the above generalization: and these two exceptions, namely the two singers Mark Volman and Howard Kaylan, formerly with the Turtles, practically ruined the evening. Normally, it would take nothing short of a small bomb to ruin a Mothers performance; at their best, they've always teetered close to total chaos, with a touch of satire here, and a dash of lunacy there. But, just as normally, their satire has always been intelligent, and their lunacy particularly inspired. The muggings and gestures and antics of Volman and Kaylan, however, were puerile. As good as their singing was—and many of Zappa's vocal lines require someone with an avant-garde set of instincts—it was submerged under a deluge of corn. For example: when you have a lyric (from a tune called "Dog Breath, in the Year of the Plague") that goes: "The air escaping from your mouth. The hair escaping from you nose ..." the surest method is not to follow any method at all, and to let the lyric itself carry whatever humor, or satire there is. But no. Volman and Kaylan gagged it up with brassy falsettos—sort of like a couple of the Supremes gone to pot—and the joke was laid on with a heavy hand.

Zappa and the Mothers of Invention are usually filed away as rock theatre. With the Fugs, and, to some extent, the now defunct Bonzo Dog Doo-Dah Band, the Mothers worked within rock as a constant criticism to it; and they embellished the sort of serious irreverence with sight gags. With bassist Jeff Simmons, drummer Aynsley Dunbar, organist George Duke and longtime Zappa accomplice, Ian Underwood, on piano, any invention for the Mothers is mainly musical. From each came excellent solos, as Zappa directed the entire group through the various, ensemble textures. Unlike most rock composers, Zappa views any long work as an entity, and however many changes in tempo, rhythm, or harmony there might be, he keeps enough of the original idea threaded through to hold it all together. Thus, any solo seems more a part of each piece. But Dunbar's solo was notable, in particular, not so much for what he did with it, but for what he didn't do. As rock has developed its own sense of self-importance, its soloists have played longer and longer, and as a result, they've sounded worse and worse. But Dunbar's effort was terse, without frills, and in no way derivative—as most rock drum solos are—of the swing-band solos in the early 1940s.

VAN MORRISON

NOVEMBER 1970
TORONTO TELEGRAM

IT'S SOME SORT OF tribute to Van Morrison that only a few people outside pop have heard of him and would have known about his concert last night at Massey Hall. That's not to say he hasn't a large following and an even larger mystique. In fact, the hall last night was packed; and each song—strange, flowing things, all rising out of the same ideas—were greeted with that hush of instant recognition. But Morrison's music is strung out in a deceptive simplicity, having fragmentary quotes from other pop songs, and little humorous flourishes that you have to listen for intently. Yet, there's still something else that adds to Morrison's removal from mass recognition. For in listening to his sound, you don't become involved in a particular personality. One cannot see his music being sung by anyone else; and when it is—as with "Brown-Eyed Girl," for example, which is his biggest hit, it always sounds strangely flat.

Most of Morrison's material last night was from his last two albums, *Astral Weeks* and *Moondance* (released early this year). This in itself is significant, for before this, Morrison had a rather inauspicious hit, "Brown-Eyed Girl," and before that, in 1965 as lead singer with a British group called Them, he was involved in three rock hits, "Baby, Please Don't Go," "Here Comes the Night," and "Gloria." The music from his last two Warner Bros' LPs can't easily be pigeonholed, or readily defined. But his performance last night at least gave some clues.

Coming out of Belfast, Ireland (he was born there in 1945), Morrison took up the sax at sixteen, and toured Europe with a rock group called the Monarchs. And last night he played sax in two instrumentals, backed by his sextet, or, as the DJ on hand called it: "The Van Morrison Orchestra." He produced some fine, choppy little runs, much along the lines of Ben Webster. And when Morrison replaced the sax with his guitar, and started to sing with his hard-edge, cutting voice, you could almost hear him thinking along sax lines.

In a tune like "Moondance," in fact, the feeling was positively jazz. The beat didn't drag as pop too often does, but shuffled along with an easy pulse. The band's role in all of this was fairly straightforward, throwing out little counter-melodies against Morrison's vocal, changing direction here and there thus adding extra interest to the piece.

What makes Morrison's singing all the more flexible is that way it contrasts and reflects the kind of songs he is writing. In his voice you can hear the raspy Irish "brrr," and in his backup groups you can hear some fine jazzmen (Connie Kay and Richard Davis played on the *Astral Weeks* LP). But Morrison's now living in upstate New York, not far from Woodstock, and there's that country roll and bounce in his newer music. In "And It Stoned Me," there was the kind of heavy emphasis on the first beat often found in The Band's or Dylan's music. After a minute or two, you found that this was a country-cum-rock tune in its outer trappings only, as the music began to slide into its own unique byways, and Morrison sang, "On the way back home we sang a song but our throats were getting dry/Then we saw the man from across the road with the sunshine in his eye." Like Dylan in the best of times, Donovan the occasional time, and the Beatles all the time, Van Morrison does something so well that no one could ever hope to do it better. And what he does is so rooted in his own personality that he's his only competition.

THE BEACH BOYS

JUNE 1971
TORONTO TELEGRAM

SOUTHERN CALIFORNIA IS A place of terminal craziness. It's Disneyland, and Alcatraz, and everything in between. One writer called it the synthesis of opposites: there's Los Angeles plastic, and Big Sur, the narcotic stare of freaks on Haight-Ashbury, and the speeding greasers, still whipping their super-chargers out of the Lockheed plant. If you believe Hollywood, Pacific America is the zenith of the race. If you believe the rest of the media, it's a place of strange madness—Manson, mass murders, Satanism, and mass arrest. However you feel, it's created a style, probably one of few American styles of the decade. And in pop music, it's all summed up by the Beach Boys.

When—and if—they arrive at the Beggars' Banquet Festival at the Borough of York Stadium this Saturday afternoon, the Beach Boys will have been ten years in the business. It's been a career so long and durable that you can divide it into various phases. But what is more significant is that while the Beach Boys have kept progressing musically, there's been such a consistency to their approach that they're still associated with their earliest phases. In short, for many the Beach Boys are still the first and foremost teenybopper act of the sixties; for me, they have been—and might still be—one of the most important groups the U.S. has produced.

First came "Surfin'" for Candix records. A local hit, it gave them a Capitol contract, and the start of a series of million sellers. For the next four years, however, their music stayed on the same level initiated with "Surfin'." The sound was brisk and breezy, with a Chuck Berry influence. The lyrics celebrated cars (little Deuce Coupes, little Hondas, T-Birds, and 409s), and the technology of cunning and sinning in California. The next step was major and resulted with the recording of *Pet Sounds* (1966). Says Mike Love, "At the time, I was unconscious myself. So the group was unconscious except for Brian Wilson, who was, I think, conscious." *Pet Sounds* was recorded six months before *Sgt. Pepper*, but was, in many ways, as groundbreaking as the Beatles' effort. Lush, intricately worked out, it reflected Brian Wilson's work with song writer Van Dyke Parks.

Wilson, who had left the touring with the group to write and produce, was getting involved with advanced production techniques that resulted in the single "Good Vibrations." The LP that was to follow, *Smile*, was never released, although much of it is in the can still. What was released, *Smiley Smile*, (1967) is the finest album the Beach Boys have done and probably one of the finest produced in the U.S. in the sixties. What *Smiley Smile* represents is probably the greatest jump in internal growth any group has made. For, by 1967, rock had entered its heavy period; British blues were popular, the Stones and the Beatles had concept LPs, Jimi Hendrix was extending rock's technical resources, and the San Francisco groups were starting to tour.

But the Beach Boys missed all that. They jumped one whole stage in rock's development to such a degree that *Smiley Smile* can be directly compared with things Crosby, Stills, Nash & Young are doing now, that Joni Mitchell, or the Byrds are involved in. Capitol Records didn't know what to do with the Beach Boys, and did nothing. They were urged to go more commercial, which they did as their recent *Sunflower* LP attests. And, because they didn't appear at the Monterey International Pop Festival, they missed the great media explorations into "pop culture." But their influence is still lasting. Several cuts on the new Paul McCartney LP reflect the Beach Boys high vocal sounds, while the tight vocal harmonies of many groups are derived from the Beach Boys' example.

The Beach Boys are always somewhere else, never in pop's mainstream. Mike Love describes it as "a non-identification with the issues." They don't get involved with politics, yet the first group recording for their own Brother Records is called *The Flame*—and the Flames is from South Africa. And sometime from now, when all the fly-by-night super-heavies have disappeared, the Beach Boys' sound—if not the Beach Boys—will still be around. There's just enough teenybopper in all of us to remember that.

JIM MORRISON

JULY 1971
TORONTO TELEGRAM

JIM MORRISON, lead singer of the Doors and one of rock's most charismatic personalities, died last Sunday night in a Paris hospital and was buried Wednesday night in a Paris poets' cemetery, his Los Angeles lawyer, Max Fink, reported. A respiratory ailment was said to be the cause of death. Morrison was in Paris working on a script for a feature movie. He had been in hospital for almost a month.

"The reason it took so long to find out about his death," Mr. Fink said last night, "was that not even his closest friends knew about it. The other guys in the group (Ray Manzarek, Robby Krieger, John Densmore) didn't know, and it was too late for them to go. Even his parents didn't go. The only people who attended his funeral were his wife, Pamela, and his manager." In 1968, Morrison's death was also reported. "But in that case," said Mr. Fink, "it was a guy who had been posing as Jim who had been killed. It had us pretty frightened at the time. But this time, sadly, it's for real." Morrison's death has cast new gloom over the rock scene, which, in the past year or so, has witnessed the deaths of the Rolling Stones' Brian Jones, Canned Heat's Al Wilson, Janis Joplin, and Jimi Hendrix.

Morrison once described the Doors as "erotic politicians." And no group ever mixed sex and violence with touches of brilliance that bordered on the primitive. In New Haven, Connecticut, Morrison was arrested onstage for having allegedly described an encounter with a girl backstage. Later he made national headlines when Miami, Florida, police issued six warrants for his arrest on charges involving "lewd and lascivious behavior in public by exposing himself and simulating masturbation" during a March 2, 1969, concert there. "But what I do," he once told me in Los Angeles, "is to turn rock into theater. The things I do are all part of a play. If the play works well enough for me, we can be free." Born in Melbourne, Florida, the son of an admiral, Morrison spent the early part of his life in various American cities. "I went eventually to Florida State University mainly because I didn't have anything else to do," he said. After college, he went to Los Angeles to attend UCLA film school, and lived in a rather rundown section of Venice, California.

At UCLA, Morrison met Ray Manzarek, then a young filmmaker and sometimes a jazz pianist. For a while they shared a flat, and Jim began reading his poems to Manzarek. The idea of the group was formed as Morrison started exploring the possibilities of singing. The Doors (named from Aldous Huxley's book *The Doors of Perception*) first played in cheap bars and cafés along Los Angeles' garish Sunset Strip. Gradually, they garnered a small local underground reputation. In January 1967, they released their first LP, *The Doors*, and a hard-hitting single, "Break on Through." They then toured to the east coast, playing at Ondine and then Steve Paul's the Scene in New York City. With the release of the single "Light My Fire" in April 1967, the Doors lost their anonymity, became internationally famous, and, as a consequence, made Morrison a public image.

Few performers in rock have attracted so much attention as Morrison. "In person," Lillian Roxon wrote in the *Rock Encyclopedia*, "singer Jim Morrison was cold, insolent, evil, slightly mad and seemed to be in some sort of drugged or hypnotic trance." Novelist Joan Didion wrote in 1968, when Morrison was at the peak of his fame: "It is Morrison who defines the group's interest as 'anything about revolt, disorder, chaos about activity that appears to have no meaning.'" In *New York* magazine, rock critic Albert Goldman described him as someone who "embodies more than anyone that free-floating longing for revolt, for breakthrough and transcendence that lies so close to the heart of the present movement."

Morrison was an artist anarchist, who often described himself as a "shaman" or sorcerer, who works on his audience's imaginations and tries to exorcise its fears. "Violence," wrote Richard Goldstein in *New York* magazine, "is his major motif. It permeates to the core of his work." In one of his early songs, "The End," he pushed himself through his lyrics past normal convention to the point where there was nothing left but "the end, my friends." In a small book of poetry, *The New Creatures*, which he personally had printed, he offered one lament: "Doesn't the group swallow me when I die, or the sea, if I die at sea?"

All this was pretty heavy stuff. For when I first met him, sitting in his Los Angeles office, the heat baking everything white, he seemed shy, reluctant to talk. It was ideas he was interested in—Wagner, Brecht, Nietzsche, neon signs. "I'm sorry," he said eventually. "I haven't much to say." He then gave me another private, loosely bound collection of what he called "my visions."

Called *The Lords*, it was nothing more than a series of sheets, each with small paragraphs, neatly printed. "Don't read it now," he said. "Get into it when you feel you want to." I took it home and forgot about it until last night. Almost every section dwells on the movies. Singing, or making music, aren't mentioned. And the last sheet has these brief lines: "Door of passage to the other side, the soul frees itself in stride. Turn mirrors to the wall. In the house of the new dead."

DAVID BOWIE

MAY 1978
TORONTO STAR

"OOOH," SAID THE GIRL, swooning ever so picturesquely, "look at that hat. Such a beeeautiful hat! I must have a hat like that." And why not? Wasn't that the reason the wearer of the hat, David Bowie, was at Maple Leaf Gardens last night? To set the style? To establish the new tone in and out of rock for the next few years? Admittedly the hat, a large, floppy affair vaguely nautical in design, appeared at the very end of an over two-hour almost nonstop performance (there was no opening act and only a brief intermission). And it was only a small addition, visually, to a show that had been alternately bathed in pastel lights or brutally left open to an antiseptically white backlit affect. But it was exactly because it was such a discreet touch, such a hint, that made it so important. You don't go to a Bowie show for the broad gesture. You go for subtleties. Even just a hat.

Outwardly, this might have been a rock show like any other. A blue-jeaned army of over eighteen thousand kids trooped through the gates while scalpers tried their best to get up to $20 for a top $8.50 ticket. Inside, everyone was met with kids hawking $2 souvenir programs and tacky $5 colour-clashing Bowie T-shirts. How ordinary! A blue-on-yellow T-shirt may be just fine for Randy Bachman, but for Bowie one expected a little something by Bill Blass, at least. Outwardly, too, there was much in the show itself that was familiar. Part of his band was on the '76 tour which brought the thirty-year-old British singer to the Gardens.

If anything, though, this show was even leaner than the one two years ago, which at least opened with a screening of the 1929 Luis Buñuel–Salvador Dalí surrealist film *Un Chien Andalou.* This show had Bowie, a first-rate collection of his bigger songs, and three changes of clothes, with each showing the singer in progressively baggier pants. Was this some sort of hint at some new-found pretension? Perhaps. Bowie's the Oscar Wilde of rock 'n' roll. His transition a few years ago from the esthete, wearing gaudy things, to the dandy of today, in rather simple gear, roughly parallels Wilde's transition from esthete to dandy in the mid 1880s. Bowie, like Wilde before him, is a man dedicated "to his own perfection through the ritual of taste," as social critic Ellen Moers wrote in *The Dandy.*

You could see it in his onstage movement, always rigid, always controlled and contrived. You could hear it in the music. As much as the band thumped and pounded around him, Bowie remained slightly removed from it all. What mattered were the small things.

BRUCE SPRINGSTEEN

NOVEMBER 1980
TORONTO STAR

THERE'S THE SOUND OF some eighteen thousand whispers here. The audience, it seems, is puzzled. Springsteen is about halfway through one of his marathon four-hour concerts, a night that's raged and rocked and gone further than anyone could expect and—what's this?—he's stopped to read a letter. The buzz grows louder. But what a letter. It begins apologetically, the author realizing that the singer is midway through a cross-continent tour (bringing him to Buffalo next Thursday and to Toronto January 20 and 21) but would he consider playing a wedding with his band?

Sure, he's big time now, a $100,000-a-night performer, with trucks, roadies and portable stages and all that. "But the ability to keep up with the wedding circuit is the kind of knowledge no performer should be without," he reads. "We'll pay $50 per player and there'll be an extra $50 for the leader." You can hear the click of the usher's flashlights, it's so quiet in the hall where on most nights DePaul University plays basketball. Might he actually do it?

Suddenly he laughs and we have the answer: No way. A few years ago, he might have done that wedding, not for the publicity, but just because it was the kind of thing Bruce Springsteen might do. (Whether he would actually do it or not was irrelevant; it was your belief that he might that mattered. Isn't that what he's always been about—belief, his own and his fans?) But he doesn't do things like that anymore. He can't. He's thirty-one and the biggest star in American rock right now—no longer the "last innocent," the dreamer of the sweetest dreams of boardwalk romance on the Jersey coast, of kids in custom Chevies. Born to Run. More than time has passed since he was last out on tour in 1978, playing small halls in small towns and universities. He has, in his own way, come of age. As he says, "I've discovered there are limits."

It's two hours after the show, and he's pacing nervously in a small concrete dressing room. There's a platter of food nearby. He looks pale and tired. "When you're sixteen or seventeen, you're never conscious that there are limits to your life, that there is something called age," he goes on, his hands fanning the air to draw out words when ideas won't come. "There are signposts. You can drive when you're sixteen and you can drink when you are eighteen—although maybe it's nineteen now in New Jersey—but, whatever, these are just signposts and ones that are telling you the way anywhere. The consideration of age is open-ended. After you're thirty, although you're still pretty young, I think you begin to realize that life is not so open-ended."

That's not the way it was, though. "Each show has such intensity it's as if it's the end of the world." I remember him telling me one wintry night in New Hampshire. We sat in an empty basement at the University of New Hampshire as he outlined his credo. "Rock 'n' roll," he said, "gave me everything and I feel I have everything to give in return. It's like a pact. A vow. And you have to honor it."

We are alone then. His faith has paid off, but with *it* has come new responsibilities and complications. He's never alone now, not completely. He's always in conferences in his room: outside there is always the inevitable line-up of DJs, friends, fans from the old days, kids who've only seen him in the *No Nukes* movie and hard-as-lacquered-nails groupies. "The last time out we were all pretty green," says Bob Chirmside, his roommate and road manager. "Now we've become a lot more professional."

This time he's playing large halls, all sold out. In fact, CHUM Radio is taking eleven busloads down to the Buffalo concert. And Jon Landau, the ex-critic who's now his manager, has been sent a fifteen-thousand-name petition from kids wanting him to go to Winnipeg.

Promoters are now worried about crowd control, not crowd size. His appearance at Cincinnati's Riverfront Stadium was its first sell out since The Who were there last December 3 and eleven fans were trampled to death. He played Milwaukee just nine days after what police call a "mini-riot" during a Black Sabbath concert. In both cases, though, the concerts went smoothly as he proved that large-scale American rock can work peaceably.

Tonight in this concrete cavern called the Rosemont Horizon, drearier because it's so new, he's clowning and kidding with the E Street Band, now leaning up against saxophonist Clarence Clemons, now down on his knees for a guitar solo, now up on a ramp waving his fist in the air, singing "Prove It All Night," "Independence Day," "Jackson Cage," "Fire," "Jungleland," "The Promised Land," and all the songs from *The River* dealing with poor folks doing the best they can. And as he moves, the crowd moves; as he sings, the crowd sings along.

The Who's Peter Townshend has talked about the rocker's nightmare, of the performer dying on stage and the crowd cheering. Springsteen talks about the dream, of being loved by the audience. And in a way he's living this dream. He's communal property.

In a *Village Voice* review of his album, Stephen Holden explains its themes in a fifties context. But in a letter to Holden, a Detroit fan named Chuck Wilbur says, "Like Michael Cimino's *The Deer Hunter,* [the album] may be an uncomfortable vision for those whose political and cultural sensibilities were shaped by the movements of the sixties."

It's Springsteen asking searching questions of himself; "I think you come to a point in your life, around when you're thirty, when you look back to the dream you had when you were twenty and you try to assess just where you stand now in relation to that dream."

He's out pacing again as I ask, "but isn't rock a young man's..."

"Yes, yes," he says. "It's like baseball. It's like all sports in that when you're thirty-five you're considered an old-timer. But that's just what you're considered. It's not true. This is why I listen to country music a lot because it allows growing up. There's an entire generation in country music that's in its forties and it's still there, you know."

Lyrics are running through my head, one saying "we're runnin' now," and "I'm a rocker baby," and I wonder, out loud, if all rockers don't have to maintain this tough guy, James Dean stud pose?

"Yes, yes," he comes back, "there is that aspect to it, but I think that's one of the limitations that's now being knocked down in rock itself. To me, age is no limit. There's (guitarist) Link Wray. I've seen him around little bars in Jersey and he's fifty-one, maybe more. He's as wild as anyone."

"You know what rock 'n' roll really is? It's a bunch of people growing older together.

It's me and my band going out to the audience tonight and growing older with that audience."

"I don't think this new album, *The River*, is any more introspective than the other albums. It's pretty much about how I'm looking at things now. Like I'm finding I'm thinking a lot about my parents (now living in California). You know, for the first twenty years of your life you don't think much about your parents outside of the fact that they're bugging you. You don't think about their lives and you don't think about their particular problems or what were their hopes and dreams. How did they succeed? How did they feel? What were their sacrifices. How did it affect you?

"When you were a kid all you wanted was to go out tonight, but when you get older you start to look over everything you really do want. And everything you dreamed."

3.

OUT OF TIME

BOB DYLAN (2020)

IN ACCEPTING THE 2016 Nobel Prize in Literature, Bob Dylan offered his readings of *Moby Dick*, *All Quiet on the Western Front*, and *The Odyssey* as examples of how the raw material of world literature has insinuated itself into his craft of contemporary songwriting.

It was a gutsy if problematic approach, when you consider the singer's awareness of how well-armoured most interpretations of these works are against any down-market thrill-seeking by the likes of a Bob Dylan—who also cited Buddy Holly as a seminal influence in his acceptance speech. The lecture, recorded in Los Angeles, was disseminated in 2017 because the singer had skipped the Nobel banquet.

A further problem was noted in the composition of the speech: "long-winded" was one of the kinder reactions. "Freewheeling" was another description.

In being awarded the prize, Dylan earned a deservedly triumphant moment according to hard-core fans. Notwithstanding, the decision earned its share of criticism. This set me to thinking about how, in the many times he'd come into my life or, rather, I was dispatched as a reporter to cozy up to his, the impetus had been doubt arising from a sense of something about him being "not right"—whether it was with the oeuvre or the ouvrier.

From "going electric" in the sixties to directing movies or finding God in the seventies, Dylan disappointed time after time, failing to deliver the expected or needed. Only later, on reflection and reappraisal, did these disappointments indicate that they were in their time revelations in the making.

Dylan never gets it right, right? Just look over his entire career: its achievements are inevitably understood only retrospectively. Released in 1975, the album *Blood on the Tracks* was dumped on, with one critic noting it was made with "typical shoddiness." The praise, which came much later, placed it among his very best work.

"I've always gotten criticism, so it doesn't affect me," Dylan told me at one time or another over the years. "Not only me, but the people who've supported me. John Hammond, who produced my first album, had lots of criticism for doing it. He was fired from Columbia Records for doing it."

For one of his earliest return concerts in his home state, Minnesota, he allowed only one interview and that was with his high school newspaper in Hibbing. "Very funny," groused a Minnesota rock critic. "Very funny."

Back to his Nobel moment: "We see only the surface of things," Dylan went on in his analysis of *Moby Dick*. "We can interpret what lies below any way we see fit." (Can anyone sense a song coming here?) "Crewmen walk around on deck listening for mermaids, and sharks and vultures follow the ship." (Cue the minor keys.)

"Reading skulls and faces like you read a book. Here's a face.
I'll put it in front of you. Read it if you can."

1963, ORILLIA, ONTARIO

"DON'T THINK TWICE" TWICE.

The second annual Mariposa Folk Festival is underway. We're sprawled this way and that way on the grass, with one or two over-observant officers of the law standing on the fringes of the modest crowd waiting for the riot—God only can imagine the excesses marijuana can whip up—when the atmosphere chills. Just about the saddest song you ever heard echoes from one of the stages.

"It ain't no use," the lyric begins, but when you look up and see the singer, the world-weariness, the bitterness, doesn't fit. His name is Al Cromwell, just in from somewhere on the Canadian east coast, I found out later. Neat-looking for a folkie and with a voice far better than most. I'm totally wrapped up by the melody and by the rejected-in-love lyrics, which perfectly describe my generally pissed-off condition.

"That's Dylan's," says someone in my sprawling coterie. "Don't think so," says this older guy. "It's older, traditional."

"He calls it 'Don't Think Twice, It's All Right'," says the first guy. "It's on his new album." *The Freewheelin' Bob Dylan*, released in 1963.

"Maybe, but he's reworked it," says older guy. "He's a scavenger. But brilliant."

Mariposa is the name given a fictional town north of Toronto by homeboy author, Stephen Leacock. He was no hick Canadian raconteur, though. Groucho Marx recommended him to Jack Benny, who loved the author.

"Mariposa is not a real town," Leacock wrote. "On the contrary, it is about seventy or eighty of them." This was surely true of the festival, too, which occupied one Orillia park or another before being booted out of town in the mid-sixties because of very bad behaviour the police had been expecting all along.

From Gordon Lightfoot to Québécois chansonniers, the festival talent was an honest and true reflection of the multifaceted Canadian folk tradition. I won't be saying much about Glenn Gould—at the time, the hottest classical pianist on the planet—skulking in his cottage near Uptergrove, twenty minutes away.

We will also leave aside talk of the First Nations people whose land we were on, before they were conned about a century earlier into moving southeast. Where, in revenge, they host a modern-day casino, getting their money back.

Dylan first heard an earlier version of the melody of "Don't Think Twice, It's All Right" from Paul Clayton, a mellow-voiced folkie who'd revamped the original into his own version, "Who's Going to Buy You Ribbons (When I'm Gone)." In the original, the question was asked about "chickens," not ribbons.

Over the years, Al Cromwell at Mariposa stayed on my mind. There was a story that he had recorded "Don't Think Twice," but the single was hard to find. He drove cab for a while, disappearing in and out of downtown gay bars, leaving a trail of fond memories and, so I am told, a small family.

1972, TORONTO ISLANDS

A FAMOUS PHOTO BY Art Usherson, a leading rock photog in his day, shows Bob Dylan and Gordon Lightfoot leaning into one another, each enjoying his gnarly icon status. They're hemmed in by a cheerful crowd, miles of smiles from everybody: it's that sort of lovely, perfect day.

There's a little kid, no higher than Dylan's waist, making a face. Another guy seems agitated, not wanting to be photographed. Too late, pal. But, hey, aren't you somebody? David Bromberg the guitarist, maybe?

The photo might as well have come from the 1870s, perhaps from a special afternoon off for minimum-wage workers at a local factory. But the picture—it's turned up in enough books already—followed a delicious instant that happened maybe an hour earlier.

It's drizzling all weekend, a lovely mid-summer soaking that leaves shirts and skirts and pants pasted on bodies. A Who's Who of folkdom is here: I was knee-to-knee with Jackson Browne and Steve Goodman in the cramped shuttle boat freighting us to the Mariposa Folk Festival's new home, Toronto Island. By Sunday mid-afternoon, an end-of-festival lassitude is settling in when a sudden, unannounced, set by Neil Young can be heard on a stage to the east, only to be overlapped with a surprise set by Joni Mitchell on the stage to the west.

In the space midway between the two stages, I'm twisting here and there to avoid the crowds running to and fro between the performers and find myself face to face with Bob Dylan, entirely unrecognized in all the rushing. Dylan stops briefly and cadges a bottle of beer from a passerby, a kid on his way to hear Roosevelt Sykes, the blues piano great, and guitarist Bukka White, and now with a Bob Dylan story to tell.

Bob Dylan has his own story, of course: "We were vacationing in the area," he says, trying to be just about anybody other than Bob Dylan. "I've been to Mariposa many times in the past. This year reminds me of the way it was ten years ago. I won't be playing though."

I don't tell him there was a workshop, the day before, on the influence of Bob Dylan.

1978, SANTA MONICA, CALIFORNIA

BOB DYLAN IS BACK on the trail as a singing country movie star, just like Roy Rogers or Gene Autry. Except.

"'Ceptin'," says Dylan, "I don't have a horse.

"People," he goes on, "simply expect music in a musician's movie. You understand. In this country, we were raised on Roy Rogers and Gene Autry. We went to their movies every Saturday night until we were eight. I'm just like them."

We're in a warehouse turned rehearsal hall, on a vile, fall day in

California when the weather is more a psychological condition than anything to breathe deeply about. He's his own advance man, even if that entails talking to the press although he insists that's nothing special. "I've never minded talking before. I just never had much to say."

So, now we're faced with Bob Dylan being just-folks. It's not easy for him. It's hard portraying him this way. (I realized when looking over my notes that I made up that "ceptin,' bit but I like it. I wonder if an editor will catch it. An editor should have caught up with the movie Dylan is talking about.)

Renaldo and Clara, the movie in question—at best a faint memory since the premiere's hostile critical reception—is a rambling, four-hour, quasi-concert-cum-fantasy documentary. Released in 1978, it's timed to bring extra oomph to the launch of an extensive world tour, the first of many in the never-ending *Bob Dylan World Tour*. Shot in six weeks during the 1975 Rolling Thunder Revue tour through New England and Canada, *Renaldo and Clara* cost an estimated $1.25 million and is distributed for $500,000 by Dylan's own Minnesota-based company, Circuit Films, headed up by younger brother David Zimmerman.

Bob Dylan knows Bob Dylan is the story. His presence at the film junket, he admits, is "the best way to make it known." It's mid-morning and he looks as if he has had enough already. Enough of what, is the question.

His eyes are red: he rubs them constantly. His face is puffy. The belt on his pale, smudged jeans cuts into his stomach. The sleeves of his black leather jacket seem too short. He keeps adjusting his worn worker's cap as he talks, pushing it back slightly farther on his head with each new question.

I sympathize. I'm in no great shape myself, having flown into Los Angeles following last-minute negotiations to get to talk to him. Originally, Dylan's plan was to talk to only two North American newspapers, the *New York Times* and *Los Angeles Times*. I'm joining that select group through knowing Paul Wasserman, Dylan's laconic public relations guy (as well as the Stones' and later U2's). Wasserman, according to the *New York Times*, is "firmly in control of marketing the Bob Dylan legend." Hmmm. The setting this morning is hardly mythmaking, as we sit in a semicircle in a downstairs space facing Dylan. Dylan is as close to the exit as possible and, after some small talk, he singles out one of the writers for revealing the location of his house some weeks ago. It's hard enough being who he is, he practically hisses at the writer. Remember, he has family.

Is something bigger happening? Even more personal? Has Bob Dylan of all people found himself, like so many celebs before him, suddenly scraping for a bit more respect and some considerate reporting to stabilize a career in down-trajectory?

Has everyone by the late seventies had a chance to peek behind the many masks he wears and found, not more masks as was expected, but a rich, thirty-six-year-old musician who has just gone through a messy, middle-class divorce, who worries about his five kids and lives in a $2 million home in Malibu?

"I sound foolish to myself trying to explain this film," he begins, in control now and measuring his words. "It's all there for anyone to see. It might seem vague... to some. But it all has meaning. It will be seen as being true. I'm not a filmmaker, really. But I don't see how anyone would find it incomprehensible. It just has to be felt, like the weather."

This is a good line and a typical Dylan line, of the sort that have created a cottage industry out of interpreting his songs. His every move, starting with "going electric" in the sixties, has been the object of scrutiny and sharp criticism. Then, speculation replaced criticism during his relatively inactive period after totalling his Triumph 500 in the summer of 1966.

"I'd been touring a long time, particularly two years nonstop, eleven months out of every year," he said. "It got to me, and I fell off my high horse. I was tired."

He'd returned with a vengeance, playing nearly two hundred shows since he started touring again in 1974 and turning down a greatest-hits album package from CBS Records, producing instead his eighteenth studio album, *Street-Legal*. "He gets these feelings something must be done," said fellow songwriter, Bobby Neuwirth.

There's a scene near the end of *Renaldo and Clara* where Renaldo-Bob's former lover, Joan Baez, along with his former wife, Sara, demand that he tell the truth. Both smile in a most kindly fashion. Both give the impression of birds of prey, circling.

Which woman does he really love? Does he love anyone at all? Just what is he thinking? They want to know the truth.

"Sure, I'll tell you the truth," Renaldo says. "What truth do you want to hear?"

There's a scene in *Dont Look Back*, the 1967 documentary of his 1965 English tour, when he tells a reporter "the truth is just a plain picture." The reporter looks befuddled, and we pity this reporter but not that much, really, because, hey, we're on Dylan's side. Bob Dylan, who has made the put-on a minor art form.

He tells another reporter he's a good singer because he can hold his breath three times as long as [Enrico] Caruso. Mr. Jones knows something is happening but doesn't know what it is: but we know, or think we do. The press is Dylan's patsy and he's drawn us to his side.

Interpreting him remains a not-so-minor industry. Kris Kristofferson calls him "a dozen different people." Dylan is a great pretender. He leads everyone to wonder just how many masks and masks-behind-masks he wears. Shifting identity is his métier, and it should not surprise anyone who's aware of the dozens and dozens of characters he slips in and out of to bring alive an array of musical styles and genres.

A recent survey found hundreds of courses at various universities and colleges concentrating on Dylan's lyrics. Allen Ginsberg called him "the most influential poet of our time."

By the mid-seventies, Mr. Mystery Tramp—the master of the

put-on—has become put-upon. *The Village Voice*, once the absolute centre of Dylanism, sent several critics to see *Renaldo and Clara*, but the reviews offered little hope for the would-be filmmaker: one writer even said he wished Dylan had died before he made it.

Is this the press's revenge after having been the butt of Dylan's put-ons for so long? Is everyone simply suspicious of his current willingness to talk after all the years of silence? Does Dylan think *Renaldo and Clara* is such a turkey that it needs a hot-air blast in the form of his interviews to get it off the ground?

Renaldo and Clara is a film about the creative process or, as he says, "It's about birth, death, and rebirth." It deals, in the live concert scenes, with the results of the creative process: the performance of the songs by Dylan himself, Ronee Blakley, Joan Baez, Roger McGuinn, Allen Ginsberg, and Gordon Lightfoot, the latter only heard offscreen singing an old Dylan tune, "Ballad in Plain D."

The film also deals with all the pressures, personal, social and artistic, contributing to this process. It is not about Bob Dylan, Dylan insists, but about someone who has lived and created the way Bob Dylan has. Dylan calls this someone Renaldo. Dylan plays Renaldo behind masks, from the grotesque one that begins the movie to the pancake makeup he wears through the rest of it. The role of Bob Dylan, however, is taken by Ronnie Hawkins, an Arkansas rocker turned Canadian pop icon. At least, this is how Dylan the writer-director-editor, in one of his genuinely quirky moods, wants us to see Dylan—who in fact purloined and then reinvented the Hawks, Ronnie's bar band, to become The Band. Hawkins plays Dylan as a good-ol-boy turned superstar, giving an interview to a CBC reporter in the lobby of a hotel and then trying to seduce a country girl into coming out on the road with him.

There is further deliberate confusion and masking of character. Sara Dylan plays Clara, Renaldo's wife in the movie. Singer-actor Ronee Blakley plays "Mrs. Dylan," and, in one of the few completely scripted scenes, she becomes nearly hysterical when accused of having an affair, and then shouts that she hasn't had sex for nearly three years.

The other major female character is the Woman in White, played by Joan Baez. In one scene, she and Renaldo wonder what it would have been like if they'd married twelve years earlier. In another, she and Clara start dissecting Renaldo's personality, agreeing that he never reveals himself. Is this autobiography on Dylan's part, or is he playing with the public's image of him?

I had spent a few days travelling with the Rolling Thunder Revue and, on more than one morning, remember coming into the motel coffee shop to find a folk legend, or a half-dozen of them, having coffee. Such as guitarist, pianist and producer T Bone Burnett over there and Ramblin' Jack Elliott at the next table. Fiddler Scarlet Rivera had been added to the amorphous ensemble, Dylan having spotted her walking down the street with a violin case.

Gossip was everywhere. The film shows the first time Sara Dylan and Dylan's former lover, Joan Baez, ever talked in twelve years. I was told this very hush-hush, as if the press might not otherwise notice. I also remember Dylan finding ways to be alone.

According to Dylan, however, the making of the movie had nothing to do with the recent break-up of his marriage, the bitter court fights over custody of the four children, or any reconciliation with Joan Baez.

"My marriage breakup?" he asks, almost of himself. "It was just one of those things, one of those things that happens in life." About Baez? Bob Dylan lived all that with her, years and years ago. I understood that scene: that's why it was in there.

The masks come down as Dylan tries to explain the problems connected with being Bob Dylan, filmmaker, and with just being Bob Dylan. It's as if, after the final curtain, the actor has come back without makeup to explain that it was just a play.

"There were non-believers in the project," Dylan tells the semicircle of rapt reporters, as his hands fiddle with a box of matches. "There were those people who were more concerned with the shows, the concerts, and there was a struggle with them on the film part of the project. It would have been a much better film if there had been co-operation. We started with a broad general outline which, we knew, would include parts of the tour. The tour, in fact, financed the film.

"We tried to get financing before we did it, but that was impossible. The financiers wanted to know exactly what they'd get for their money. Some wanted all music. Some said it had to be only ninety minutes long. Some wouldn't have let it run long in their theatres if it didn't succeed."

He knows *Renaldo and Clara* may not have broad popularity. He knows it's too long, knows why it's too long and doesn't care. "You know how I make my albums? I just make them. And who's on them is just whoever's available at the time. The film was like that. There was no struggle at all."

"A lot of the tunes from the movie might have made a good LP, but my record company [Columbia turned Sony] doesn't want one. It wants an album of new songs which should come out next year. That's what I'm thinking most about these days, the new songs and the tour. We finished the movie last spring and I've stopped thinking about it.

"I didn't make the movie for critical acclaim. But I do care what happens to it. If it's still around in ten years, I'll know it'll have done well. Actually, if it's acclaimed, I'd worry I'd just have to live up to my reputation as a great filmmaker. And I don't want to add that to the other things I have to live up to."

The movie's forty-seven songs, from "Hurricane" to "Tangled Up in Blue" to "Catfish" to "Isis," are tightly edited while the fictional, play-acting sections between them often owe their style to Andy Warhol. Howard Alk, who helped Dylan edit the forty hours of raw footage, points out that "some stuff was left in just because it looked and sounded so good. That part where the show is being set up and crates and amplifiers are being brought in. That's there just because of the sound. It sounds so real."

Like many of Warhol's works, this film is a moving object in its reality or at least in its picture of reality. Dylan ties the images together the way he links word images in his lyrics. Just as an idea can turn on a word in a song, an idea can turn on a picture in *Renaldo and Clara*. His directing—"if you can call it that," he says—was based purely on instinct.

"The subconscious took over in the making of this; it's not a movie at the conscious level, but one that came from my notion of the subconscious. In a lot of ways, it didn't meet our expectations. But I feel some confidence to make some more movies. I was under incredible pressure doing this and I'd bring in some outside help on any other. For the next one, which I'm planning to start next fall, I want more definite characters. I don't think I'd do a script. Maybe just an outline."

Dylan's explaining the difficulties he faced in financing his movie and barely blinks when asked how he can spend so much time talking about money, when he was "the archetypal symbol of all the anti-capitalist feeling in the sixties."

"Well, this is America," he laughs, attempting to slough off the question.

But that isn't good enough. Why is it, he's asked, that there are so few blacks in his movie? What exactly is his opinion of blacks? His eyes flash. Where does this question come from? This, he seems to be thinking, is not the simple PR job it was supposed to be.

"I didn't think of blacks in any way," he says, a trace of nervousness in his voice. "I don't look at people, colour-wise."

Well, okay, will there be blacks in the band he's taking to Japan and Australia this month?

"Two," says Dylan, "possibly three people who are black will be in the band."

As much as he has talked, then not wanted to talk, about his activities in film, it's clear he's much more comfortable talking about music. "Being on the road, playing," he says at one point, "is a much bigger kick than making movies."

In fact, one of the problems with the Rolling Thunder Revue, he says, was not the filmmaking but the band. "For the first part of the tour," he says, "the band ended up playing five or six hours every night. It got tired working for so many people. I don't want a band to work that hard. If it does, I want it to work that hard for me."

The tour passed through a lot of out-of-the-way places, rekindling Dylan's interest in making close contact with his audiences. "Actually, I'd like to play in small halls all the time—to five hundred people or even one thousand. The problem with doing it that way on the tour was that expenses got too high," he says, relieved at the new line of questioning.

From what I've heard over the years, Dylan has never been unaware of the music industry's ego-bruising capabilities. He's always read the music industry trade sheets, checking on the progress of his singles and albums. In fact, the one scene in *Renaldo and Clara* that's dealt with unambiguously is the one where he's meeting with a biggie at Columbia Records and they are discussing how to maximize the marketing impact of his song, "Hurricane," written for the jailed boxer, Rubin "Hurricane" Carter.

"I know who I'm reaching with my songs," he says, suddenly intent on making a clear, precise point. "I don't know anything about age groups, although they'd be of my own age, I guess. I look out from the stage and see everybody—policemen, priests and criminals—all sitting side by side. I know who they are, because I've never been confused about who I was."

Why then, he's asked ever so gently, did he change his name? He was born Robert Allen Zimmerman on May 24, 1941, in Duluth, Minnesota. When he was six, his family moved to Hibbing, a town near the Canadian border, where his father was a partner in a hardware and electrical supply store just off the main street.

"Can you tell me why anyone has changed their name?" he shoots back. "Why not? Do I feel guilty? Most people who've ever been on a boat have changed their names."

Was he bothered about being Jewish? The question is asked in a whisper.

"I didn't know Zimmerman was a Jewish name," he says. "Is that what it is? Why did Bob Dylan change his name? It's an honorable thing to change your name. Women do it all the time when they marry."

But that just brings up his attitude toward women. Didn't Sara, the "mystical wife" in his song to her, tell a court he struck her in the face? Doesn't Dylan as Renaldo in the movie play pretty free and easy with the women in his life? Doesn't Dylan the director at one point show all women as whores?

"Oh god," says Dylan, turning his head away. "Renaldo really doesn't have an attitude toward women. His attitude, basically, I guess, is that they're material objects. He has a problem with his identity evolving."

There's no question about identity, evolving or otherwise, with Dylan the musician, however. He says he doesn't listen much to new music because "the music I want to hear has to come from a particular point of time, from a particular place. It's polka music or blues music, all the music I heard as a kid. Unless the music is based on that, I don't like it. But that's just me."

The Sex Pistols? "Never seen the Sex Pistols," he says. The Rolling Stones? Aren't they rock at its most basic?

"The Rolling Stones represent an attitude toward rock 'n' roll," he says. "I can't think of any new musicians who're really rock 'n' roll except maybe Robert Gordon and Link Wray. When I listen to music, I listen to who I've always listened to—Mother Maybelle, Woody Guthrie, the Carter Family and, yes, Elvis."

To him, the music that matters is the music that lasts, just as he hopes *Renaldo and Clara* will last, even if it's not accepted now.

"You can still listen to something by Woody Guthrie after all these years and feel it holds up," he says. "My songs have held up. I sing them all the time and they hold up. Maybe I wouldn't feel like singing

'Blowin' in the Wind' all the time. But it holds up. The arrangements of the songs always change. We have some new arrangements now so that you might not even recognize the songs. But the songs hold up. And me. A song only makes sense when I sing it. I'm only a servant to the songs."

He ends there. Suddenly. Waiting outside is a delegation from Japan. He has been given a list of questions they want to ask, things like: Do you have any concern in Buddhism and Oriental thought? He stares at each question as if it might be fine print in a contract.

He looks toward the now-open door but doesn't move. For what seems like several minutes, an amazing thing happens. Here's Bob Dylan, surrounded by agents, reporters, and friends, and no one has anything to ask him.

"So," he says. We're standing near the couch.

"So," I say back.

"I'm going to be around a lot now," he says. "I'll be touring a lot, playing everywhere. I was surprised by the turnouts when I first started touring again with The Band a while back. People had remembered. But if they don't keep remembering I'll just keep going. I'll go back to the clubs. Or making movies."

1979, NEW YORK

DYLAN'S BORN-AGAIN PHASE, as it's called, heads to New York where it's needed most. Propelled by a concert tour, as all things always are with Dylan, it leaves in its wake a fan base utterly perplexed and a music industry looking for a word like "perplexed" to describe its concerns.

Where exactly is an evangelical Christian Bob Dylan leading it? What does it mean at the dawn of the era of Madonna? It is certainly not the religious content itself that has the hipsters worried, but its sincerity. Don't follow leaders, they say. Isn't that from Dylan's

"Subterranean Homesick Blues"? Watch the parking meters. Oh, get born, keep warm.

I spend the day before the concert wandering around the Village—Cafe Wha? on 115 MacDougal Street and Gerde's Folk City on 11 West 4th Street—aware that I am chasing the ghost of Dylan past. It's still early afternoon, but everyone gets riled when asked about Dylan and religion. Now Fred Neil, someone would say (or Tom Paxton or Phil Ochs), they didn't sell out.

I myself tried selling out to God. And so, as one who at one time contemplated taking orders in the Anglican or Episcopalian Church, I was far less horrified by Dylan's conversion to Bible belt Christianity than most were.

Backstage the next evening, he explains: "It was inevitable," he says. "But everyone goes through something they are forced to go through. There was Picasso and his blue period, Elvis going into the army. It happens to everybody. It's the same with my music. It's Bob Dylan music. It's not disco. It's not reggae. It just happens to be what I'm doing at the time. It's not even rock 'n' roll. People expect—

"Every so often, I'll think about the past. When I started out. Where I started. I'll think about different places down the line. And different situations, and different people that I've met. Just wondering how I got where I am now. But people always drop out and other people always drop in."

Dylan in his dressing room is almost vulnerable.

"I don't listen to much music now," he says, in an abrupt shift in the conversation. "Don't have much time. I listen mostly to old records. That's all, maybe I'm jaded. I don't know."

"Hey, Bobby! Could ya do me a favour, eh, boy?"

Bob Dylan squints at the bottle of Drambuie in front of him then up at the electrician, a broad-beamed, bulky gent in his late fifties who's just wandered into Dylan's temporary dressing room in the bowels of Madison Square Garden.

A favour? Dylan eyes the massive role of heavy-duty wire coiled around the man's arm and shrugs. Sure. Why not?

"There's a fan of yours in New Haven," the electrician went on. "So, hey, Bobby, could I get an autograph, please?"

Bobby sniffs. The guy fetches out a crumpled sheet of paper, plunking it down in front of the Drambuie. "To Jan from New Haven," he orders.

Dylan starts writing with great sweeps of his ballpoint pen. "How do you spell Haven?"

"How far did you get in school?" asks the electrician.

"Not very far," Dylan mumbles.

"I guess that was far enough, though, eh, Bobby?" the guy says. "Uh, there's one other thing."

Dylan glances hard at him.

"She—Jan—makes up these etchings and she wants you to have 'em."

"Sure," says Dylan, "if they're for free."

1990, BEST WORST DYLAN SONG EVER

"OKAY, BOB, take one . . . and . . . !"

"Wiggle, wiggle, wiggle, wiggle like a—"

"Uh, Bob?"

"Wigg—"

"Okay. Stop. Thanks. Uh, Bob, your handwriting can be difficult. The lights in the control room maybe, too. Uh, well—but, 'Wiggle' is not on the list of songs I've got here."

"Ah, man, that's just a word, wiggle. Wrrrrrrr-iggle. It's a placekeeper. The real words come in the moment. 'Spontaneous bop prosody,' is what Jack called it."

"Jack, Bob? What Jack?"

"Which Jack?"

"Yeah, exactly, which."

"Jack as in Daniels, Duluoz, Kerouac. All 'bout the same sort of Jack. OK, again. Wiggle, wiggle—"

"Mmmm, stop."

"Wigg—"

"Please. Two wiggles in a row? It's not exactly 'Desolation Row.'"

(Sounds of the band breaking up.) "Want to break, Bob? Need a pencil?"

"Remember 'Rainy Day Women'? That came to me on the spot, eh, Koop?"

Keyboard player: Al Kooper. "Bob first called it 'A Long-Haired Mule'—"

"—and 'a Porcupine Here,'" Dylan adds. "Then it changed. Changed. We know what we're doing here in Hitsville. Always did. So, so again."

Wiggle, wiggle, wiggle like a bowl of soup.

IT'S NOT A LONG-SHOT bet that fans of Bob prefer to believe that something akin to the above took place when Dylan recorded "Wiggle Wiggle" as part of *Under the Red Sky*, his twenty-seventh studio album released late in 1990. A Who's Who of rock 'n' roll turned up for the sessions, including Kooper, George Harrison, Elton John, Slash, David Crosby and Stevie Ray Vaughan.

But while some celebrity goofing around is evident—Dylan himself admits it was sloppy at times—the playing is usually bright, loose, and aggressive, the tune "Wiggle Wiggle" in particular. It comes screaming out of the box, hard-core as Dylan gets. So why is the song considered to be among the lowest of the low points in Dylan's creative life, inevitably named as one of the Top 10 worst things he recorded? (For the record, it's got a good beat and you can dance to it. Enough said.)

Rock lets in lots of strays, words not given sanctuary anywhere else. Take Iron Butterfly's "In-A-Gadda-Da-Vida." Does it matter that it was supposed to be "In the Garden of Eden"? (The singer apparently slurred his words.) Isn't it better that it may not mean that? Or there's the Beatles' "Ob-La-Di, Ob-La-Da." Jazz had Cab Calloway's "Hi-De-Ho."

My point: we love that stuff, the more outrageous the better. And it's as central to rock practice as mumbling—one of Mick Jagger's pointers on achieving rock-singer stardom—or word garbling that adds some delicious ambiguity. (Singer Jann Arden told me she thought Jimi Hendrix sang "excuse me while I kiss this guy" in "Purple Haze," not "kiss the sky.") It touches on rock's connection with Dada and performance art.

Dylan himself resorts to raw sound for effect. On some performances of "Just Like a Woman" you hear him utter: "... huh, oh, I-I-I came i heeeeeere—a-huh-ah-huh-ah-huh ..."

But yet: this is Bob Dylan and the word is "wiggle." Twice.

And sung more. This is seriously transgressive.

Rock is about repetition and repeated repetitions; about common-use language, slang, gibberish, creative obscenity, sly innuendo. John Lee Hooker groaning "yass, yass, yasss" is about as salacious as music can get. Rock revels in sexual expletives, grunts, groans, and much more sublime silliness. Add to these attributes the "incongruous, trivial, mediocre, banal, insipid, maudlin, abominable, trite, redundant, repulsive, ugly, innocuous, crass, incoherent, vulgar, tasteless, sour, boring" as listed in *The Aesthetics of Rock* by Richard Meltzer.

"Wiggle Wiggle" is not without a broader precedent. Indeed, several songwriting traditions—and we know Dylan loves tradition—are filtered through it. The main one derives from Tin Pan Alley and Broadway-Hollywood tunesmithery. Any pro songwriter in most of the past century would have a good children's song up his or her sleeve. (You never knew when Gene Kelly would come looking.)

A funny, nonsense lyric—another craft going back a century or more to "Shoo Fly, Don't Bother Me"—could become the song of the year: I cite "Mairzy Doats" (and dozy doats and liddle lamzy divey). It was a monster success in the mid-1940s, selling close to five hundred thousand copies in sheet music in weeks. (It was a test to see how fast the unprepared listener would get equine-signifying substratum).

Besides, banality in the hands of genius can have a depth of feeling lacking in anything more literate. Witness "I've Got a Crush on You," Ira Gershwin's lyric for brother George's drowsy, sexy tune that rhymes "sweetie-pie" with "hear me sigh" for one of the great emotional highs in Tin Pan Alley history.

It can also be argued that "Wiggle Wiggle" reflects Dylan's debt to the beat poets, particularly Allen Ginsberg, as much or more than it does his roots in folk. If, that is, there's that much of a difference. In his memoirs, Dylan recalls meeting Thelonious Monk in a Greenwich Village club one night and telling the pianist that he was at another joint up the street playing folk music. "We all play folk music," Monk said.

Out of Ginsberg's epic "Howl" pours a jazz staccato of word images: "tea head joy ride neon." Out of "Subterranean Homesick Blues" dances an entire life portrait in three snappy lines: "Oh, get born, keep warm/Short pants, romance/Learn to dance, get dressed, get blessed." Out of the supposedly silly "Wiggle Wiggle" comes the apocalypse and no less:

"Wiggle till you're high/wiggle till you're higher/Wiggle till you vomit fire/Wiggle till it whispers, wiggle till it hums/Wiggle till it answers, wiggle till it comes."

Of course, what works as a rock lyric doesn't often work on the page. (If it did, Chuck Berry would have locked up a Nobel Prize for Literature half a century ago.)

"The relationship between the work that has to do with the eyes and the work that has to do with the ears is naturally not the same because the eye isn't an ear," writes John Cage with typical gnomic simplicity. In *Poetry of Rock* (1969), Richard Goldstein, former critic for *The Village Voice*, notes that "in transposing these lyrics into verse, I discovered that mere linearity can destroy a rock lyric."

Indeed, any lyric in any form is written to be performed. Every song title opens the music's curtains in theatrical fashion, every lyric gives director's cues to the performance. Take Drake's "Hotline Bling." The title alone subtly yet perfectly conflates ideas and images culled from modern Toronto in the headlines, from emergency hotline help services to upscale shopping along Bloor Street, a charged scenario which in performance suggests telephone sex talk. Hot lines indeed.

Going back to rock's earliest days, we find "Be-Bop-a-Lula," Gene Vincent's greatest hit. Just sing "be-bop" and the entire song pops alive, demanding a kinetic theatrical response. With "Wiggle Wiggle" coming about halfway between Vincent and Drake, we hear the slippery and lubricious way Dylan sings about wiggling "like a gypsy queen."

It's tempting to suggest that detractors are those who—how can I say this?—don't like booty-shaking rock 'n' roll (or booty-shaking, in general) and grudgingly tolerate it in Dylan's music due to the work's otherwise literate nature. Indeed, "Wiggle Wiggle" hasn't any of the bookish demands that "Tangled Up in Blue" does with a line like "... a fishing boat/Right outside of Delacroix."

So "Wiggle Wiggle" represents a terrible intellectual letdown and is, perhaps, another signal that Dylan was entering one of his failed states, like his earlier born-again phase. (Not that the singer himself recognized such things. For him, his interest in Christian revivalism was an artistic phase as he told me backstage at Madison Square Garden.)

Compounding the letdown theory is the fact that *Under the Red Sky* followed *Oh Mercy*, his twenty-sixth studio album from 1989, which was deemed a huge comeback success. Then there's the detraction theory. *Under the Red Sky* also followed the 1988 release of *The Traveling Wilburys Vol. 1*, with Dylan, George Harrison, Roy Orbison, and yet another all-star cast. The second official Wilburys release, *The Traveling Wilburys Vol. 3*, released in 1990, followed the appearance of *Under the Red Sky*. (Yes, No. 3. Don't ask, it's complicated.) So, was Dylan too involved with the Wilburys to focus on *Under the Red Sky*?

The big hit from *Wilburys Vol. 3* is "Wilbury Twist," considered by the Fobs to be even worse than "Wiggle Wiggle." Could it be they get crazy at any possible connection between Chubby Checker, the original Twist king, and their guy? How downscale! Then again, if you want enigmatic, try Checker (Ernest Evans) and forget Dylan. Yet, any journeyman travelling bar band needs a song like "Wilbury Twist" as part of its repertoire. It's part of the dance hall tradition. And Bob Dylan, you may have heard, has a thing about tradition.

After the initial pounding it took, *Under the Red Sky* saw a revival in its critical fortunes and its very loose nature had it revalued as a tossed-off gem. Those who supported it remind us that the entire album was dedicated to his four-year-old daughter, Desiree Gabrielle Dennis-Dylan, whom he calls Gabby Goo Goo. So sure, a child might see the "wiggle" in "a bowl of soup" or wiggling "like a rolling hoop." As for the "big fat snake," that's the kind of scare antic that kids love. Dylan sounds like a knowing father.

Short words—silly, dumb, disgusting, et al.—often invite suspicion from those who fear that few letters contain little information, that something in the inherent ambiguity is being pulled over their eyes. Weren't the Wobblies the radical American labour union the Industrial Workers of the World formed at the start of the last century? What kind of deep game is Dylan playing here? But you can't keep a good—or bad—short word down.

Rappers like KRS-1 reverse-spell cuss words and you get kufin' to fudge censorship. Then there's Norman Mailer, the novelist, witnessing fug, his censor-castrated cuss word, come alive with each live appearance by the gloriously scruffy Fugs, the New York group. Redemption for Mailer.

So too redemption for Dylan.

When I first heard "Wiggle Wiggle" years ago, a lot of the lines, including "wiggle like a swarm of bees" passed right over me. Returning to the song, I began to think Dylan might have a simile problem. Then I heard about Tania Munz's book, *The Dancing Bees: Karl von Frisch and the Discovery of the Honeybee Language*, which had me thinking more than twice about Dylan's bee line.

Frisch, a winner of the Nobel Prize in Physiology or Medicine in 1973 and who died in 1982, researched bees under the Nazis' close scrutiny. He was one-quarter Jewish, barely forgivable. Frisch revealed that the honeybee's "waggle dance," is in fact a hugely significant aspect of bee life as the dancelike motions by an individual bee incorporate a complex set of signals sent to the rest of the bee colony about the location of succulent, pollen-rich flowers and distance to the destination.

This is where Dylan really gets scary. He's keeping up with insect ethology.

THE BRITS (2020)

AS URBAN LEGENDS GO, the one insisting Paul McCartney was dead was a doozy. Not only for its durability, but for the degree of credibility it was given in the later 1960s by otherwise rational people and lots of journalists. Proof of Paul's demise was found just about everywhere, but central to the legend was the image of a grave on the cover of *Sgt. Pepper's Lonely Hearts Club Band*.

The British Invasion didn't begin or end with the Beatles, but the band expanded its perimeter to welcome pop art and mysticism into a perceptual scramble that fascinated me as much as the music did. Pop fantasias took over all forms of expression. We saw James Bond and *Dr. No* on the big screen, *The Prisoner* on TV, and literature became rife with global conspiracies and stories of psychological manipulation—like the hugely popular novel *The Magus*.

The Invasion saw thousands of bands from the United Kingdom arrive on North America's stages and hit-parade charts in the sixties and early seventies, scattering glossy magazine layouts of bony models in minidresses in their wake and introducing new words to non-Brits like "wanking" and "bollocks."

Although the name sounds sillier with each repetition, the British Invasion was brilliant, and it was also crude, sexy, and sexist—and just about everything in between. Ignoring the fantastical non-musical elements running through the British Invasion, from comic craziness to dead-sure mysticism, was just as crazy as entirely embracing them.

It was the antithesis of an earlier Brit invasion, the rather snooty Arts and Crafts movement from the turn of the twentieth century, when a cultural wave in design and decorative arts swept into the European mainstream and across the Atlantic Ocean. (Weirdly, an eighteenth-century version also occurred when the florid Italian opera invaded England with strutting dandy castrati and major hair—a parallel ripe for a PhD thesis.)

By 1965, the Beatles led the way in what became a truly unparalleled moment of music super-saturation. The British run of hits had begun in 1962 when two British singles climbed to the top of the Billboard charts: "Stranger on the Shore" by Acker Bilk, a clarinetist with a wobbly vibrato, and "Telstar" by the Tornados, a British instrumental group.

By 1964's end, the Fab Four had fifteen Top 20–selling discs. Their leading rivals, the Dave Clark Five, had seven. Overnight, it became all Beatles—and all Brits—all the time. Radio stations would play "She Loves You" for two hours straight, day and night. Brit bands clocked thousands of shows across North America in a year. TV dance parties suddenly had cockney-speaking hosts. It was fab, all agreed.

Such an all-pervasive musical style might find an equivalent in the jazz/swing era, which blossomed on Broadway and in Hollywood in the 1930s when George and Ira Gershwin were in full swing, Duke Ellington ruled Harlem, and Cole Porter was just hitting his stride.

Broadway might have three hundred shows open at once. And Broadway glittered harder-than-any-diamond for a reason: everyone needed a shot of happiness. The Depression of the 1930s left some twenty-five percent of potential workers without a job. "I can't give you anything but love, baby," lamented Billie Holiday.

Britain's outlook entering the sixties was no less grave. Having won the war, England was losing the peace, as the cliché went. By 1951, Clement Attlee's exhausted postwar government was out of power. Then, Winston Churchill's second attempt to govern failed in the mid-fifties. Anthony Eden's missteps led to the Suez crisis, which was resolved in a way that was galling to him (and to the country, as a whole): American intervention.

There was an odd disconnect between the spirit nurturing rock in the U.K. and that of America. The U.S. was at war with itself, going tribal, with Civil Rights movements and antiwar demonstrations pushing the white political class further and further to the right—and the momentum was blamed on rock 'n' roll.

In 1962—when the Beatles broke with "Love Me Do"—Dean Acheson, former secretary of state for Harry Truman, told the crowd at West Point: "Great Britain has lost an empire and not yet found a role." He didn't see, or couldn't hear, what Great Britain was doing in the economy of illusion, how it was chivvying up industries to take people's minds off their grey days. In England, rock felt like part of the popular imagination, stoking it and commandeering it, growing feistier with each new album. Journalist and historian Neal Ascherson even suggests that the British post-1939 interest in Europe waned "as British high and popular culture grew in self-confidence."

British cultural business was turning Thomas Hardy's line on its ear: the "power to preserve is an illusion" now meant that preserving illusions is a power on its own. The illusion of Cool Britannia was as coolly calculated as the length of the Beatles mop-tops, selling North America the innocence of the British schoolboy look.

And this illusion, like any great circus act, was way too interesting to ignore.

THE *SGT. PEPPER* COVER, with its dead-celebrity vibe designed by painter Peter Blake and wife Jann Haworth, became the Rosetta

Stone of pop iconography right from the album's earliest appearance in June 1967. Rock conspiracy theorists had a field day. Look! Wasn't that Paul's left-handed guitar made of yellow flowers? And wasn't that Paul's old rugby trophy on the grave? Wasn't Paul the only Beatle turned away from us in the back-cover picture of the four of them together?

Notice how Paul walks shoeless across the cover of *Abbey Road*, preceded by John in a doctor's smock and followed by Ringo in formal undertaker's suit, and George dressed in gravedigger's denim. And what about John's assertion that the walrus—a Scandinavian death symbol—was Paul?

Such a preposterous pursuit wouldn't have been thinkable if it hadn't metamorphized out of the overwhelming presence of the Beatles everywhere in our lives, even when not wanted.

I was working for the *Toronto Telegram* by then. It was an old-school, conservative broadsheet daily, now long since mould'ring in the archives of York University in Toronto. The *Tely* was not the sort of publication likely to give time to nonsense of this kind.

Yet it did—occupying a good part of the newsroom for a good part of the day. Hard-nosed editors usually longing for a decent murder-suicide before the late edition found they couldn't ignore it. *Rock was such a screwball thing*, they thought, *weird shit like this could happen, no?*

The theory was that McCartney had died in 1966, before the making of *Sgt. Pepper*, and been replaced by a strikingly alike lookalike who could play bass and sing falsetto. The Beatles (those saucy rascals) had even cleverly introduced this newcomer to us. He was Billy Shears:

So let me introduce to you, the one and only Billy Shears…

Other papers were after this story. Others had it confirmed. There'd be a press conference. The press conference was cancelled. Then a woman phoned our newsroom from Scotland to say that she'd just located a grave marked Paul McCartney. "I'm too old to believe in this kind of thing," her voice crackled over the long-distance landline. But exactly. Who wasn't?

So, to get to the bottom of Paul's possible death once and for all, I phoned George Martin, *Sgt. Pepper's* producer. He assured me that Paul was alive and well. I phoned Paul but, being un-dead, he was apparently not up to answering questions on the matter.

Then I got a call from a DJ in Rochester, saying he'd decoded the entire mystery and had found a phone number and an address—an address on someplace called St. Clair Avenue. Did we have such a street up there in Toronto?

Oh, boy, did we. St. Clair Avenue runs east-west through the centre of the city, right through Toronto's toniest neighbourhood, Forest Hill. So, we phoned the number and thought we'd uncovered the psychedelic coverup of all time because it turned out that a certain Billy Shears had once lived at a house with that very number.

I say "we" because I was no longer at the centre of this case. Increasing numbers of the *Telegram* newsroom huddled around the story as it progressed.

We bellowed into the phone. "Once lived there? Where's he now?"

"That's hard to say," said the woman. "I'm only his auntie. He moved to England and hasn't been heard of since. He was a big fan of that band."

"That band?"

"You know, the what's-their-name, the Beatles."

By now, a half-dozen *Tely* reporters were crushed around the phone. We'd done it! We knew the truth. Paul was dead. The Beatles had replaced McCartney with this Billy Shears.

"But you'd best phone his mum," she continued. "She lives in Etobicoke." Etobicoke was the city's urban sprawl on the west side, more blue collar than not.

Billy's mother was sweet. She corroborated everything Billy's aunt had told us. By now we were panting hard, imagining our names in TIME, when suddenly she sensed something was wrong.

"This Billy Shears you're talking about," she said, "you know he's black, don't you?"

WELL, THEN.

BEFORE THE BEATLES CREPT into my consciousness, I was already hooked by a singularly English something—a view of life: caustic, scornful, incredulous, roaringly hilarious—mostly, the roaringly hilarious. I had first found it in the early fifties on the radio. Canadian radio in pre-rock times meant hockey and *The Fisheries Report* from Newfoundland and Labrador (follow the cod) and re-broadcasts of American radio.

The American radio felt more like home, or rather it felt like California or New York, places I wanted to be my home. It was intimate and upscale. George Burns and Gracie Allen were funny and pleasant and quietly sophisticated. Like my uncle Lou and aunt Mamie. They had a swell house, you could tell, and so did Uncle Lou, who was in the hotel business for a while, had a pool and was a natty dresser.

No one rushed in radio's America, no one lacked for money nor wanted for work. Relax. Light up a Lucky. Why, it was said that on *Amos 'n' Andy* blackface radio black Americans sounded happy. And white.

And then, one afternoon, after some exploratory dial-twisting, I arrived accidentally at a fissure in the ether and through it came the most wonderful chaos, careening like a circus wagon around my bedroom, spilling out all sorts of daffy characters, weird old ladies and soldiers and chief magistrates and such like, everyone with their own funny voices and jokes.

Eventually, this chaos revealed itself to be *The Goon Show* with Spike Milligan, Harry Secombe, and Peter Sellers.

ORCHESTRA: [Nautical musical link]

SELLERS (AMERICAN ACCENT): And now…

FX: [Waves against wood]

GREENSLADE: Seagoon and Bluebottle travelled by sea. To avoid detection by enemy U-boats, they spoke German throughout the voyage, heavily disguised as Spaniards.

SELLERS: As an added precaution, they travelled on separate decks and wore separate shoes on different occasions.

SEAGOON: The ship was disguised as a train; to make the train seaworthy, it was done up to look like a boat and painted to appear like a tram.

MILLIGAN: All rather confusing, really.

Milligan, chief writer; Sellers, the man behind the voices; and Secombe met on Sundays at Grafton's, a London pub. All three had been orbiting the BBC, which finally brought them together for a program recorded live in front of a modest studio audience. To warm the audience up, Sellers played drums while Milligan—who was once in a jazz group—played trumpet. (Secombe, who cowrote the pilot with Sellers, spent his later years in religious broadcasting.)

The arrival of tape machines at the BBC put an end to recording each program live onto a sixteen-inch transcription disc. Suddenly, sounds, words, or squeals of joy could be sped up, replayed, layered against others. Dials could be twisted, knobs pulled, tape sliced, diced, and reassembled.

Milligan could start playing the studio like it was a huge instrument. *Sgt. Pepper's* future started right here.

SEAGOON: Also on board were Major Bloodnok and his regiment. When we were ten miles from Algiers, we heard a dreaded cry.

ECCLES [OFFSTAGE]: Mine ahead woohoowoo! Dirty big mine ahead!

BLOODNOK [APPROACHING]: I say I say I say, what's happening here, why are all these naughty men cowering down on the deck, the cowards?

SEAGOON: There's a mine ahead.

BLOODNOK: Mine...?

FX: [Footsteps running away—*splash*]

Dada, the radical art movement from the 1920s—think Marcel Duchamp's impudent urinal-as-art-object—went out of its way to cross up accepted logic. A lot of Dada is found in the Goons, from disregard of literal meaning to the theatricality of the absurd. ("Like everything in life, Dada is useless," said Dada co-founder Tristan Tzara. Also: "I won't explain myself because I hate common sense.") But, a sea mine? Isn't that pushing a bit too far? Dangerous sea mines left over from the Second World War were still found in shipping lanes, well after the war, so how could something so unfunny end up so fall-off-the-bed funny? As with Dada, a lot of the Goons' comedy was gallows humour.

FX: Sounds of battle and, surreally, a squawking chicken (added for British rural listeners, it's explained).

KAPITÄN MORIARTY: Ah there you are. The British have broken our line.

ERWIN ROMMEL: Curse! All our washing in the mud again.

KAPITÄN MORIARTY: Listen, Herr General, it is serious. We must retreat, otherwise the British will lose.

ROMMEL: You're right. It's a shame to disappoint them after all the trouble they've been to.

I had a feeling for some of this, picked up from the British kids who'd been resettled in our scrubby suburb west of Toronto. They were brought to Canada by parents looking for a new life. There were German families, too. A number of the new houses were yet unfinished and the doors to the basement living quarters dotted the roadside like mine entrances.

There was Michael and his sister, Patricia, who lived for some time in their basement. Mike and I talked endlessly about sex, lying about all the girls we claimed were desperate for it and for us. We embellished each fabricated fornication with stories of increasingly dexterous displays of agility. I realized after a bit that we were starting to sound like a Carry On flick. I also realized I was beginning to say, "I say."

Jeremy's parents had an apartment in a town nearby and sounded like the rich people in British movies. And Wesley, chunky and hearty as a British character actor specializing in factory-worker roles, lived in a tiny place that sat, weirdly alone, in the middle of a farm field at the end of a long, long, grassy lane. His parents loved it, happy in their tight little British island.

I wasn't alone with the Goons or in my need for a British fix. Elliott, a kid my age, short but wiry, lived around the corner. One day, he took me up to his room to make a deal. From a deep, dark hiding place at the back of his closet, he pulled out a small stack of British "girly" magazines.

I can't remember the titles of these glossy mags, each like the other—*Naughty Bits Explained* and *Bums* and the like—with two or three women on the black-and-white cover, trussed up like the star victim at a S&M soiree in a latticework of lace, bra straps, and corsets hitched to stockings. Their heads and arms thrown back and cone-shaped bras as threatening as a pair of American MIM-3 Nike Ajax missiles.

Soon, Elliott and I had concluded a blowout trade: my dirty books for his trussed-up lineup. (He got the better of the deal, I feel, the sight of one pimply temptress from Everton being much like another to me. My cheap novels at least gave directions, like "melon-sized" bra-opening and when "too-tight" jeans are never too tight.)

Magazines. Newspapers! Exactly: my search for further life in the alt-Brit universe of my youth brought me to a long-running column in the *Daily Express* by Beachcomber, a nom de plume held for five decades by humorist J. B. Morton. Stuffed-shirt military figures and discombobulated lawyers and justices were favourites in the cast of recurring characters. Then, there were the Twelve Red-Bearded Dwarfs:

"The Case of the Twelve Red-Bearded Dwarfs, Part 9" was held before Mr. Justice Cocklecarrot, a Beachcomber regular who could have been a Goon:

A scene occurred after lunch, when the dwarf was asked whether he had ever served in the navy. He burst into tears and said, between sobs, "Ever since I was a little fellow—well, I mean, ever since I was even smaller than I am now—I longed to be a sailor. I always wore a sailor suit. But my eyesight made my dream impossible of fulfilment. And now, of course, it is too late. There has always seemed to me to be something wonderful in the surge of the waves and the roar of the wind. Then there is the comradeship. I tell you, after such ambitions, it is difficult to resign myself to being pushed through doors by ladies like Mrs. Tasker, for no apparent reason."

At this point Cocklecarrot intervened impatiently and the dwarf left the witness box, still sobbing. A lady who shouted, "I'll adopt the little dear," was asked to leave the court.

Actually, "things British" were in the air much earlier. There was the renewed and somewhat reinvented Royal Family. It was now made-for-TV, just as my family made itself ready-for-TV, with our first television set arriving at my parents' place for the purpose of watching Elizabeth II's coronation ceremony on June 2, 1953, broadcast live by the CBC via the BBC from Westminster Abbey in London.

A chosen few neighbours, as rigorously vetted by my mother as any of the Royal Family's invitees, were invited to dress up a bit (with the women in hats) to drink tea and nibble at my mother's signature sandwiches, made with alternating thin layers of cream cheese, a lurid green hotdog relish, an unidentified tinned meat or salmon, and then a mustardy hotdog relish—all rolled up and sliced into colourful pinwheels.

To a kid, these hors d'oeuvres-from-a-can were heavenly, and they were all gone before the crown was on the young queen's head. Everyone left feeling satisfied that the Empire was still in able hands. A splendidly produced commemorative magazine—the Crown Jewels posed like other Brit pin-ups—remained among the most cared-for relics in our house long after my mother wasn't there anymore. I probably still have it.

In a way, I was better prepared for the televised coronation than my parents, staunch Anglicans though they were in their faux-Tudor home with its leaded windows. (The Great Depression was poised for a return tour, at least in my mother's imagination. She claimed that she alone through her secretarial work brought an end to the last one, unlike my lazy uncle Ed).

The CBC did its part to strengthen our status as a colonial outpost, as did the upscale magazines and newspapers issuing a column generally billed as a "Letter from London" to bring us up to date on the madly gay doings in West End theatre. Regardless, we mostly saw the U.K. through the eyes of its filmmakers, whose movies ended up on Canadian TV.

The closest Hollywood got to our house was the Roxy Theatre, a repurposed Quonset hut two miles along the upper middle road. Saturday afternoons at the Roxy were for kids: serial westerns, the Three Stooges. Nights were for double bills. Cars lined up for hours on the 1957 night when they showed *And God Created Woman*—it was airlessly hot until well past midnight.

The Roxy showed comedies, like Dean Martin or Jerry Lewis, or westerns in Technicolor, whereas the televised British flicks—made before rationing had ended—had a gloomy energy that seemed capable of mayhem, like Frank Launder's 1950 schooldays comedy, *The Happiest Days of Your Life*, or a delicious, dropping-bodies-off-a-bridge malevolency like *The Lavender Hill Mob* (1951), or the unfinished sexuality of the Carry On series. When the Beatles made the rounds of British TV, you could see the debt they owed to those earlier movies. In 1963, for instance, they appeared in straw boaters and striped blazers to do an old music-hall song.

The Goon Show's nine-year run on the BBC Home Service ended in 1960, but for decades its illogical logic seeped everywhere throughout Brit culture. From *The Pink Panther* to *Beyond the Fringe*, *Monty Python's Flying Circus* and the "black roof country" of Cream's "White Room," with its "tired starlings" (tired starlings!), the Beatles' *Magical Mystery Tour*—and on to the music of Queen and Genesis and the invention of what was termed, hopelessly, psychedelic rock.

Between one decade and the next, new technology transformed British moviemaking, moving swiftly from monochrome in 1960—*I'm All Right Jack* with Peter Sellers—to the theatrical opening credits of James Bond's *Dr. No* in 1962, the film's style reflecting an evolution in the cultural palate from "too real" to deliciously unreal.

This transformation wasn't about cameras intruding into real life: it was about real life operating like a film set; or at least, our desire for real life to operate like a film set. What was left of reality was found in *Dr. No* and *From Russia with Love*, rejigged on an enormous scale to create bad guys of previously unimaginable badness running evil empires that were far more evil than the piddly and powerless Soviet Union.

In 1964, the British Invasion crested: it was everywhere you listened or looked. Twelve of the fifty bestselling songs in North America were British. The top two tunes were by the Beatles, and by April, Beatlemania had saturated popular culture and the Fab Four held the top five spots in most Canadian and American hit parades.

(Also selling discs like crazy were the Dave Clark Five, Gerry and the Pacemakers, Manfred Mann, Billy J. Kramer and the Dakotas, and the Searchers. Brit bands' prices were doubling, quadrupling, up one hundred percent—based on radio airplay, especially this new thing called FM radio, and record sales.)

Goldfinger (1964) became the template for the Bond series and the staggering commercial success to follow. Bond instantly became a brand of meta-theatre, right down to his high-end watches that we too could, and still can, wear.

Sgt. Pepper's Lonely Hearts Club Band was its own form of meta-theatre, released in 1967 and overtaking the Beatles' real lives with a fictive universe of their own contrivance. The album cover showed photographic replicas of their real selves next to wax reproductions of their real selves, all standing around a grave.

Why don't we make it as if *Sgt. Pepper* really existed, Paul mused, and it may have been a never-never land relived for him; but for John Lennon, it was more likely the surveillance environment of *The Prisoner* where Patrick McGoohan's fictional Number Six is trapped in an inescapable world. (In *Sgt. Pepper*, Lennon aligns with several versions of Number Nine, most notably in "Revolution 9" on the 1968 white album.)

Although we feel we're in a play, we are anyway. What begins as surveillance finishes as adoration.

I WAS THE LAST one to move out of a ramshackle shared apartment in the late sixties. As a doctoral music student, I was barely surviving and my tools of entertainment were a novel and a black-and-white TV show, *The Prisoner*.

Events in the novel *The Magus* are manipulated by a well-dressed industrialist named Conchis, an enigmatic Greek island lord who emerges as equal parts Aristotle Onassis, Picasso, and analytical psychologist Carl Jung. Conchis imagines life itself can be manipulated in its entirety, the way a film director or music producer can manipulate events in his particular theatre of operation, or the way the Beatles began to play the recording studio the way they'd once played their instruments. The God-game, as Conchis calls it, should have no limits.

("Then you shouldn't involve ordinary human beings in it," says the naive Brit, Nicholas Urfe, who realizes he's become Conchis's subject.)

The Prisoner was created by British actor Patrick McGoohan, an original choice to play James Bond. The now-iconic show was set in a mysterious, pretty village for retired spies to nurse their fear and to be spied on by other spies. The series had its surreal touches, including an all-seeing eye, and included mind-eating futuristic drugs and brainwave-reading MRI machines.

McGoohan saw *The Prisoner* as part of his own war against the creep of authoritarian technology. The penny-farthing bicycle, its enormous front wheel eventually rendering it obsolete, was the series' logo.

NUMBER SIX (PATRICK MCGOOHAN): Where am I?
NUMBER TWO: In the Village.
SIX: What do you want?
TWO: Information.
SIX: Whose side are you on?
TWO: That would be telling. We want information.

Then one day, my phone went dead.

There might have been a perfectly good reason for that. The small group of us who'd lived together for a few years were parting ways and cancelling the phone in the process. But, still, I was staying on a bit and the phone contract was okay for a few weeks.

(There might have been an even more interesting reason for it. Like being surveilled by the Royal Canadian Mounted Police or, to be clearer, being informed I was being surveilled by the Royal Canadian Mounted Police—as was John Lennon.)

"There is nothing wrong with the phone," said the redhead from next door—my lone visitor to the flat. "It's just bugged." Just? Red, I should explain, was an unemployed mother of two carrot-topped kids and the wife of the most mysterious man on earth. His long hair was as orangey-red as his kids', his skin just as pale, and he never slept. He arrived home at two in the morning and left two hours later. Their talk could be heard through my bedroom wall.

Red said they didn't have time to have a phone installed, so she had to use mine.

"Yeah, sure," I said, "and the cops are outside."

"Right there," she said, pointing to a dented, brindle-coloured Ford van. Kendal Avenue, where I'd been living, was lined with old maples. I fell asleep as soon as the office workers and students paraded off to work. A nice place to be stuck in a truck. "But I've done nothing but phone my girlfriend in Florida," I griped.

"That's all?" Red said. "They've been listening. You'll see. The next thing you know, your phone's going to start working again." The next thing I knew, my phone started working again. The Ford van was gone.

"See?" said my neighbour. "The fuzz don't need to stick around anymore."

The fuzz? I'd never heard any real, live person say that. About a half hour after Red returned to her flat, our landlord, a skinny guy with long hair who drove cab on the side, rushed to his taxi and squealed off. I went back to packing books into boxes. Some time later, there was a crash. The cab had run into the front of the building and the landlord, looking pale—well, he always looked pale—was walking around it, then disappeared into his bleak little flat.

No sooner had his door slammed shut then Red's husband appeared, from the back of the building it seemed, dazzling red hair flowing behind him as he dashed into his flat. Next morning, he was sitting on the steps outside, his head as close-shaven as any army recruit's, looking like a new man.

The landlord didn't emerge for days. Later, I heard about a bust involving a drug pickup made by cab in front of infamous, anything-goes Rochdale College—not far from our Kendal Avenue flat. Stories varied, as they always do, but this one always included a figure with flaming red hair.

THE YEAR SGT. PEPPER taught the band to play, we were going to Expo 67.

Everybody was going to Montreal that summer, some because it was Canada's one hundredth birthday being celebrated by thousands of American draft resisters and some because they were curious about the province that might separate from Canada, but most because the summer was sweet, warm, and welcoming.

Besides, there wasn't much else to do and we weren't going to worry about it.

So, three of us piled into an ancient Renault and started out along Harbord Street in Toronto. Barely two blocks later, we saw Bonnie, who said she'd come along too. Her boyfriend, Terry, was already there and it might be fun to surprise him.

Hours later, as we came into Kingston—not even halfway to our destination—we thought it might be more interesting to head south instead of east. We had about $70, all told, and one charge card.

We ended up in Miami, Bonnie without Terry. Then on a plane; then on a beach in Nassau. I played pool at a seaside shanty called the Pass Me Not, figuring I was a mark, and the Beatles played "With a Little Help from My Friends."

The Renault died on a Florida highway on our way back and everywhere we went, we heard the music from *Sgt. Pepper*.

The album was released in late May 1967. Throughout June and July, every radio station played it nonstop. By August, everyone had a copy or knew someone who did. Listening became a ritual. Hearing it was inevitable. Just walk up or down any main street.

The backdrop wasn't promising. Europe saw the beginnings of violent protest. Revolution. The dreaded Richard Nixon was creeping to the American presidency. War poisoned Vietnam. Charles de Gaulle ignited separatist dreams in Quebec with his infamous proclamation: "Vive le Québec Libre!" And yet, in the press it was the psychedelic summer, which would give the entire sixties its most rosy memories. We didn't see it coming, of course, but utopia was about to become nostalgia.

Other albums, many dozens, in fact, before and since, were posited as being artistically superior. The Beatles themselves recorded a few of them: *Rubber Soul* and *Revolver*, for starters. Other albums—many, many others—cost more and sold more. But *Sgt. Pepper's* soon found a unique place in pop music, not unlike, say, Stravinsky's *Rite of Spring*. Here is a point of reference for everything else. Here is a model and test case. Here is something inescapable, love it or loathe it.

And we were expecting it—sort of. The Beatles were up to something in the winter of 1966. They'd given up touring the year before and tried to drop out of sight, involved in individual projects. George Harrison went to India twice to study with Ravi Shankar and John Lennon went off to Spain to film *How I Won the War*.

They'd begun it in November the year before and through John Lennon's insistence and with producer George Martin's help, they'd recorded it over and over until it was textured perfectly. "To this day, they believe it was the greatest single they ever did," David Pritchard, a Beatles radio biographer, told me.

"The idea," McCartney said later, "was to do a complete thing that you could make what you liked of it. Just a little magic presentation. Normally, 'a new Beatles epic' would be just a collection of songs or a nice picture on a cover, nothing more. We wanted to make it something more. A complete show."

Sgt. Pepper is Day-Glo bright, assured and charming. *Revolver* was dark and provocative and fearless. *Revolver* was about the Beatles as a band of musicians: *Sgt. Pepper* was about another kind of band.

The superlatives kept on rolling in. *Sgt. Pepper* sold 2.5 million copies in the months following its release, and who knows how many additional millions in the years since. More people have heard the entirety of its forty-second, final piano chord than have spent forty seconds with Brahms. I can keep on going.

But almost from the start, numbers were a mug's game when it came to *Sgt. Pepper's* because it was an atmosphere of its own making, a ready-made time capsule.

The album's impact grew far beyond whatever its sales may indicate. Its reputation is sweeter by the year and has even managed to obscure what may have been the Beatles' finest work, *Revolver*.

Sgt. Pepper has more in common with Richard Nixon and Watergate than any flowery ballad crafted by Donovan. It connects with spy thrillers and *Chariots of the Gods* pseudo-science and not all that much with what has happened in rock.

THE TWO MOST DIRECT musical responses, the Rolling Stones' fabulously fake *Their Satanic Majesties Request* and the Mothers of Invention's bitchy *We're Only in It for the Money*, both misfired. Both aimed at the band when the real target should have been the fans; both aimed at the music when the target should have been the reaction to the music.

Because back then we weren't just playing the album. We were playing with it, as if it were an early version of Trivial Pursuit.

Lennon pooh-poohed any possible mysticism: "All that symbolism exists in people's minds," he warned. "If an intellectual sees intellectual crap in it, it's there." And McCartney to this day is casual about this aspect of it; about the games people played and how that remarkable album cover came about.

But we listeners were anything but casual about the connections we made among the famous faces on the cover, the lyrics, and the bits and pieces of trivia—including the Ontario Provincial Police badge on Paul's uniform.

"We came up with a list of our heroes"—McCartney now shrugs—"like Oscar Wilde, Marlon Brando, Aldous Huxley and Lenny Bruce.

Everyone had their choice." Well, not really. John Lennon nominated Adolf Hitler, but was talked out of the idea. "It was really to say who we liked," says Sir Paul. "It was about time we let out the fact we liked Aldous Huxley. That wasn't the sort of thing we'd talked about before. No one had ever asked us in an interview."

That was the point: the Beatles, the most public group of men on the planet, were total mysteries to most of us. And with the release of *Sgt. Pepper*, it was collectively decided that they should remain enigmatic. We would have it no other way. We preferred not to know.

Years later, I talked to John, Ringo, and George—and Paul, but only briefly—and found each, in his own way, among the least enigmatic people I have known. With George, talking was unnecessary. His melancholy could be felt across any room.

Right from the start, *Sgt. Pepper* attracted its share of critics. John Gabree, in *DownBeat*, the jazz magazine, said that the band had "never been in the vanguard of popular music." Richard Goldstein drew an enormous deluge of outraged letters to the *New York Times* when he reviewed the work as "Beatles baroque, an elaboration without improvement."

But that wasn't the point. Everyone lived *Sgt. Pepper*. For there was the piece which ended it all, "A Day in the Life." Even Goldstein admitted to the staggering impact of this two-part song. A precursor to today's leaner, pared-down sound. It began, "I read the news today, oh boy," and ended with "I'd love to turn you on."

A generation lived between those two lines that summer.

NOTEBOOK #37, PG 14.

I'M AT THE HOUSE manager's office at the Rock Pile, a compact, mid-Toronto performing space, taken over by the promoters and their crowd. Led Zeppelin is in-loading its equipment through a door to the backstage. It's August 1969. This was a little-known band back in February when it played the same venue. But the through-the-roof sales of their debut album over the intervening months have made them the biggest thing on the planet.

The problem is, the contract for the 1969 gig had a return clause paying only a pittance compared to what the band would henceforth command. So, the real problem becomes band management. It—Peter Grant, that is—wants a lot more cash or no show.

For the moment, the band is not setting up. And there's a mob of fans waiting outside for the first of two shows. The "why" to the question is answered when the phone rings. The fee has just gone up, doubled, tripled: still a bargain.

"No way I'm paying that," one of the local money men snaps into the phone.

The click down the other end of the line was audible outside. This was back when you could smartly cradle your handset to show your displeasure.

Sudden panic. Quick huddle. No option: they'll pay. The return phone call finds the price even further up into the stratosphere. Down slams the phone again.

"No way," says the promoter.

Ditto all the above action to reach utter capitulation. The show is a killer.

NOTEBOOK #42, PG 14.

I'M AT AN OVERLY sauced French restaurant with an overly sauced Joe Cocker. Why, I wonder, do so many Brit managers remind me of keen-eyed English public-school dropouts getting by on their accent, looking for cash accompanied by a woman? By reputation, Cocker's current manager Peter Grant is as mean and tough and smart as they get. He defines flash, that smug after-effect of posh.

Flash sits at the head of the table in one of those romantic, old-style faux French restaurants, where faux peasant food comes gift-wrapped. The Cocker entourage is seated along both sides of the white tablecloth as Flash surveys the wine list.

The singer himself and his nymphette-consort with the kohl eyes look miserable. "We just want a burger," he says sotto voce, leaning over to me.

"What's your most expensive wine?" Flash asks the sommelier.

"Bordeaux? Cahors?"

"You worry about what you want to call it," says Flash. "All I want is the most expensive."

NOTES (IN SCRAPBOOK)

THEN THERE'S IAN DURY, on a transatlantic call prior to a North American tour. We're deep into post-punk, late-seventies disco and Dury's single, "Hit Me with Your Rhythm Stick," has just knocked the Village People's "YMCA" off the top of the charts. To my mind, "Hit Me with Your Rhythm Stick" is one of the greatest naughty songs in rock history. Imagine Noël Coward writing for John Travolta. Rhythm stick? The mind totters considering the infinite meanings.

But Dury doesn't want to talk about that. All he can talk about is coming to Toronto and playing Massey Hall. His voice is seductive and silky, a great radio voice.

"I can't tell you what this means," he says, telling me what it means. "This is where the greatest jazz concert ever happened. I couldn't never have thought I would get there, to be there on that stage, to play there—"

The May 15, 1953, concert with Dizzy Gillespie, Charlie Parker, Bud Powell, Charles Mingus, and Max Roach is often called the greatest jazz concert ever.

THE ROCK PROMOTOR HAD replaced the Broadway producer as the driving force in live entertainment. Yet Sid Bernstein might best be described as a Broadway guy who just so happened to get hooked on the Beatles. Others, like Bill Graham, the promoter behind the Fillmore dance hall, were rock crazies in their own ways. But not Bernstein, whom I'd meet for a bit of an afternoon whenever I was in New York.

I knew a lot of guys in the music business named Sid; many have a certain edge to them. But not this Sid. Sid Bernstein was a dreamer, not always the best thing to be in New York in the early, hard-bitten days of rock 'n' roll. I like to believe Sid Bernstein was a real-deal New Yorker, like the waiters at the old Palm steak house over on Third Avenue. Sometimes, we'd meet in his office. After, it was mostly over lunch at a second-floor steak house in the theatre district, Frankie and Johnny's maybe. Homey place.

Sid had an unstressed, handsome face which had some dignity. He was one of those people you want to like. He was about as wide as he was tall—lunches or dinners inevitably meant a steak as big as a catcher's mitt—and he loved to schmooze. And all that mattered to him—ever—was bringing the Beatles back together again. And so that's all we talked about over lunch.

Sid Bernstein was no *freier*, no pushover. A Manhattan-born baby, he'd been adopted by Yiddish-speaking Russian immigrants who had a background in theatre. (Bill Graham, likewise no *freier*, was in fact born Wulf Wolodia Grajonca and sent to France from Berlin in 1939 to avoid the Nazis, growing up in the Bronx, but eventually working out of San Francisco.)

Stationed in France during and after the Second World War, Sid started a club for thirsty and nostalgic Yankee soldiers. Back home, he opened a place in the Bronx called the Trocadéro to tap into the craze for Latin cha-cha-cha. He booked Judy Garland and other acts into Carnegie Hall and he began managing rock 'n' rollers starting with the Rascals, called the Young Rascals at the time.

Sid then hit pay dirt. He booked the biggest act in the history of big acts by bringing the Beatles to America, first to Carnegie Hall in 1964 and then to Shea Stadium on August 15, 1965, and on August 23, 1966, just as the band had decided to quit touring. The first Shea concert remains one of rock's pivotal moments.

The memory of it stayed with John Lennon the rest of his life. After this, everyone wanted to be a Beatle for a time. That 1965 afternoon, that sheer pandemonium, wasn't just an extension of Beatlemania back in England. This was the future of all of rock 'n' roll.

You didn't want to get Sid Bernstein started on Shea. "And you know I really didn't make any money from it," he'd say. From that time on, he used all this charm, guile, or whatever else was left to book the Beatles again. To no avail. His $1 million offer to them for a 1967 show was turned down, as were many further efforts on his part, leaving him heartbroken if unshaken in his pursuit of that one last Beatles show.

After a while, there was no more Beatles and no inclination on anyone's part to reverse history. Nothing changed when Sid took out a full-page ad in the *New York Times* in September 1976, offering the band a concert that would have global reach and the possibility of a massive international aid effort as the payoff. Come on, guys!

A Beatles reunion. It was in the air.

Once, when I talked to John on the phone—inevitably about his new album release—I dutifully asked if he ever imagined the band getting together for any reason. (The question was always in the air.) I knew he hated the idea more than any of the others did. And he didn't say no, no, absolutely not. He thought it was a maybe, a definite maybe.

Perhaps passing John's reaction along to Sid added to the Bernstein conviction that the door was not absolutely, utterly, and forever shut. Who knows when that happened? Anyone needing a way of pinpointing rock's last day should discover the moment when Sid Bernstein gave up on getting the Beatles back together.

I'm reminded that art forms attempting to decree their own collapse ensure in doing so their continuation, if only in a different form. John Lennon knew that. The Beatles had to end, if whatever the Beatles meant was to go on.

Sid didn't get that. Sid the promoter wanted a crack at the last show. He wanted to be offstage at Shea Stadium to watch the band one more time.

JOHN LENNON & YOKO ONO (2020)

THE OLD ONTARIO FARM John Lennon settled in is just less than an hour west of Toronto. One of the shorter ways of getting there took you, as it still can be done, some distance along Dundas Highway, a two-lane rural road going back at least several hundred years, but, more importantly for me, back to my Grade 1 and Grade 2 studies in a wood-frame schoolhouse that saw secondary service as a community hall.

Getting home from school—after the yellow school bus got me there—required a walk along the highway's gravel sides. I loved it, even when the temperature tanked. Dawdling in all seasons, kicking rocks or ice clumps or throwing fall chestnuts at doors—at old Mr. Whaley's door once, a crime I'll never live down—I came to know stretches of the road and each unrepaired pothole.

I could recognize just about every tree along the road and name the families down the lanes and driveways—the Prices, the Collards, the rarely seen businessman who landed in jail charged with his wife's murder. It was a road for cars, not people, and not a nice drive even at that. There was—is—a huge dip that iced up just before the Credit River crossing. Before this was a curve where a car hit and killed a kid who I sort of knew, the boy—Howie Turner—a year older than me, on his way home with two others from school.

So, there I was twenty-something years later, in 1969, on Dundas Highway again. Only this time I was in my Jeep Cherokee on assignment for the *Toronto Telegram*, folded up in 1971 and its subscription list sold to the rival *Toronto Daily Star*.

The *Tely* was conservative and monarchist and desperate for readers. And out there, as if beamed down from Mars, was a Beatle, a real, or semi-former real Beatle, tucked away in the cozy winter landscape, buzzing around on snowmobiles among the rolling hills separating century homes.

There was John Lennon.

I drove along, through relatively benign weather, conflating scenes from *Holiday Inn* with *Help!*: roaring fires and lots of sparkle and silly romps in the snow with John instead of Bing Crosby. And colour. After *A Hard Day's Night*, the Beatles were always in colour. Except in my mind, John was always shown in grainy grey-and-white snaps from his Liverpool school days, the sarcastic, bitter teenager shipped from home to home, from Julia, his mom, to his aunt Mimi, furious at his father for leaving them all, and blaming himself.

Beatlemania had coloured all of that in, like the colourization of an old movie. But on his own, John Lennon, stuck in the stark Canadian winter, seemed fallen back to earth in black and white.

The afternoon before, at the paper in Streetsville, an older editor showed me a heavily crayoned old black-and-white photo of Edwin Alonzo Boyd, the infamous but Hollywood-handsome gang leader of Canadian crime in the fifties. Lennon had reminded him of Boyd, said the editor, who'd done some reporting on Boyd's escapades. Both looked like hoods.

Boyd had been rumoured to have holed up in an old farmhouse somewhere along the Dundas Highway. The rumour was false because Boyd was slippery. He escaped the hanging two of the other gang members could not; Boyd hadn't killed anyone. He eventually changed his name, moving out west where he died after a peaceful life.

Lennon was denied entry into the U.S. in May 1969 due to a minor drug infraction in London where he had copped a plea. The entourage headed to Toronto for an overnighter at the King Edward Hotel, where I first met them, and then to Montreal starting May 26, for the famous/infamous Bed-in for Peace, in room 1742 of the Queen Elizabeth Hotel.

In mid-September, the couple returned to Toronto, now as the Plastic Ono Band, for a hastily arranged appearance at Toronto's Varsity Stadium where they were blown off the stage by Little Richard. "I'll show 'em what a headliner is," Little Richard said backstage and went on to prove his point with the show.

Although staged about a month after Woodstock, the day-long Varsity Stadium concert—Chicago, Bo Diddley, and Junior Walker and the All Stars appeared, too—nevertheless claimed its own measure of fame, foremost for being Lennon's first public repudiation of the Beatles and for Ono's performance in her signature bag.

I remember it for my disappointment in Gene Vincent, now puffy from booze. Lord. Vincent was more Elvis than Elvis at one time, whining "Be-Bop-a-Lula," while stem-to-stern in tight, black leather, shirt collar perpetually touching the back of his head. Talk about hoods. ("Be-Bop-a-Lula" brought Lennon and McCartney together when Ivan Vaughan, a friend to both Beatles, coaxed Paul to hear the Quarrymen, Lennon's band. Paul arrived just as Lennon was singing "Be-Bop-A-Lula." After Paul played guitar for a bit backstage, Lennon asked him on the spot to join the band, his, John's band, as he never let Paul forget.

The truth is, the concert was a downer. Jim Morrison of the Doors was drunk, and not in an interesting way. Backstage, the Plastic Ono Band was surrounded by burly guys in expensive suits who would have looked in place outside an overpriced strip club. Three months later, then, Lennon's arrival back in the city, even with the promise of a festival to dwarf all rock festivals—and for peace yet, a fine, righteous excuse for a festival—met with a measure of skepticism.

The Vietnam War banged away louder across Canadian newscasts. A mid-May 1969 student protest at Berkeley, California, had witnessed California highway patrolmen, ordered in by Governor Ronald Reagan, firing birdshot from shotguns and blinding one man in the process. I already had a good many draft-dodging friends.

Even the Cold War hadn't vanished entirely, although it seemed suspiciously overwrought in what little memory of it I had. I slowed down as I drove by Janet F.'s old house, just south off Dundas Highway, and remembered the tour she gave us years ago down the cellar into the family bomb shelter. I remember seeing some stacked cans of pork and beans. Janet was super-brainy, and her family read a lot. They knew something, we supposed. But pork and beans?

World-saving was a fine idea, but not the kind of idea that would have come naturally to John Lennon, rock's great snarky, questioning, ironic presence. Lennon-for-peace was a big deal for *Rolling Stone* in 1969, but not in most daily newspapers, still run by hard-nosed, old-school editors sitting grumpily around the editorial desk. These guys longed for Frank Sinatra's return the way the French had longed for de Gaulle's. Lennon's peace plan was, to them, more sixties bullshit, however transcendental. And as the days went by, news out of the festival seemed increasingly nonsensical.

"What's this about flying saucers?" said Doug Creighton, the city editor at the *Tely* at the time. "Are you telling me they have flying saucers?"

Me: "Yes." (Keeping up with the story, I'd interviewed a lawyer who'd signed on to the festival—Lennon was paying the bills, so money seemed to be no hassle—who was making himself at home in a just-rented office with leased chrome-and-beige leatherette furniture and explained that it was reasonable to think that if anything might attract attention from outer space it would be this festival, so they were preparing plans for landing facilities for interstellar craft as we spoke.

Creighton had red hair and a ruddy face that went redder whenever he was pissed. Which was much of his time at the office. He looked at me in silence, but as if his head, now a brilliant, radiant crimson, was about to explode.

Me (aiming to clarify): "No. I mean, they don't actually have them. But they've talked about them coming. Not John or Yoko, exactly, but others." I start riffling through the notes. "There really are plans to provide landing-pad thingies or whatever you provide for flying saucers."

Ronnie Hawkins's farmhouse, where Lennon and Yoko were encamped, was up a lengthy driveway on a gradual hill from the main back road. Dirt-brown ruts were left behind the cars heading up or down the driveway. Ronnie was an entrepreneurial show-business wizard combining a genius for survival with lots of "good ol' boy" charm and hokum. He also knew something of rural winters, having arrived in Canada from Arkansas in the fifties. The stretch of farm property his aunt owned outside of Fayetteville, Arkansas—I visited with him once for his quasi-autobiography, which we co-authored—could have been found next door, so alike was the countryside.

Canadian painters love those looming, winter days, the foreboding ones arriving just before we're locked into ice for a month or two. Artists have taught us how to look at their unsettled nature, near-frozen streams half-covered with blueing ice and at the yellowish, early-morning skies that herald afternoon storms. And the sudden nightfall.

All this suited Lennon, who'd been out snowmobiling and was in scuzzy Bolshevik post-Beatle mode at the time, gaunt-eyed, skinny as a rake, dressed as if he were about to take out the trash. This was part honeymoon, he told me.

Hawkins loved the indirect attention but kept his bullshit-detector turned on. I'd heard that for days now the Lennon-Onos had been running up prodigious phone bills, which had Hawkins grousing. He'd been left holding the tab before—many, many tabs and many times. Ronnie knew he'd bought into too many high-priced hopes of advancement offered by his highly placed buddies.

But this was a whole different scale of things. Hawkins understood what a worldwide, career-boosting opportunity had just landed in his backyard. He'd held on for dear life on enough weird rides in his life and figured he'd grab hold of this one too and see where it'd take him or leave him.

But Ronnie was discreet. He's off elsewhere as John Lennon and I talk, facing one another seated on the old couch. Yoko Ono is across the room with Rabbi Abraham Feinberg, their heads only inches apart, everything between them a whisper. The "Flaming Red Rabbi," Feinberg's nickname, which he wore like a service badge since he'd visited Hanoi, was under the scrutiny of what was then called the Royal Canadian Mounted Police Security Service, which already had a fat dossier on him and a file on Lennon. (And Elvis Presley, for that matter.)

"I don't think we're being naive," I am able to hear her say. "We want to change the world. Is that naive?"

John is now off the phone from talking to another media outlet.

"I was pretty cynical as a Beatle. I was a full-time cynic, you know," he tells me. "Now there's some direction to things. Peace is the just thing in the future thousands of years—and not just for the next generation. Too many people have got hooked on material things. That's why we got dropouts and hippies. I mean, what good is it if I can watch twenty TVs with twenty suits and have twenty cars? I mean, these are what other people consider success.

"Yes, the festival will be expensive," Lennon goes, now thinking about money. "It's cheaper than a life, though. It's going to cost. It's cheaper than the alternative, no peace."

Everywhere you look, there's a hunkered-down atmosphere to the house. A lot of watchful bodyguard-type guys were hovering around, silhouettes against the snow like a scene from *The Godfather Part II* outside Michael Corleone's house. Standing. Waiting. Guarding.

Already there's been a little rough stuff. Frank Lennon, a *Toronto Star* photographer not related to John, got a buzz-off, take-a-hike pushing around from Heavy Andrews, a downtown tough guy who had an office in the Le Coq d'Or, the Yonge Street tavern where Rompin' Ronnie and the Hawks— later The Band—were practically the house band. (Yes, you always used the bilingual double definite article when talking about the Le Coq d'Or.) Heavy obviously hadn't received the message that this country sojourn was all about media.

Waking up Americans about peace was a goal, says Lennon, meaning setting up shop not that far from the American border. People in Buffalo, New York, will hear about this. "That's not all we're here for, though. We're trying to get up this peace festival we've been talking about. We're taking our time about it, starting with the 'War Is Over' posters. It's all about selling it. We'd like to have our peace campaign pop up on the TV like all the other ads. We want advertising to take over.

"I don't want to be a leader in this. Yoko doesn't, either. We want everyone else to see us and get in the game. I know there are a lot of people who think we're naive. They may be right. So, let them take over."

The living room we're in is arranged in old Ontario country fashion—Wanda Hawkins, Ronnie's wife, is a genius at just about everything—where living rooms are rarely used other than for weddings or funerals and where people face each other, but always at a certain distance. I try to listen in on Ono and Feinberg across the room. From the beatific look on the rabbi's handsome face as he leans closer and closer to Yoko, he would seem to have been imagining her as a Chagall, imagining an angel floating in the air above another old man's fine, handsome head.

John was yapping away for another caller. And as I sat back watching the flow of people—promoters, gofers, flacks and hacks, and security—in and out, I noticed a strange thing. No one hesitated even for a second to approach John. Everyone increasingly kept some distance from Ono and the rabbi. It was hard for any of them to forget her and her bag, on stage at Varsity Stadium. You didn't need to know anything about Fluxus, the New York art collective where her bag-ism was born. The grandchild of the 1930s Dada movement, Fluxus—Ono was den mother to the movement in her studio at 112 Chambers Street inherited little of Dada's cosmic cheekiness. That bag had serious power.

An entire shift in dynamics could be felt, not just in the power of the personalities in the room, but why they were in the room, and the shift was to Yoko away from John. Each time she minimized her importance—people say I'm naive—the more power she seemed to accrue to herself. She told me that from her first meeting with John, in November 1966 at the Indica Gallery in London, she knew "he was so important for so many people and that wasn't going to stop." Nevertheless, this was her "War Is Over Campaign," which John only took on.

Here was a woman famous for her nudity—with a plush figure of the kind favoured by men's magazines—whose clothes seemed designed to obviate a sexual gaze. Floppy hats, bulky clothes, loose sweaters—she managed to be distinctly indistinct—like the peace festival itself, I was beginning to realize. From the Montréal Bed-in on, this has been their "honeymoon," as John called it. The accumulation of press photos and TV news clips show soft, sweet images of the adorable couple in diaphanous white with a diffuse, pale, winter light flooding their hotel room.

Lennon looks groom-like: wraith-like and skinny and worried. Ono's sexuality—the thickness of her hair, her sensual face—radiates in every instance. I was told by a producer of *The Way It Is*, a CBC current affairs television program that covered the Montreal Bed-in, that he was forever tucking a bit of her gown over some suddenly exposed flesh.

"On or about December 1910 human character changed," Virginia Woolf wrote famously (from the perspective of 1924). I remember this (checking it later) watching the John-Yoko dynamic, the Yoko-John dynamic. Something was beginning to change here, other than something between a married couple. For John, the festival was an extension of his practice and ego. Yoko saw it as part of her ego and practice. But more than the power shift between them, it felt as if the reasons for rock had changed. Lennon was putting rock to one use, trying to make it work as a sales job. Ono, in her soft, singsong voice, was putting it to another: to turn personality into a performance and vice versa. And more and more, rock seemed to be following her model, not his. The performance of personality would be rock's way through the seventies.

Another phone call come and goes, and John wants to make one of his own, asking me for the number for Capitol Records, his label, Apple's, distributor in Canada. "This is not that weird a thing, not really," he assured me. "Think of it as a new thing to sell, a new product, so you have to have a new way of selling it. I've been selling all my life. I have to know how the record's doing," he says. "Cold Turkey." "I have to worry about records and things, still. For how else will I be able to make me money? Eh? How else?"

John was checking out record sales with his local distributor, Capitol Records. I punch buttons. I imagine that the record company guy I ask for will hang up on me because he'll say, "This is a joke, right? John Lennon doesn't do stuff like that, check record sales." And that's exactly how the call goes. Before John can come on the line it goes *click*—dead. We have to call someone else I know at Capitol, who does talk to John Lennon. "Cold Turkey" is selling.

Less than an hour later, I'm back on the highway heading to the office. The story doesn't make it to the front page, and the *Tely* itself doesn't exist past 1971. The festival itself died when John and Yoko lost interest. John worried that Allen Klein would try to turn it into a Beatles reunion.

Because with startling suddenness, the Beatles had become past tense.

Hours after John and Yoko decamped from Ronnie Hawkins's place, they had a short, prearranged meeting with Marshall McLuhan, the communications seer. McLuhan began talking and thinking big about ideas and about television in the abstract, and patterns making TV popular. Lennon didn't have to think in the abstract. The Beatles were their own abstract. John was in the flesh the very sort of idea McLuhan was pulling out of thin air.

"As soon as you find the pattern you break it," John Lennon told McLuhan. "Otherwise, it gets boring. The Beatles pattern is one that has to be scrapped. If it remains the same, it's a monument, a museum, and one thing this age is about is no museums. The Beatles turned into a museum, so they have to be scrapped or deformed or changed."

K.D. LANG (2020)

SHE'S NO LONGER AN INGENUE, but k.d. lang's career-defining album, *Ingénue*, is still played on the radio, possibly because the 1992 release of the single, "Constant Craving," resonated so deeply as the torch song for the LGBTQ+ community. Rereleased in 2019, "Constant Craving" remains one of music's great laments, a great tradition going back to Henry Purcell's luminous "When I am laid in earth," or "Dido's Lament" as it's best known, from his late seventeenth-century opera, *Dido and Aeneas*. "Dido's Lament" stops time. It seems to exist outside of any particular history. More and more, "Constant Craving" feels that way.

Ingénue provided the soundtrack for lang's protracted indecision about coming out, which nevertheless came to a very public conclusion with the cover story of the June 16, 1992, issue of *Advocate*, a Los Angeles–based gay magazine, where she talked openly for the first time about being gay.

It was soon clear this was not just another reveal in the brilliant sleight-of-mind of k.d.'s made-up life. Like showing up for the 1985 Juno Awards, the Canadian version of the Grammys, in a wedding dress. Like kicking her red-meat-eating country fans in their hamburger buns with her "Meat Stinks" commercial—protests over which led to the cancellation of her concert in beef-raising Owen Sound, Ontario.

She had teased concert audiences about the rumours, which refused to be anything but rumours. "I've heard those stories," she'd say. Okay, she'd murmur confidentially, the time had come to "fess up, to come out, right here and now." An anticipatory hush would fall over the crowd. Yes, k.d. would say finally, yes, it's true! "I am a Lawrence Welk fan." As the laughter washed back across the stage, she'd stand there grinning, the spotlights catching her high cheekbones just the way she wanted. Even this was now part of the show, something that continued outside the music, before and after she made it to the stage.

The true grit of her coming out in the teeth of the AIDS crisis, an era of gay bashing and celebrity gay-outing, said something about the way several generations thought about sex. But there was more to it than that. Oh, the one-woman rodeo, the cow-punk princess extraordinaire was saying something about Canada.

So, even if everyone seemed to know k.d. was gay, no one had in fact said so, least of all k.d. herself. lang only seemed willing to describe how laborious the entire process of coming out was becoming. Much heavy going was involved, evidently. "Maybe a great magnet pulls all souls toward truth," she sings in "Constant Craving."

I found myself drawn to her almost painful decision, while working on a story for *Chatelaine*, then Canada's leading women's magazine. ("Miss Chatelaine" was *Ingénue*'s other single.) Despite the magazine's slightly suggestive mistress-kept-in-a-chateau name, *Chatelaine* represented feminism's more conservative impulses.

Complicating matters was that our conversation came with the understanding, on the part of both parties, k.d. and me, about what *The Advocate* piece was about. Complicating matters further, our talk took place on the landline in my neighbour's kitchen in an isolated, century-old farmhouse across the county road from my equally isolated, equally old place. A winter storm had slashed my phone line, and everyone else's on my side of the road, but not the Stevensons' side of the road.

So, I had trudged through a blizzard to make the call. I felt I was looking frivolous—calling a big, music-business star in front of them—because I knew Bob and Betsy had lost two of their sons to accidents when they were still young men. The Stevensons said little and had no opinion on k.d. lang as far as I knew. Yet, there they were listening in as k.d. lang and I did this slow dance along the long-distance phone line.

Me: "So what's the problem with coming out?"

Her: "I don't want to hurt anyone."

She meant her mother.

I'll never forget the calm of her voice, soothing against the snow rattling the Stevensons' windows. I felt as if I were talking to a girl I was courting, who really wasn't sure if she wanted to go out with me or not. Minutes in, I was quite in love. On the one hand, coming out is no big deal, she told me. "To tell the truth, I'm not sure what to do. You could say *Ingénue* was a catharsis. It was about something I had to forget, all right, but that doesn't make the forgetting any easier."

Seated near the Stevensons' woodstove, rocking on its feet amid blasts of winter against the smokestack outside, I was reminded that k.d. knew something about country living. In 1962, her father, Fred Lang, bought the town pharmacy in Consort, Alberta (population 714) and moved his wife, Audrey, and four kids there from a town south of Edmonton.

Kathy Dawn, the youngest, was only a year old, but it was quickly clear that her passion was music. Her mom, a second-grade schoolteacher, used family allowance checks to pay off a second-hand piano and cheerfully drove Kathy once a week to piano lessons at the Theresetta School in Castor, ninety kilometres away. But Kathy quit lessons when she was ten, frustrated that the nuns wouldn't let her play her free-form mashups of pop, jazz, and whatever else came into her head. As it turned out, she never learned to read music, playing everything by ear.

Not that music was everything. Fred taught his daughter lots of other interesting stuff too—like how to handle her own twelve-gauge shotgun. He left home to be with another woman when Kathy was twelve. In high school, she was a shy kid who sometimes developed fierce, secret crushes on her teachers—most of them women—because, with their city origins and university degrees, they had exotic backgrounds by Consort standards.

But then, Kathy was becoming a tad exotic herself. She tried out for the school's all-male basketball team and made it. At eighteen, she enrolled at Red Deer College to study music and voice but quit within a year and hitched up with several small performance art groups in Edmonton and Red Deer. One of her performances was a thirteen-hour re-enactment of heart surgery. In another, she wore a blonde wig and sang Nancy Sinatra's "These Boots Are Made for Walkin'," sending up Las Vegas–style bimbo singers everywhere.

In the process, she was putting some distance between who she was and who everyone thought she was. Whatever Kathy Dawn was feeling inside, no one ever knew from her "acts." In 1981, she stumbled on a way to achieve a semi-permanent distance.

She landed a role in a repertory musical, *Country Chorale*, playing a country singer in the manner of Patsy Cline, the queen of hurtin' music who died in a 1963 plane crash. When the musical was over, Kathy went right on playing the role. She set to work as a country singer in the clubs of Edmonton, imitating the keening sorrow in Cline's voice. This is how I first saw her in a club with her band, the Reclines.

Kathy Dawn had found an alter ego. And why not country music? It was the perfect symbol of her childhood in Consort, where country was just about the only music around. Kathy rebelled against it and loved it, all at the same time. But if she was to be country, it would be country on her own terms. She was twenty-one years old: while others were growing up, she was making herself up.

In 1982, she appeared at the Edmonton studio of record producer Larry Wanagas. A perky, offbeat, tomboy cowgirl with a voice the size of Nashville, Kathy Dawn was there to audition with a "Texas swing," twin-fiddle band that rented rehearsal space from Wanagas.

"She was astounding, the band wasn't," Wanagas told me. Within a year of that audition, his Bumstead Records had released her first single, "Friday Dance Promenade," followed by an album, *A Truly Western Experience*. But not before the newly renamed k.d. and Wanagas had sorted things out. She thought she might become a jazz singer; he wanted the big time, so forget jazz—no one wanted a kid jazz artiste. An act was what they wanted. Wanagas packaged k.d.'s wildest ideas in the comfy duds of Patsy Cline's kind of country. k.d. even proclaimed herself to be Patsy Cline reincarnated. She wore cowboy boots—but with the tops hacked off. And those old-fashioned, wire-rimmed glasses she wore? Pure country—except they didn't have any glass in them. The act ignited a small explosion.

Losing one's identity in a role seems to be a Canadian thing. Ottawa singer Sneezy Waters (aka Peter Hodgson) grew so absorbed in his role as Hank Williams that he told me he sometimes had trouble separating himself from the Nashville icon.

A 1984 cross-continent tour ended in New York City's Bottom Line club, where she was signed by the American label, Sire Records, famed for the discovery of Madonna and the Talking Heads. In 1987, the torchy, big-voice heartbreakers on k.d.'s second album, *Angel with a Lariat*, earned her a Juno and, later, a *Rolling Stone* Critics' Choice award. Suddenly, k.d. was hip—dining with Liza, chums with Madonna.

Next up, *Absolute Torch and Twang* (1990) brought a Grammy, two Junos, and three Canadian Country Music Association awards. And heartbreak—her affair with a married woman was ending. She was devastated. That was when she began writing the songs for *Ingénue*. The re-released, remastered version has extra material taken from her 1993 *MTV Unplugged* appearance. In 1993, k.d. lang was inducted into the Canadian Music Hall of Fame on a Junos show by Anne Murray, who marveled on camera at lang's evolution from cowgirl punkette to cabaret chanteuse. Then it was k.d.'s turn to say something.

"Only in Canada could such a freak as me be receiving such an award," said k.d.

The Junos usually make for better TV than the Grammy Awards. And with k.d., here was celebrity TV in its rawest, natural state. By embracing her own feelings as an outsider, she was playing to an inner Canadian sense of somehow being a country of outsiders, unconventional in the eyes of the world and fixated on such national monuments as the Ski-Doo, poutine, and the decorated goalie mask. Here was confidential TV, an awareness of a shared Canadian moment.

The truth was—and is—that k.d. is as Canadian as you can get in her need for love and affirmation. Her well-publicized caprices, such as cutting her shaggy hairdo by her own hand and performing barefoot on stage, only added to this love affair. Having moved south decades ago, she's in rainy Portland, closer and closer to Canada again. She does have a place in Calgary too.

Official Canada, the one with its strings pulled by the national capital in Ottawa, would have us think of Canadian history as generations of rugged men against the rugged landscape. This is the "Us versus the Great Out There" narrative. The Canada I grew up with, the country seen from one particular kitchen window near the stove that kept my mother's water for tea hot at all times, had a woman's feel to it. This Canada was a "Woman's World," to quote Canadian singer Sylvia Tyson. ("Feminine" is not the right word here, too loose at the edges, and "feminist" goes too far in the other direction.) Into this world, men came and went. My father, a piano teacher, kept to his studio in our basement during the day.

lang shares a good many things with Anne Shirley of *Anne of Green Gables*, starting with a rural childhood, an uncertain identity and a tough-love mother figure. Anne and k.d. might both have lived down the street from the young woman in Alice Munro's *Lives of Girls and*

Women, who takes pride in being the "hired hand" around the family place. k.d.'s father, called her his "buddy" and his "little boy-girl." k.d. calls herself "a boy girl." Young women found throughout the work of Canadian authors such as Margaret Laurence, Margaret Atwood and Carol Shields have prepared us to feel the intensity of k.d. lang's introspection. ("I would love to be called Cordelia," says Anne. "It's such a perfectly elegant name." Anne was craving constantly long before k.d. was craving.)

"Miss Chatelaine," one of *Ingénue*'s two hit singles, is about a shy kid from the Canadian Prairies coming to terms with being k.d. lang—a cover story, a star and the most famous pair of lowercase initials since poet e. e. cummings. It's not a song about fame found. It's about innocence lost. Only in Canada, they say.

DAVID BOWIE (2020)

THE NIGHT IN 1975 I found myself meeting David Bowie, the Thin White Duke was, by his own later account, coked to his eyeballs in a cave-like hotel suite in Albuquerque, New Mexico. Bats would not have been surprising.

The Thin White Duke tour was officially titled "Station to Station," Bowie's reference to Christ's twelve faltering stops on his way to Calvary and crucifixion. The singer's thinly veiled fear of a druggy down-spiral and death had fuelled decadent, pro-Nazi comments—theatrical statements, as he described them later.

In town to film *The Man Who Fell to Earth*, Bowie had (again by his own and others' later accounts) pretty much vanished into himself. He kept going over and over the first thousand or so words of an autobiography which had trapped him before it went anywhere.

His back was to me when I came in, his feet stretched down the length of the lounge. He looked back over his shoulder and gave me a skeleton smile, gaunt eye sockets sunk in a skull face smooth as marble.

Now what? I frantically tried to remember where I'd left the hallway door. I couldn't avoid staring at his bony body while aware that his handler—an anxious young woman, simply dressed—seemed prepared to spring from the edge of her seat.

Bowie loved playing the stranger in a strange land. He was pushing, exhibiting, parading his very Englishness, knowing how bemused and shocked Americans were by Europeans in general and the Brits in particular, an idea confirmed by his life spent in recent months in Los Angeles, in the valley of the kitsch when kitsch had lost its charm.

We talked about Springsteen briefly, whose career was then in the ascendency and thus unavoidable.

"I'm a fan of certain of Springsteen's songs," Bowie said, making the word *fan* sound like a grenade thrown into the conversation. "But to me, the excitement about Springsteen is a perfect example of a culture trying to find archetypes. Rock audiences today don't enjoy the clichés which, to me, produce the excitement."

Music, he went on, was his painting materiel, not his picture. Music allowed him to paint himself. Bowie was drilling down deeper into his own dreamland, playing constantly in his head like a nonstop movie. The stark lighting everywhere, white and antiseptic, "reminds me of Kerouac's vision of America, of William Burroughs's," he went on. "To me it's all a fantasy. I'm really a comic, indulging in my fantasies of what should be, not about what is." The tour soon to follow would include a screening of Luis Buñuel and Salvador Dalí's *Un Chien Andalou*, a 1929 surrealist, lurid dreamscape impossible not to watch. Bowie had a great band this time around and the music—not his greatest, admittedly—was connecting with the crowd. But not Bowie. He seemed removed, as I wrote at the time, trapped in his dream.

THE WHO AND THE BAND (2020)

IT'S AN EARLY SPRING night in the hills north of Toronto, with everyone but me asleep in the farmhouse as the wind whips in from the northeast off of Nottawasaga Bay. I'm upstairs listening to all the fury outside while trying to catch up on my packing.

There's more spring still in that howling than winter and the temperature isn't dropping. This old house won't be cold for some time now. So, I can dawdle as I go through some of my memories. I'd come across a charcoal sketch of a muscular pony, defiantly facing into the winds of an earlier time. I'd found it during an earlier wintry spring, when I was in Denver with the Who. It was a terrible time for the band, coming only five months after the death of eleven fans on December 3, 1979, in the crush of people trying to get through a closed stadium door at the concert. The guys in the group didn't learn about the disaster until after the show and could only honour the lost fans at their concert in Buffalo the following night.

The 1980 tour was their return to the stage and both Denver dates sold out. I'd been warned how much stress the band had been under—even just to stay together. Keith Moon, the drummer, had died a year earlier, a casualty of the band's spectacular liftoff.

Fuelled by power chords, rock opera, films, synthesizer, and bull-headed energy, the Who were unmatched by any band of their generation. Everything about the Who was singular and focused in the extreme. In subverting rock's basis in the blues, they were rock's avant-garde before rock grew punk on its own. "You can't get philosophical if you're in danger of not surviving," punk artist Judy Nylon opined. Well, the Who were rock's only multimillionaires seemingly damned not to survive.

Everything about those two Colorado concerts was stashed in a green garbage bag, with the bubble-wrapped pony taped to the top. I was easing my way through a storage room packed halfway up its walls with these bags. There were countless publicity glossies and other things of questionable provenance and pedigree. How did I ever get a battery-driven Jim Carrey statuette heralding the movie premiere for *Liar Liar*?

There were reels the size of hubcaps that were once used for radio broadcasts, along with audio tapes, microcassettes, mini-cassettes, VHS cassettes, and DVDs. It was a rarity to have time to listen to old tapes. My sense of loss is at its most acute, I've found, when I'm in the place I'll miss, at the house, or with the people. Loss wasn't the problem here. As a journalist, I'd covered rock for some fifteen years by that time and I had a sense that many more years, nearly twenty as it turned out, were yet to come.

I'd found the pony in the town of Cripple Creek, where I'd gone for a break from the mood in Denver. I'd left behind an atmosphere sucked airless by rage, an impression I found impossible to shake.

Although not blamed for the tragedy in Cincinnati, the Who had been cited in dozens of articles about the "violence" of rock 'n' roll. Hence, the press was regarded with conspicuous malice by the security hired for the shows. From years of backstage passes, I was used to steroid robo-security guys itching to do damage. But these guys were scarier.

Just the sight of me waiting at the edge of the hallway for the band's arrival and wearing my "Access All Areas" badge—which I merited for reasons I never figured out—pushed security wrath to its zenith. "All Access" is the ultimate entry. It's what the star's dad gets. It's what whoever's holding the drugs gets. One steroid king checked my badge repeatedly hoping, I suppose, that it had fallen off and he would be justified in murdering me on the spot.

Then, there was the noise factor. The Who were not just loud. They were proudly loud, even after Cincinnati, after anything: loud was their badge. Pete Townshend is a master of noise. He studied art under the famous German-born artist Gustav Metzger, who would spray a canvas with acid, leaving it to shred and curl. "Destroy a canvas," he'd say, "you make shape." Metzger described his anti-authoritarian practice as "art which triggers its own destruction."

The anger was the bigger show. Any such therapeutic aftershock was lost on the security goons. Rage was like heat in the air. The city felt on edge, for whatever reason, if there was ever a reason. Lost between my hotel and the show at the McNichols Sports Arena—since razed—I rolled down my window at a red stoplight and signalled to the guy in the passenger seat of the truck next to me. I waited while he rolled down his window and with a big "Welcome-to-Mile-High-City" smile, showed me his gun.

The fact that I remember that atmosphere so clearly came as a surprise.

It was a period of my life that I was sorting through, partly discarded and not expected to return. Stuff piles up in a quarter-century. Word got around. One university, two colleges, and two schools of journalism made inquiries about the thousands of interviews I had squirrelled away. (To whet their appetites, I'd drop hints about the tape where Patti Smith suggested I join her for our interview under a big fur coat or blanket. Well, a fur something.)

I was moving back to the city, likely forever, and hauling my notes, proposals, books, and tapes with me. I was learning how to close the door on my memories. I'd learned this from my father, one of the few things I felt he wanted to teach me.

One day, he said he wanted to be taken on a drive to the rickety, wood-frame, waterfront cottage he'd had since the 1920s, where I'd spent all my summers as a child. It was unchanged. It never changed. After a short walk around the cottage and a look-see into each of the rooms, my father went out the front door, turned the lock, patted the door once and said, "That's it." Before I could finish asking, "Are you sure?," he was up the hill and heading to the car parked in the trees. It was the hardest, toughest thing I ever saw him do, this man who never raised his voice to me or my brother, who loved a Chopin legato more than anything. He never went back.

Sometimes, I'd pick a random interview tape, spin through it a bit, and then: listen. Who's that saying the next album was going to be recorded in Nashville? That drawl? Kris Kristofferson. The names I remembered, the content not so much. Listening anew, I could hear there were lame exchanges and monumentally embarrassing moments: How many times did I forget a name while talking to a megastar? Did I really ask Ringo to call me back? (Christ, I even said "ring" me back.)

There was something else in those tapes, I was beginning to recognize, something quite wonderful. What an enormous mashup of music was created back then, an almost joyful bust-up of barriers that forced a looseness of definition—a situation unimaginable now, not so many years later, with our targeted audiences and personal playlists. Because it wasn't just the music that the tapes reveal, to whoever is listening, but what happened before and after the playing was done.

FOR A GENERATION WHO once believed itself to be communally inclined—antiwar, pro-pot—rock was about a lot more than rock alone. As I read the names scribbled on my cassettes, it was clear other things were soaring even as rock came to dominate everything.

Jazz was reinventing itself with musicians as disparate as Charlie Haden and Keith Jarrett, classical music was saving itself through tonality, country music had stopped whining, reggae was becoming world music, and urban music—Black culture by another name—was poised to take over the music business. All this and Herb Alpert, too.

The drawing of the pony came from Cripple Creek, site of one of the last great gold strikes of the nineteenth century, where I'd headed when I was sensing a general need for the band to take a break. Driving the I-25 south to Cripple Creek and then west on the US-24 was, for me, an homage to "Up on Cripple Creek," one of the greatest cryptic songs in rock 'n' roll, written by Robbie Robertson for The Band.

Robertson was a kid-genius guitar whiz who played with Ronnie Hawkins's band, the Hawks, back in my Toronto hometown when I was teenager. He played like an angel and looked like one too; far too handsome for his own good.

I had a connection with him. The guitarist in a band I played piano for had (insanely) rejected Hawkins's offer to join the Hawks. I knew this would be the closest to making it that I would ever get as a piano player. Years later, as a journalist, I caught up to Robertson, who proved to be affable but famously oblique when it came to his work. "Maybe I was reading about it" is how he explained a song to me, one time.

What struck me was that it wasn't the music from The Band's 1969 song rolling over my mind as I headed for Cripple Creek, but the words stripped of sound. Drummer Levon Helm's Arkansas country-boy singing underlined every syllable. The result was augmented reality. The result was that the modest hills my rental car climbed to Cripple Creek seemed a whole lot higher because Helm described "that mountain," an understandable exaggeration by the homesick old miner offering the song.

Rather, it's how Robertson was able to convey his way of seeing it, as a movie, following some guy on a lonely odyssey in his truck.

"Just following him with a camera is really what this song's all about," Robertson has said.

I bought the pony sketch at a nice, touristy place. I assumed its ancestors worked in the mine shafts in the 1890s, as they did in England, but it turned out that they worked open-pit mines in Cripple Creek. The great gold rush of 1893 drew thousands of prospectors and circuses and whores and professional strike breakers, all temporary professions.

Cripple Creek, close to being ghost town for much of the twentieth century, remains modest by any standard. Bob Womack, who discovered the local riches, died dead broke in 1909. Although $500 million had been extracted from the ground, the small miner was overrun by big-business interests.

The Band song's greatness isn't heralded on any sort of civic tribute. After about an hour of looking around, I pulled over by an empty shack, one of many, to sit on the car's bumper and fight like hell the compelling insanity of stepping into the shack itself. Sound was stifled there, the days still too cold yet for many migratory birds. Crazy dreaming never felt far away.

I have a theory about ruins. Larger ruins—old castles or peasant homes or even crumbled-down walls—contain a babble of imagined stories in the contemporary imagination from the days when they were busy with many people and many uses. Smaller places in isolation are the opposite, like an abandoned hunter's shack my daughter and I came across in France once, or the entrance to an old mine. Sound seems excluded: you can't imagine why anyone would have spoken.

I WAS A KID before the omnipresence of rock 'n' roll, so it was only one of many genres in my life. I soon understood—somewhere in that seam of time after Elvis and before the Beatles, as Chuck Berry spent his bitter twenty months in jail—that rock music mattered in a different way than other music. This didn't make it better, or lesser. But it mattered differently. And in a sense, this connected musicians at a time when jazz players thought rockers were goofs and classical composers preferred not to have an audience at all.

In his brief memoir of Greenwich Village life in the 1940s and 1950s, Anatole Broyard said, "It was as if we didn't know where we ended and books began"—he was a bookstore owner for a time—"books were our weather, our environment, our clothing. We didn't simply read books, we became them. We took them into ourselves and made them into our histories."

My circumstances were different. I was born into a musician's family. My parents collected classical albums that were each multiple 78s—Arthur Rubinstein, Jascha Heifetz, children's histories of Mozart and Beethoven—which were played a lot, scratched a little, and kept forever out of the way of the prying fingers of children. Safe until music-loving guests arrived. They were heavy in the hand, breakable and black, with mysteriously designed labels and a hole in them.

We recognized that was over with the arrival of sleek, long-playing recordings. The LP with its glamorous cover, seductive liner notes and much, much extra music. With the LP, and those cute 45-rpm mini-discs, so much sexy, modern plastic, the recording moved to a place once occupied solely by the book. The arrival of a new book didn't prompt the need to immediately talk about it, but a new record did.

Books had their place. Records occupied the rest of the space. Books seemed to have been put together by people who had a higher purpose beyond our understanding. That wasn't always true with recordings. We felt we knew what they were up to.

A middle ground between book and LP was training ground for a new category of writer that I'd come across: the critic. There was the British theatre critic, Kenneth Tynan, and Pauline Kael, the American film critic, and Richard Goldstein, rock critic at *The Village Voice* in the sixties. They seemed to be reinventing or reimagining what they were writing about as they went along. This uncertainty, this probing, this second-guessing was electrifying. Talking about records took on a kind of loose urgency.

The act of explaining records—Cecil Taylor or James Taylor, it didn't matter—added enormously to why they mattered or didn't. Elucidating pieces of consequence was also a way of explaining who you were—a necessary and very urgent thing to do. And so it went. As rockers learned a manner of playing in their own style, listeners developed a manner of hearing in their own style. On both sides, intensity and extremes were always desired.

DRIVING BACK TO DENVER for the second of the Who concerts, I was aware of the dramatic potential of writing on the dramatic extremes of place, purpose and sound: the sensuous, deafening Who, the shrieking silence of Cripple Creek. But I don't think I found a forum for it, at least not while day-to-day events took precedence in what seemed to be the Who's final days.

"People around the group don't want to admit this is happening, but this is the end of the Who," Townsend told me. He'd stopped boozing and he was introspective. "They may not be as ready to make that radical change in their life, but that's tough. I've come too close to death, to really dying, to fool around anymore. I want control of my life and I'm not in control of it in this band."

The conversation took place in an elegant hotel suite. Nothing on earth would have made him fit in there. Something of the early-sixties London mod was still about him. He had been up early—easier to do since he wasn't drinking. He used to drink up to a bottle and a half of brandy every day. He said he'd had dinner with David Bowie, and he was saying how he had to watch everything he did, or "they" would misquote him. Bowie always worried that "they" wouldn't understand.

"Well, I don't know who he means by 'them,'" Townshend said. "I do know that if you tell the truth and only half of it is printed, at least that's something." Indeed.

"I remember when after the Cincinnati disaster, our manager, rightly or wrongly, decided not to make a statement that evening. There was a load of card-carrying reporters who went back to the phones and made up statements. I know how they felt. They were waiting outside a fucking hotel for five hours trying to get a story on which their careers rested. They knew people wanted a story so they said what they thought we would say."

The Who, as it turned out, was far from breaking up. I now realize that picking out "WHO: DENVER 1980: PT/RD" from my stash of cassettes was predetermined as a date of some significance. Rock changed in the early eighties, as did all the arts, due mainly to technology. Wave after wave of new technologies rewired all the systems.

One result was more music than ever: music's omnipresence, endlessness, and timelessness. This potential was not lost on the creative generations who came up with club mixes lasting entire evenings or the droning minimalism of Philip Glass or Steve Reich.

But another result—ironic, to say the least—was higher-than-ever levels of sound pollution, levels that suggest an invisible plague. The health risk of noise pollution due to road traffic is forty percent greater than the air pollution created by that traffic, according to findings by the World Health Organization. WHO, what irony!

So, we worry about the physiological damage of high decibels to kids' ears but overlook the psychological numbness caused by music without end and without definition.

Back to Townshend.

"The reason the Who has had such good press for so long is that we've been good copy, we've been both articulate and sensational. The Who is a better example of a rock 'n' roll band than the Rolling Stones because we are more diverse while also being more ordinary. We are not the glamorous, dangerous figures that the Stones are. In the past, we attempted to look that way, to look rebellious, but that wasn't us. Even Keith Moon, he wouldn't have pulled a knife on anybody."

Or a gun.

JIM MORRISON (2020)

LOS ANGELES. The thing is, the cop just wouldn't have cared. He could let me walk or not. He was kind of bored and I did look temptingly strange with my longish hair—so maybe I should come for a ride.

A ride downtown to the station? *Oh no*, I thought, *no rides*. I was going to explain that I was waiting for—but that wasn't going to be any good, either. To say the least. That would be worse. No, to mention Jim Morrison's name wouldn't likely help my cause at all. Cops weren't likely readers of *Billboard* magazine, but they sure knew about Jim Morrison. The spectre of the Doors singer, all leather and capable of showing whatnot to whomever and wherever, just might conjure up visions of riots and indecent exposure, of sex and all things un-American.

No rides, and no Jim Morrison.

"Just hanging around, officer," I averred, and it worked.

I loved this about L.A. at the time, from the mid-sixties on. Everything about it was right there, right in front of you. Obvious. The right-wing newscasters were obvious. That unknown starlet advertising herself on the billboard over Sunset Avenue was obvious about her ambition. No shame. The station on the rent-a-car you got from LAX would be playing the most banal pop song, which anywhere but here would sound doubly banal, but here was rather iconic.

So. Saying "just hanging around" earned me a pass. Obviously. Or maybe it was the heat. A blast of heat filtering through the smoggy haze made things tense, made things seem to slow down to a shimmer.

When Morrison ambled to his office door, the heat seemed to make him move oddly slower. He was smaller, less demonic than any of the 8 x 10 glossy photos would lead you to believe. He was unshaven and wearing dirty blue denim clothes. I began to think of Ricky Nelson in comparison. "Poor Little Fool"—now, there's iconic.

But here was Jim Morrison. Through his poetry, films of the Doors in concert, their famous and infamous performances, he had become a surgical pin in a press agent's nervous system. The geometry of publicity, of one little item taking on absolutely mythical substance, had ballooned his name into King Kong proportions.

As descriptions of him in performance reached out into permutations and combinations. As each writer *click-clicked* their way toward another obscuring distortion, Morrison the "Sex-Death, Acid-Evangelist of Rock" was encrusted with image after image.

James Douglas Morrison, twenty-five, son of an admiral in Washington, self-defined Lizard King, sat waiting. Mike Jahn, author of *Jim Morrison and the Doors*, seemed to only gratuitously include The Doors' other members: organist-bassist Ray Manzarek, drummer John Densmore and guitarist Robby Krieger. Jahn referenced Morrison's "brooding expression, primeval sneer and leather pants combined with Nietzsche and Artaud" to create the "most charismatic sex symbol in the U.S. today."

In a way. Morrison had become sort of a Rorschach test for writers. For *The Village Voice*, he was "the first major sex symbol since James Dean died and Marlon Brando got a paunch." And for the defunct Hearst publication, *Eye*, Morrison was a "demonic vision out of medieval Hellmouth." So it went.

After what is gingerly described as the "Miami incident" of the previous winter, in which the singer did—or didn't—reveal a lot more than just his voice, the *Miami Herald* dubbed him "King of Orgasmic Rock." Even gossipy Joyce Haber in *Hollywood*, sensing that something was happening, named him "Swinging Door."

But this morning, nothing was happening. That's why the cop acted as he did: he was caught in the heat's undertow. Sleepily, Morrison blinked across his desk. Things weren't relaxed, but they were absolutely still. As if we had been in this room since it was built. Still, it wasn't just the cool darkness inside that made me think of him as a shadowy figure.

"Just what do you want?" asked the Lizard King.

Relinquishing thoughts of Miami and other sub rosa topics like sex, death, cops and why-did-you-cut off-your-beard, I armed myself with something more substantial: "Your theory of theatre-of-rock. Let's talk about that."

"Okay. All rock's theatrical."

"Yes, but—"

"But what?"

"Well, I mean, I heard that you mean the Doors, as a group, you understand, aim at something theatrical while on stage?"

"The theatre, hmmm," he said. "You mention a review of *Waiting for Godot*. That theatre is nothing more than keeping people entertained in the dark for several hours. Now, that's what the movies do. That's what a lot of live theatre does. Not the Living Theatre, of course, they're excellent. That's the kind of theatre I mean. Rock's like that a bit. Instead of merely having an actor up there giving forth some interior monologue, he's able to demonstrate in physical terms what's occurring in his mind at a given moment. Any performance is theatrical, really. My idea of theatre—or rock—hasn't progressed very far, though. It's sort of wishful thinking. Before I get into that,

I'll probably involve myself in film. To really be into something like that, you really have to involve yourself with it. When the Doors perform, we all act as catalysts on each other."

NEIL DIAMOND (2020)

I KNOW A WOMAN WHO was friends with Neil Diamond, or rather, is friends with his wife and who (my friend, that is) always described him in the most workaday of terms—as just another modern businessman who happened to travel a lot. Neil this, Neil that, oh what a funny guy, Neil. The truth is he sounded rather dull when he wasn't being Neil Diamond, which was struggle enough because—to an outsider and listener he never seemed to know what that meant exactly.

Neil Diamond never seemed to fit in anywhere, not into the grubby business of rock 'n' roll nor into the vintage Las Vegas/Frank Sinatra ethos, or whatever. The truth was Neil Diamond never seemed to be entirely of his own time or any other time, for that matter. Forget ageless: He was era-less.

And yet, his career will likely be defined by two of the most era-defining events in modern popular culture. One was *The Last Waltz*, The Band's 1976 farewell concert. The other was the 1980 remake of *The Jazz Singer*. (You can add a third event to the list, the part he didn't get—or want or rejected, take your pick—in the 1976 remake of *A Star Is Born* with his pal, Barbra Streisand, who appeared opposite the gnarly Kris Kristofferson. Worse versions of the story can barely be imagined.)

Seeing Diamond backed by The Band was puzzling at first, to say the least, to those of us at the show. Onstage, he appeared in jacket and slacks as if he had walked in from maybe a pool party, looking to wind down with an old-fashioned and a Camel. Backstage later, he seemed to have disappeared entirely. Everyone else was schmoozing in clusters (my favourite moment being when drummers Ringo Star and Levon Helm were next to each other).

Helm was initially flabbergasted that Diamond was invited, but guitarist Robbie Robertson explained: "Neil is like Tin Pan Alley." (Helm surely was aware that Robertson had produced Neil's *Beautiful Noise* album.) Here was the least hip-looking singer of his era at the celebration of a craggy, Canuck hipness that had had its day. (Yes, Canadian. The event was at the Winterland Ballroom in San Francisco on American Thanksgiving Day, but, with Joni Mitchell, Ronnie Hawkins, and Neil Young on stage, the night really felt like Winnipeg. I even developed a crippling cold that night to prove it.)

Urban legend has it that Diamond, coming off stage, challenged Dylan by saying something like "top that." Dylan, due on next, reportedly replied, "By doing what, falling asleep?" Years later, Diamond claimed he joked with Bob Dylan by saying "those are my people out there" when clearly, they were Dylan's. I believe Diamond's version. Talking with him over the years, I can't imagine him being cocky with anyone, let alone Bob Dylan.

"Dry Your Eyes" was the song in question, co-written with Robertson, which cleaves to a narrow melodic range repeated so often it's practically a chant. In its way, though, the persistent re-statement suits both the growing urgency of its antiwar lyric and Diamond's blue baritone, perpetually raspy from a lifetime of unfiltered Camels. That was extraordinary enough. But the voice—utterly, unmistakably Neil Diamond—froze the crowd into awareness.

Hipness could not have mattered less.

The nearly universal rejection of his remake of *The Jazz Singer* had less to do with Diamond, although he appears monumentally uncomfortable throughout the film, or even the music—most of which was his, and thus had zip to do with jazz. Rather, the ominous cloud of negative word of mouth had its roots in the unrivalled chutzpah of merely using one of the most storied titles in music, movie, and Jewish history with still-strong memories attached to the 1927 original featuring Al Jolson.

Diamond's discomfort really began way before his movie, his first movie and first acting role, had its premiere evening. I was with him for a slice of time then, specifically at his tux fitting—gotta look smooth—at his Hollywood office, a cozy townhouse behind a row of dwarf trees just off Melrose Avenue.

"Really, I'd rather have no one see me, just sneak in some back door," he said, as the fitting finished. Looking smooth was his way of calming his nerves, a not unreasonable thing to do given the bad vibes.

First of all, the rumour was that Barry Manilow was the first choice. Then, according to the *Los Angeles Times*, Diamond's "high anxiety about his dramatic film debut" resulted in massive changes, from the screenwriters to the musical choices to the firing of first director, Sidney J. Furie. And, as co-star Lucie Arnaz later said, "The press on this film is the worst I've ever heard of."

"I see myself as a George M. Cohan," Diamond told me, trying to gain back some control on the spreading dissent. "You know, he was really the first songwriter who was also a performer."

"I hadn't acted before," he went on, "so I phoned Barbra and asked her what I should do." That's Barbra as in Streisand. Barbra, being a friend, likely didn't say that comparison to Al Jolson probably wasn't the best way to start a performing career.

Jolson lived for the stage and embodied the ideal of sweat and heart-pounding and no-shame flow of feelings that animates musical theatre. Diamond's métier is the opposite, designed for the intimacies of the microphone and the recording studio.

"Jolson?" said Diamond. "Yeah, I saw the original, but I don't think it influenced me too directly. It's the tradition that the music started that matters more than anything else. In my movie, there's a song called 'On the Robert E. Lee.'" I (later) realized that Jolson had one like it.

Any Jolson-Diamond comparison shouldn't be about ego. Jolson's self-centeredness was without rival, yet he could be terribly insecure and would turn the water on in his dressing room so as not to hear the applause for the act then on stage.

Diamond readily saw himself as larger than life. "We were in a limousine" was how he began his description of how a song came to be written. *We*, I wondered, *who is we? His band? A posse of songwriters?* No, as it turned out after several more we's, it was evident he was speaking about himself.

Jolson never seemed young. Neil Diamond, at least from a distance, has rarely seemed anything but youthful. He presents the odd phenomenon of the adult adolescent, the grown-up replica of the teenybopper star.

At his shows, I found myself wondering about his aging fans' newfound, inner adolescence, goofily happy smiles on their faces and hands swaying in the air. A man in front of me, wearing a $2,000 bespoke suit and the weary-eyed look of someone in the money markets, was waving his arms frantically during the vintage crowd-rouser, "Brother Love's Travelling Salvation Show." Next thing I knew, he was giving the peace sign—giving two of them in fact, a double Nixon farewell. Several aisles over, "I Am ... I Said" inspired a heavyset woman with grey hair to wave her orange Bic lighter in the air, shedding light on a song that oozes not a little schmaltz.

Musically, the Diamond oeuvre is somewhere between lusty ballads around a cottage campfire and Las Vegas. He sings about being forever in blue jeans, but has a spangled stripe down his pant legs. This makes him the perfect companion for audiences old enough to know Michael Bublé sure isn't Frank Sinatra yet, at the same time, not having been around long enough to understand what Frank Sinatra was all about in the first place.

To watch this crowd file into a show in their finest, you might as well have been outside a Broadway theatre at the latest revival of *Cats*. Inside was another matter entirely. They got younger. Inside, they shed one inhibition after another, snapping up pricey, all-colour programs and, in general, doing silly concert-going things people their ages aren't supposed to do, at least not in public.

Diamond knows this. He knows this is not The Band's crowd, for sure. Or Dylan's. They're the new middle, forever finding ways of staying forever young. Viagra Nation. This is why he calls them "kids." This is where his genius kicks in. He knows about all the inhibitions and how to expose them. Midway through his two-hour marathon, he jumped up on the piano and soon had everyone in the seats behind and to the sides of the stage up on their feet to a loose version of "Dancing in the Street." ("Dancing in Their Seats," he called it.)

"Did you have to pay for those seats?" he asked.

"Actually, this is the most difficult song I have to do," he said at one point. "I have to sit down in these pants." Actually, the pants weren't that tight and the best the line got was a giggle. If Tom Jones had used it, you would have heard something akin to a growl. Al Jolson, of course, would never have said anything like it at all.

ACKNOWLEDGEMENTS

SPECIAL THANKS TO Carol Ann Goddard, whose insights and cooperation encouraged me throughout the project. Thanks as well to Sam Hiyate, Doug Richmond (Anansi), and Nicholas Jennings, whose advice was invaluable.

Courtesy of Carol Ann Goddard

PETER GODDARD (1943–2022) was a leading Canadian music, arts, and cultural commentator for more than five decades. A trained ethnomusicologist, he covered everything from rock 'n' roll to fashion, including classical music, movies, video, advertising, opera, and visual arts.

After serving as music critic for *The Varsity* newspaper at the University of Toronto from 1965 to 1967, he became the first on-staff popular music critic in Canada at the *Toronto Telegram* until the newspaper closed in 1971. He was freelance music critic for the *Globe and Mail* in the late sixties and joined the full-time staff of the *Toronto Star* in 1972, where he remained for over thirty years. During this latter period, he contributed music columns to *Maclean's* and *Chatelaine*, as well as cultural pieces to *Saturday Night* and *Le Monde*. In 1982, he won a National Newspaper Award for criticism, the first Canadian critic of popular culture to do so.

Goddard wrote about a wide range of pop and rock acts. *Ronnie Hawkins: Last of the Good Ol' Boys* was cowritten with Hawkins in 1989. In 1973, his *Frank Sinatra: The Man, the Myth and the Music* appeared. *The Rolling Stones: The Last Tour* with Philip Kamin (1982) was a national bestseller. He also wrote a futuristic fiction, *The Sounding*, in 1988. Some of his other books (with Philip Kamin) have focused on the Who, David Bowie, Genesis, the Police, Michael Jackson, Duran Duran, Cyndi Lauper, and Bruce Springsteen. In 2017, his biography of Canadian pianist Glenn Gould, *The Great Gould*, was published to critical acclaim.

J. A. WAINWRIGHT is the author of six novels, five books of poetry, two critical biographies, and an opera libretto. He is McCulloch Emeritus Professor in English at Dalhousie University where he taught for thirty years, including a class on the lyrics and music of Bob Dylan.